OCR Religious Studies

Revision Guide

H573 1/2/3

Peter Baron

Daniella Dunsmore

Andrew Capone

Cirencester College, GL7 1XA
Telephone: 01285 640994

Contents

Ten Steps to A* Essays

In each section of this guide there is a list of potential future questions. You need to practise these using the following ten steps, without taking shortcuts. The end product is a **TIMED ESSAY** in forty minutes without notes. It is essential you build these steps carefully, using **DIFFERENT** questions- no need to do all the steps for every question, just ONE step for ONE question. You do three questions out of a choice of four, in three hours, for each of these three papers.

1. Practise creating a **THESIS** statement with one reason after the word 'because'….for example "situation ethics is the best approach to issues surrounding euthanasia because it is flexible".

2. Practise writing an opening paragraph with a **THESIS** statement and a brief outline of your approach to justifying it with this one reason. For example: "situation ethics is the best approach to issues surrounding euthanasia because it emphasises quality of life over sanctity of life, and adapts any potential rule to the consequences and to the needs and wishes of the individual'.

3. Practise writing an opening paragraph with **THREE** reasons justifying briefly your thesis. For example 'situation ethics is the best approach because it is personalistic, stressing individual needs and wishes, it is relativistic, meaning everything is made relative to the one fundamental norm of love and it is pragmatic, meaning that the end always justifies the means'.

4. Practise a **FIVE** paragraph essay structure, as an outline, that only seeks to analyse and develop the **THESIS** you have outlined. Identify some key quotes to use and a one key applied illustration to briefly ground the argument.

5. Now expand your paragraph structure to **EIGHT** paragraphs, with the alternate paragraphs of the main body of **SIX** paragraphs presenting a contrasting, evaluative point of view.

6. Practise writing **CONCLUDING** paragraphs which express the **THESIS** statement slightly modified or qualified by potential objections to it. This is because **NUANCE** will arise out of good analysis and evaluation.

7. Practise writing a full essay with brief summary notes containing one or two key quotes and more than one **SCHOLARLY** view to illustrate or object to your own **THESIS**.

8. Practise writing a **TIMED** essay in forty minutes without notes. Try revising this question from your **SUMMARY** sheet last thing at night and first thing in the morning (as this develops your memory).

9. Take the **HARDEST** question you can find in any section and try a different approach - ask **QUESTIONS** about the question in your opening paragraph. These help you impose a line on a difficult question - the bulk of the essay is then spent answering your own line on the question rather than wandering around aimlessly in your answer.

10. Practise marking a friend's essay against the **SIX** levels of assessment. Compare with the **MARKED** answers on the peped website.

It is essential you practise writing under timed conditions if you are to achieve an A*.

Philosophy of Religion Paper H573/1

Introduction to Philosophy of Religion

The specification sections 1-3 begins by examining Philosophical Language and Thought and explores **PLATO**'s and **ARISTOTLE**'s contrasting theories of knowledge, as well as **DUALIST** (two parts as in body/soul) and **MONIST** (one united whole) attitudes towards the soul.

Three of the most common arguments for God's existence are then explored (the **ONTOLOGICAL**, **TELEOLOGICAL** and **COSMOLOGICAL** arguments) and their challenges as well as the nature and problems surround religious **EXPERIENCE** and the question of suffering.

Usually in year 2, sections 4-6, the **NATURE** of God is studied and how, where that nature is revealed, it influences our attitudes towards God's omnipotence, benevolence, omniscience and eternity. We then examine the classical forms of religious **LANGUAGE**, including the **APOPHATIC** (from the Greek verb 'to deny') **VIA NEGATIVA** and the **CATAPHATIC** ways (from the Greek word cataphasis meaning "affirmation") of **ANALOGY** and **SYMBOL**.

We then look at the effects that **LOGICAL POSITIVISM** of the 1920s had on the meaningfulness of God-talk in the forms of **VERIFICATIONISM** and **FALSIFICATIONISM**, and the responses that arose to counter them.

Philosophical Language and Thought

Key Terms - Ancient Philosophical Influences

- **ALLEGORY** - A story where the characters and events have a deeper hidden meaning

- **CAUSE** - The reason why something exists

- **DOXA** - (Greek) Opinion; according to Plato we gain only opinion from experience

- **EFFICIENT** - The agent or agents that **cause** something else to exist

- **EPISTEME** - (Greek) Knowledge; according to Plato we knowledge through reason, but according to Aristotle we gain knowledge through experience

- **ETERNAL** - That which is timeless and unchanging

- **FORMS** - Or theory of Ideas argues that non-physical (but substantial) **Forms** (or ideas) represent the most accurate reality. When used in this sense, the word form or idea is often capitalised.

- **NECESSARY** - The belief that the Prime Mover cannot not exist

- **TELOS** - The final end of things, what they are made to do, the reason why they are brought into being

Structure of Thought

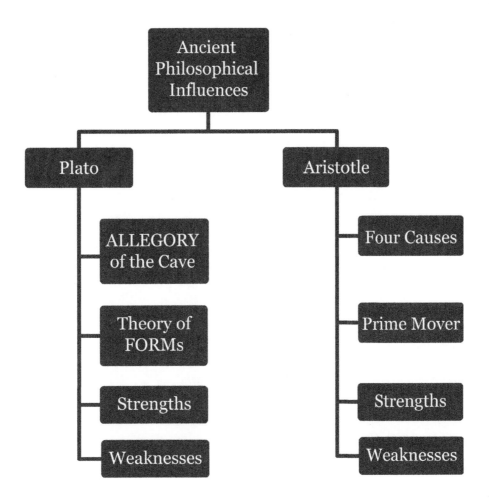

Plato

The Allegory of the Cave

Plato in the **REPUBLIC** presents the **ALLEGORY** of the cave in the Republic to illustrate that experience can only give us **DOXA** and that **EPISTEME** can only come through the knowledge of the **FORMS**.

The Symbols of the Allegory

- **THE CAVE** - The physical world of experiences in which we are born, live and die

- **THE PRISONERS** - Normal people who experience the world and take what they experience as reality

- **THE SHADOWS** - Things that we sense in the world through sight, hearing, taste etc.

- **THE PUPPETS** - The **Forms** which exist in a temporal world of ideas; they are the ideas that we recognise in the things we experience, e.g. love, truth, beauty etc.

- **THE JAGGED PATH** - The journey of the philosopher from ignorance to knowledge

- **THE SUN** - The Essential **FORM** of **Goodness** which is the highest of all **Forms** and is responsible for giving life to all things and through which all other **Forms** can be known

The **ALLEGORY** teaches us that while we think we are gaining knowledge from the **PHYSICAL** world, we are in fact learning nothing but opinion which is constantly changing.

In the same way that the prisoners are chained in the cave and only experience **SHADOWS**, we are chained to our reality and only experience the temporal particulars of this physical world. The **FREE PRISONER** gains true knowledge by crawling up the jagged path and seeing how the puppets cast shadows on the wall. So we must free ourselves from our reliance on this world, become philosophers and accept that the truth (true knowledge) lies in the abstract **FORMS**.

The Theory of FORMs

Plato argues that all things that we experience in this world are poor imitations of the true **FORMS** which exist abstractly in the World of Forms. When we experience **PARTICULARS**, for example trees, cats, acts of affection, we experience a fleeting and changing example, but in the example we are "recognising" the true **FORM**.

The fool would comments: "Ah, look at all these different trees: elm, oak, ash, there are so many different trees in the forest."

The philosopher comments, "Look at all these different examples around me, they all appear different but share some similar qualities: they have trunks, branches and leaves. They all possess tree-ness and are all poor imitations of the perfect **FORM** of tree."

The **FORMS** are **INHERENT** ideas which are **ABSTRACT** and **PARTICULARS** (eg an elm tree) are temporal, and so do not contain any true knowledge.

The Essential **FORM** of the Good was the way Plato was able to respond to **RELATIVISM**. Through the **FORM** of the good that anything can be known and it is by this **FORM** that we can behave in moral way (eg justly). For Plato, things were only good if they were clear **REFLECTIONS** of their **FORMS** especially when filled with **GOODNESS**. The **FORM** of the good is like a light – hence the sun association in the **ALLEGORY** – which shines through the **FORM**.

For example, the idea of chair-ness is reflected in an example of a new and comfortable chair which more closely reflects the **FORM** of the chair. However, over time and misuse the chair becomes squeaky, torn and broken, and not much **GOODNESS** shines through the **FORM**. However, the **FORM** of chair never changes; it is **ETERNAL** as are all the **FORMS** e.g. maths, love, justice.

Strengths - the Forms

1. **DEMOCRITUS**: All things in the universe can be constantly divided until we come to non-divisible blocks (atoms). While Scientists thought they found them (atoms) they were wrong as they can also be divided.

2. **PLATO**: Reason enlightened us to what experience failed to find.

3. **HERACLITUS**: The world is in constant flux meaning that it was constantly changing. The famous quote: "you can never step in the same river twice" highlights this view. Plato: Experience gives only changing opinions; the world is one of shadow, not absolutes.

4. **PARMENIDES**: If you take a snapshot image of an arrow in flight, at any given point the arrow is stationary. Plato: The **eternal** World of **Forms** is fixed and unchanging; all **Forms** that ever existed did so **eternally** and nothing came into or went out of existence.

Weaknesses - the Forms

1. **THIRD MAN ARGUMENT**: Plato says that the FORM of a man is still a man. Therefore, if all men need a FORM of man, and the FORM of man is also a man, then the man AND FORM of man together need a FORM, which we might call the FORM of MAN+. But the FORM of MAN+ is itself a man, and so the series continues ad infinitum.

2. **EXTENT** of the World of **FORMS**: It seems bizarre to think of such **Forms** existing **eternally**. If would suggest that there are **FORMS** of every conceivable past present and future concept, even things that have not been invented yet and things that are clear negations of things.

Aristotle

Four Causes - A Teleological Worldview

The four causes are the **MATERIAL**, **FORMAL**, **EFFICIENT** and **FINAL** causes.

MATERIAL cause - The material cause of what a thing is **MADE** of, like wood, metal or wax. T

FORMAL cause - The formal cause is what a thing **IS**. All things come in a **RAW** state, like a block of wax or iron ore, and are then worked into a particular form such as a candle or a nail.

EFFICIENT cause - The efficient cause is the **AGENT** that brings a thing about. It must be moved from that **POTENTIAL** state to the **ACTUAL** state of being a statue by an agent

FINAL cause - The final cause is what a thing is made to do, its purpose or **TELOS**, the ultimate end for any object. Living objects like trees and animals have their own purposes to survive and reproduce.

Prime Mover

Arguments for the Prime Mover

If all things are made of matter in a particular form, then the world itself is also made of material with a form. Motion is a change from **POTENTIALITY** (the raw material) to **ACTUALITY** (what it actually is, its form). Therefore, the world must have been moved from its raw material into the form of the world by some Prime Mover. Further, all things which are moved from one state to another must ultimately be moved by some Prime Mover.

All things have an **EFFICIENT CAUSE**, a cause for them to exist at all, and a purpose or **FINAL CAUSE** for which it exists. It then follows that the world itself needs a cause and has some purpose. The world also has a **TELOS** and so there must be some Prime Mover that attracts the world towards itself thus fulfilling its purpose.

Characteristics of the Prime Mover

The Prime Mover must have certain characteristics by definition of its nature as Prime Mover:

PURE ACTUALITY – The Prime Mover cannot itself be moved otherwise it would not be the first mover at all. Therefore, it must be pure actuality incapable of being moved itself.

SIMPLICITY – Given that it is pure actuality, the Prime Mover cannot be a complex being like humans, as complexity implies complex form and motion.

GOOD – The Prime Mover cannot change and so cannot be improved. This being the case, the Prime Mover must be perfect, incapable of improving, and so must be **PERFECTLY** good.

Strengths - Aristotle's Teleology

1. **EMPIRICAL** - Aristotle's approach is the **EMPIRICAL** approach to science and the experimental method of understanding the world - the **SCIENTIFIC METHOD**.

2. **SCIENTIFIC PROGRESS** - The scientific method is to experience the world, observe it, make a **HYPOTHESIS** of how things work, test it, and revise the hypothesis. Sometimes this process revolutionises how we think about ourselves: the sun no longer orbits the earth (Copernican revolution) and the Darwinian revolution suggests humankind evolved, rather than being created by God from 'the dust of the ground' (as in Genesis 1 & 2).

3. **EXPERIENTIAL** - Experience is the only tool we have as everything we do in life relies on our experiences, from the first instincts to reach for our mothers, to our desires to travel and build space ships.

4. **REASONABLE** - If we think rationally about Plato's and Aristotle's theories of knowledge, there is far more that we can relate to in Aristotle's approach. It is more rational as it does not exclude experience.

Weaknesses - Aristotle's Teleology

1. **INCOMPLETE** - Aristotle's theory of knowledge was not complete and his own deductions based on his experiences were not always correct.

2. **UNRELIABILITY OF EXPERIENCE** - Aristotle's observations were the first steps in our understanding of many things including medicine and technology, however, he himself made incorrect observations about things that could easily be discerned, for example the number of legs on a fly.

3. **SUPERIORITY OF REASON** - The example of Democritus and the a-toms exemplifies the problem of experience as a substitute for reason. Reason can consider abstract ideas in a way that experience simply cannot.

4. **CAUSATION CAN'T BE INFERRED** - When postulating the existence of the Prime Mover, Aristotle infers its existence from the four causes. However, as David **HUME** later argue, you cannot infer a causal connection between two things; you can only describe the apparent connection.

Key Confusions - Plato & Aristotle

1. Plato's Theory of **FORMS** and the **ALLEGORY** of the Cave all part of Plato's Theory of **KNOWLEDGE**. If a question asks about the **FORMS**, the Allegory can be used to support and justify what the Forms are. Likewise, if the question is about the Allegory, the question expects some explanation of what it aims to explain: the Forms themselves.

2. Do not confuse Aristotle's **FORMAL** cause with Plato's **FORMS**. Plato's Forms are **ABSTRACT** ideas that give rise to all things that we experience in the world. The **FORM** of tree for Plato is the tree-ness we recognise in the

various examples of trees that we encounter in the world. However, for Aristotle, upon encountering various different trees, oak, elm, ash etc. we see the similarities and then label those different examples with a similar form by a term, i.e. tree. Aristotle's method is **A POSTERIORI**, from observation and experience.

Possible Exam Questions

1. Critically compare Plato's Form of the Good with Aristotle's Prime Mover.

2. "In their attempts to make sense of reality, Plato relies too much on rationalism and Aristotle relies too much on empirical observation". Discuss

3. Assess Aristotle's argument for the Four Causes.

4. "Aristotle's reliance on empiricism has many weaknesses". Discuss

5. Evaluate whether Plato's rationalism is superior to Aristotle's empiricism in making sense of reality.

Key Quotes

'The sun is not sight, but the cause of sight itself.' Plato

'But the primary essence has not matter; for it is complete reality. So the unmovable first mover is one both in definition and in number.' – Aristotle

'All metaphysics, including its opponent positivism, speaks the language of Plato.' – Martin Heidegger

'The Platonic idealist is the man by nature so wedded to perfection that he sees in everything not the reality, but the faultless ideal which the reality misses and suggests.' – George Santayana

'The ideal ruler is a philosopher-king, because only philosophers have the ability to discern the Forms'. David Macintosh

Soul, Mind and Body

Key terms

- **ANIMA** - In Aristotle's De **Anima**, the **anima** is the soul of a person

- **DUALISM** - the idea that mind and body are distinct substances

- **HYLOMORPHIC SOUL/BODY UNITY** - Aristotle's interpretation of **monism**, that the body and soul are a unity and cannot be separated from each other (Greek, HYLE = form, MORPHE = matter)

- **IDENTITY THEORY** - The theory that all mental activities including emotion and intelligence are centred in the brain

- **MATERIALISM** - the idea that mind and body can be explained by physical or material interactions

- **MONISM** - The belief that the body and soul are one and the same and that the soul cannot exist independently of the body

- **TRIPARTITE NATURE OF THE SOUL** - In Platonic **Dualism**, the belief that the soul is made of three parts: reason, spirit and appetite

Structure of Thought

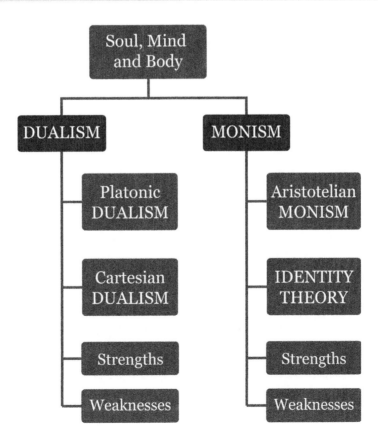

Platonic Dualism

In Phaedrus

Plato presents the analogy of the charioteer to illustrate the **TRIPARTITE** nature of the soul.

REASON: THE CHARIOTEER The highest part of the soul linked to the role of the guardian in Plato's perfect society; the rational soul is the part of the soul that thinks, reflects and learns. I

SPIRIT: THE WHITE HORSE The emotive part of the soul linked to the role of the auxiliaries in Plato's perfect society (the **auxiliaries** are the warriors, responsible for defending the city from invaders, and for keeping the peace at home. They enforce the convictions of the **guardians**, and ensure that the **producers** obey).

APPETITE: THE BLACK HORSE The lowest part of the soul linked to the role of the workers in Plato's perfect society; the appetite is the part of the soul that desires, craves and motivates.

If it can be demonstrated that people's behaviour reflects the tripartite soul, then it can be argued that the soul exists as a **SEPARATE** entity to the body (**DUALISM**).

In Republic

Plato presented a version of the **MYTH** of **ER**, a soldier who died in battle but whose body did not decompose. He witnessed souls emerging from the sky, rewarded, and the ground, punished, and then choosing **NEW LIVES** before drinking from the river of forgetfulness only to be **BORN AGAIN**.

This process myth was borrowed from the **REINCARNATION** beliefs of **PYTHAGORAS**. Plato called it **TRANSMIGRATION** of the soul, as the soul moved from one body to another. When in the ethereal plane they also gained all knowledge of the **FORMS** before forgetting them again.

In Phaedo

Plato presents his three arguments for life after death:

Argument from **OPPOSITES**: All things are in constant motion between two extremes, e.g. all different temperatures are a flux between hot and cold. All opposites are extremes and Heraclitus' **LOGOS** prevented any extreme being surpassed. We can observe these opposites in life and so we can be certain of them. In the same way that things move from hot to cold and then to hot again we must accept that we move from life to death and then to life again.

Argument from **RECOLLECTION**: All knowledge comes from the **FORMS** which are eternal ideas that we cannot experience. When we are in the World of **FORMS** in between lives we know them intimately, and then we forget about them. When on earth, our experience recollects the **FORMS** that we see in the examples we encounter. When I see a tree I recollect tree-ness from some previous existence - proof that we pre-existed.

Argument from **AFFINITY:** Plato identifies two kinds of existence, the physical and the non-physical. All things that we encounter physically have a **NON-PHYSICAL AFFINITY**. For each tree, there is the non-physical tree-ness Likewise, for each life there is the non-physical self. **CEBES** challenges this by giving the example of the music played that ends when the instrument is destroyed, but Plato insists that the affinity of a person is an eternal affinity.

In these arguments, Plato is presenting his case for why life after death cannot be refuted but instead must be accepted as a reality. It is based in the nature of **DUALISM** and is embedded in the theory of the World of **FORMS**.

Cartesian Dualism

For Descartes the soul is a **SPIRITUAL** entity that resided within the body. The soul exists throughout the body and operates in all parts of it. The part of the body, however, which was most associated with the operation of the soul, is the **PINEAL GLAND i**n the base of the brain. From here, the soul moved the body around by way of directing the spirit through the ventricles and arteries and thus operating the body like some super marionette.

Descartes chose the pineal gland because the pineal gland otherwise had no purpose in the brain, and because, while the rest of the brain was divisible into two halves, the left mirroring everything on the right, the pineal gland appeared **INDIVISIBLE**. In this way, Descartes was building an **ANATOMICAL** picture for the soul's interaction with the body.

One way of better understanding Descartes' view of the soul's interaction with the body is to compare it to the cardiovascular system (this is **NOT** an example given by Descartes).

Strengths - Dualism

1. **CHILD DEVELOPMENT** - Of Platonic **DUALISM** - Anthony **KENNY** supported the idea that the psyche develops in his observation of the tantrums of toddlers. They know they crave and have the emotions to cry but have no intellect to know how to control those feelings.

2. **REALISTIC** - In the same way we can support Plato's argument for the **FORMS**, we can support Plato's rational approach to the self and the dualistic psyche. Many would argue that there is a part of us that is separate from the body that makes our character.

3. **EASTERN PHILOSOPHY** - Many eastern traditions have adopted reincarnation as part of their belief system. These can be used to support Plato's argument for the World of **FORMS**. In fact, the work of Dr Ian Stevenson on reincarnation is modern scientific evidence to support the belief in reincarnation. He recorded thousands of **REINCARNATION** accounts which, though not conclusive of anything, stand as evidence to support Plato's claims.

4. Cartesian **DUALISM** supports Plato's dualism and helps us to see how the body and soul can interact in a measurable way.

Weaknesses - Dualism

1. **UNPROVABLE** - Plato's two arguments of recollection and affinity are all part of the argument for the World of **FORMS** which Aristotle challenged. If this theory of knowledge can be attacked it undermines the whole argument for **DUALISM**.

2. **HERESY** - **DUALISM** is rejected by the Catholic Church and considered heresy at least in the sense that **GNOSTICISM** is a heresy (the view that body is evil, the soul good). The Catholic Catechism states that the soul is the **FORM** of the body and they were created and are, one.

"Because man is a composite being, spirit and body, there already exists a certain tension in him; a certain struggle of tendencies between "spirit" and "flesh" develops. But in fact this struggle belongs to the heritage of sin. It is a consequence of sin and at the same time a confirmation of it. It is part of the daily experience of the spiritual battle", Catechism 2516.

3. **SCIENTIFICALLY FALSE** - of **CARTESIAN DUALISM** - the reality is that much of Descartes' ideas were demonstrated to be false and in fact poor science. The pineal gland is the part of the brain that secretes Melatonin and in no way can it house or direct a soul.

4. **CATEGORY ERROR** - Gilbert **RYLE** accused Descartes of committing a category error in which he categorises the body as one type of stuff and the soul as another. He gives an example of a visitor at Oxford who asks to see the university and is guided around the campus and sees the dorms, the registry office, the fields etc. But then he asks "where is the university?" It is a category error to think that the university is more than the sum of its parts. In the same way Descartes is wrong to think that the person is more than the sum of its body. There is no other self or soul that makes the person.

Monism

Aristotelian Monism

ARISTOTLE presented his ideas concerning the soul in his work **DE ANIMA**. In the work, Aristotle discusses the nature of the relationship between the body and the soul all stemming from his earlier argument for the **FOUR CAUSES**. Aristotle argues that the body and soul make up a **HYLOMORPHIC** body/soul unity. For Aristotle, there is no separate soul, but rather, the soul is the **FORM** and purpose of the body, the body in action. This can be seen through his explanation of **POTENTIALITY** and **ACTUALITY** and then of **CAUSE** and **EFFECT**.

The human being is matter in some form fulfilling some **TELOS**. Then the soul is the **ACTUALITY** of the body. Aristotle gives the wax stamp example to emphasise the unity between the body and soul. The stamp cannot be removed from the wax as they are one unity. Likewise, whatever it is that makes the **SOUL**, the appearance, shape, character, personality etc. it is all part of the physical person; the soul is the form of the body, the actuality of the flesh.

- **First potentiality** – our material self.

- **Second potentiality/first actuality** – our formal self.

- **Second actuality** – our purpose or **TELOS** being engaged.

The soul is **ANIMA**tion: the person engaging with their **PURPOSE** which is determined by their **FORM** and doing what they are supposed to be doing. As Aristotle said, if an **AXE** had a soul it would be **CHOPPING**; if an eye had a soul it would be seeing. We have a soul, and that is to engage with **REASON** and live the **GOOD LIFE**.

Therefore, there can be no question of the soul existing disembodied as the soul is the **ANIMA**tion of the body. It is not a separate thing that can exist separately. The body and soul are a **HYLOMORPHIC soul/body unity**.

Identity theory

IDENTITY THEORY is a belief that a person's self-identity is linked directly to their physical body. It is a **MATERIALIST** approach formed from a series of scholarly ideas and beliefs:

BODY OR MIND? John **LOCKE** - John Locke presented the thought experiment of a prince and cobbler who wake up in each other's bodies. The prince presents himself to the palace but is sent out as he appears as the cobbler. The thought experiment asks us to consider what the person is: the **PHYSICAL** person or the **MIND** inside. It asks us to consider whether or not a person could even theoretically switch bodies, or whether we identify the person's self with their physical person.

BODY OR PERSONALITY? Phineas **GAGE** - Phineas Gage was a 19th Century railroad construction foreman who suffered the fate of having a metal pole through his brain. While he survived, he was forever changed as a person, from being approachable and friendly, to being short -tempered and easily angered. This suggests that the **CHARACTER** of a person, or their soul, is directly linked to the **PHYSICAL BRAIN** itself, not some spiritual substance.

BODY OR GENES? Richard **DAWKINS** - Richard Dawkins argues that the body is a survival machine for the **GENES** passed on/surviving within us. They last forever if they are successful and they determine everything about our character and person. We should therefore not consider ourselves special in any particular way as we are governed by our genes and the idea of a life after death is simply a **MEME** that our brains have created in order to cope with the reality of our fate.

Strengths - Monism

- **TRUE TO SCIENCE** - Of Aristotle's **MONISM** - Aristotle's interpretation of the soul as the **ANIMA**tion of the body fits well with all modern scientific attitudes as the soul can be seen in light of the brain's activity and personal identity. It does not force the believer to accept an abstract world or a spiritual dimension.

- **TRUE TO THE BIBLE** - John **HICK** supports Aristotle's **MONISM** when he argues that the only self we can know is the **EMPIRICAL** self. He argues that God has made us as a psycho-somatic **soul/body unity**, and that the **RESURRECTION** of Christ was a purely bodily resurrection. This may be supported by the letters of St Paul when he describes resurrection as being with a **'SPIRITUAL BODY'** (but what does Paul mean?).

- **TRUE TO PSYCHOLOGY** - Of **IDENTITY** - Identity theory can be demonstrated by observing how people's behaviour is affected by psychology and a **PHYSIOLOGY (**body form). When we observe people's characters changing on account of drugs and alcohol we are witnessing a change to the character which supports the idea that the **SOUL** is in fact the **CHARACTER** formed by the physical brain.

Weaknesses -Monism

1. **UNPROVABLE** - Of Aristotle's **MONISM** - Aristotle's Monism is itself difficult to demonstrate beyond doubt. Aristotle did not give a clear indication if there was life after death. He seemed to have allowed for the possibility for the **PRIME MOVER** to maintain a person's intelligence but this was never developed.

2. **DOESN'T EXPLAIN MOTIVATION** - Of **IDENTITY THEORY** - Stephen **DAVIS** argued that Identity theory

only explains the workings of the brain, and not the motivation of the brain. He discusses the brain may be **NEUTRAL** and that the **SOUL** is what guides it.

3. **THE BRAIN AND MIND REMAIN MYSTERIES** - The reality is that we know little about the brain and how it actually works, so everything we claim about how the brain works and how it interacts with the body and forms the character is pure speculation. Elements, such as perception itself (what you see now) remain **METAPHYSICAL**.

Confusions to Avoid

1. The analogy of the **CHARIOTEER** does not describe how the **PSYCHE** drives the body. The charioteer is not the psyche and the chariot is not the body. The charioteer and horses are the whole psyche in its tripartite nature (**REASON, SPIRIT, APPETITE**).

2. **PLATO**'s **DUALISM** might be improbable/unprovable; but it is not inconsistent. Following Plato's reasoning it is acceptable to conclude the existence of the World of **FORMS**. To undermine the whole you need to attack **DUALISM**, or the arguments for the Theory of **FORMS**. Similarly, we cannot prove reincarnation. Given the nature of the spiritual realm you would never be able to, so absence of evidence is not evidence of absence.

3. **ARISTOTLE** was a **MONIST**, **NOT** a **MATERIALIST**. Materialist approaches, including **IDENTITY THEORY**, are suppositions and speculations, not proofs. It would be wrong to assume that it has proven anything concrete about the nature of the body and soul. In fact, there is arguably more evidence for **REINCARNATION** than **IDENTITY THEORY**, both from the number of believers to the work of Dr Ian Stevenson (see Strengths of **DUALISM**).

Exam Questions - Dualism & Monism

1. Assess the claim that disembodied existence is possible.

2. "The body is separate from the soul." Discuss

3. "The concept of the soul is best understood as a metaphor." Discus.

4. Assess whether the soul is best considered as reality or as metaphor

Key Quotes

Consciousness can be thought of as the culmination of an evolutionary trend towards the emancipation of survival machines as executive decision-takers from their ultimate masters, the genes.' – Richard Dawkins

Descartes split thought from existence and identified existence with reason itself: How different from the approach of St Thomas, for whom it is not thought which determines existence, but existence which determines thought! – John Paul II

I shall often speak of it as 'the dogma of the Ghost in the Machine'. I hope to prove that it is entirely false, and false not in detail but in principle. – Gilbert Ryle

Arguments for the Existence of God - Reason

Key Terms

- **A PRIORI** - Before experience

- **A POSTERIORI** - After experience

- **ANALYTIC** - Self-evident knowledge, known **a priori**

- **CONTINGENT** - Something that does not need to exist but depends on something else to exist

- **DE DICTO** - By word/definition

- **DE RE** - In reality/the real world

- **NECESSARY** - Something that cannot not be the case

- **PREDICATE** - The **predicate** is the part of a sentence (or clause) which tells us what the subject does or is eg God (subject) exists (**predicate**)

- **SYNTHETIC** - Matters of fact, descriptions of how things are, known **a posteriori**

Structure of Thought

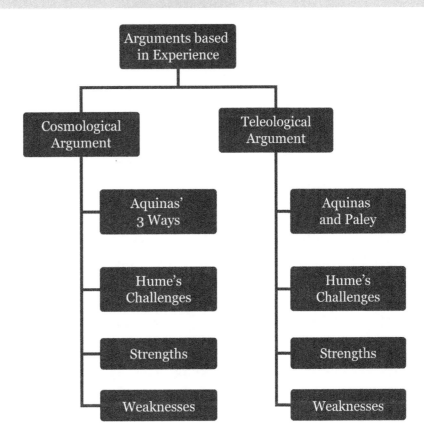

15

The Ontological Argument

Anselm's First & Second Version

Proslogion Chapter 1: Dealing with the Fool

ANSELM reflected on **PSALM 14**: 'The fool has said in his heart "there is no God"'. He set out to demonstrate that God's existence can be proven **ANALYTICALLY**, as a matter of reason, from what we mean by God. God existed necessarily and that this could be shown **A PRIORI**.

Proslogion Chapter 2: Ontological Argument Version 1

Premise 1: God is a being than which nothing greater can be conceived.

The God of **CLASSICAL THEISM** is the **MOST POWERFUL** being possible even in imagination -God is a being such that no greater being can possibly be imagined.

Premise 2: It is greater to exist in the mind and reality than in the mind alone.

ANSELM implies existence is a **PREDICATE** of God's nature (meaning it is included in the idea of God himself as an **ESSENTIAL** property). A painter conceives of a painting and has that idea in his mind but not yet in reality. When he paints, it the picture is greater. Therefore, it is greater to exist in the mind and reality than only in the mind.

Conclusion: God must exist.

If it is the case that God is a being than which nothing greater can be conceived and existing in the **MIND** and **REALITY** is greater than the mind alone, then if God only existed in the mind, he would not be the greatest possible being, as theoretically, a God that **DID EXIST** would be **GREATER** than a God that **DID NOT EXIST**.

Proslogion Chapter 3: Ontological Argument Version 2

Premise 1: God is a being than which nothing greater can be conceived.
Premise 2: **NECESSARY** existence is greater than **CONTINGENT** existence.

If we consider the relationship between **NECESSARY** and **CONTINGENT** things, we find that **NECESSARY** things are greater as they cannot not exist, whereas **CONTINGENT** things depend on others and can conceivably not exist. Therefore, necessary existence is **GREATER** than contingent existence.

Conclusion: God must necessarily exist.

If God is that than which nothing greater can be conceived, and necessary existence is greater than contingent existence, then surely God must be necessary, as between a **NECESSARY** God and a **CONTINGENT** one, the necessary God meets the criteria of being that than which nothing greater can be conceived. So God must exist.

Gaunilo's Response

In Behalf Of The Fool, **GAUNILO** responded to both premises of the first version of Anselm's argument, and so sought to undermine its logic.

Premise 1: God is a being than which nothing greater can be conceived.

Gaunilo argued that it was possible for a person to understand the definition **ANSELM** gave without committing oneself to accepting its existence or even reality. He gave the example of the rumour of a **MAN**. If I describe a man in full detail, I would use my understanding of 'men' in general to form the image in my mind. But if I were then told that this man did not exist, it would not affect my understanding of the description. In the same way, I can understand what Anselm means by 'a being than which nothing greater can be conceived' without **COMMITTING** myself to **BELIEVING** it is a real thing.

Premise 2: It is greater to exist in the mind and reality than the mind alone.

Gaunilo challenged the use of existence as a **PREDICATE**. He argued that one could not simply define God into existence by saying that God's perfection required God to exist. He gave the example of the **PERFECT ISLAND**. If I were to describe an island that were perfect in every way, I could well imagine it. Gaunilo was arguing that that existence **DE DICTO** (by definition) could not lead to existence **DE RE** (in reality). Ultimately, existence is not a **PREDICATE** and so we cannot list it among God's attributes. **KANT** argued the same in the eighteenth century.

Apologetic

Anselm replied to Gaunilo by pointing out that it was impossible to compare God to an island as the island is a **CONTINGENT** thing and God is a **NECESSARY** one. Ultimately, the argument's premises only work for God and for no other thing.

Strengths - Ontological Argument

1. **DESCARTES** argued in Meditations that existence was a **predicate** of God in the same way that three sides is a **predicate** of triangles. Descartes argued that God's nature was perfection and that existence was an attribute of perfection. God's existence needed to be discovered rather than proven.

2. **ALVIN PLANTINGA** supported Anselm in his response to Gaunilo's challenge. Plantinga pointed out that the use of the island could not possibly undermine the argument as there was no intrinsic maxim that could make an island perfect, since it was a **CONTINGENT** thing. God on the other hand was a **NECESSARY** being (in theory) and so it is perfectly reasonable to imaging a perfect God. A perfect island is illogical, a **PERFECT** God is not.

3. **CHARLES HARTSHORNE** argued in Anselm's Discovery that it was true that existence certainly adds something to the properties of a thing. Discussing the symptoms of a sickness could never compare to actually having it. The existence of the sickness adds to the understanding of it and so we can view the existence of God as something more than just the **DE DICTO** definition.

4. The first part of **ANSELM**'s argument aimed to show that the man who says there is no God is a fool. This still applies even if we do not follow Anselm so far as to prove that God must exist necessarily **A PRIORI**. Even the atheist must accept the definition of God, **DE DICTO**, as the creator of all things. This is what we mean by God.

So it is reasonable to postulate that God is not a **SUBJECT** of the universe. God is not within the universe to be discovered. God is not Zeus on Mt Olympus or Thor casting lightning bolts.

As creator God would be **TRANSCENDENTALLY OUTSIDE** the universe. Yet there is no way we, as **TEMPORAL** beings, can have any knowledge of what is in existence at the far reaches of the temporal universe, let alone outside the universe.

Therefore, if a man says in his heart "there is no God" and believes it with all sincerity, then he is a fool. All he can ever say is "I cannot know if there is a God".

Weaknesses - Ontological Argument

AQUINAS argued in Summa Theologica that God is not **SELF-EVIDENT** to us and as such we can never know God's nature. The **ONTOLOGICAL** Argument assumes that we can know God's nature ourselves. This is impossible.

IMMANUEL KANT argued i that existence could not be a **PREDICATE**. The statement 'God exists' is of the logical form S is P, that is **SUBJECT** is **PREDICATE**, e.g. grass (subject) is green (predicate). Upon finding an example we can observe it **A POSTERIORI** and answer either 'yes' or 'no' to the question 'is grass green?' To discover if grass exists we find some and then investigate. But upon finding the grass we need look no further at it, as we have shown it exists already. Therefore, existence does not operate like other properties that we need to investigate within a subject. (such as shape or colour). So existence is **NOT** a predicate of a **SUBJECT**.

BERTRAND RUSSELL argued in Philosophy of Language that when we talk of the existence of things we talk about something, that thing has descriptive features or predicates. We search for an X to match these predicates and then state 'yes, there is an example' or 'no, there is not'. This is a process of **INSTANTIATION** (providing a specific, real world example of an abstract idea). When we discuss existence we are seeking to instantiate it. We cannot say a thing exists if we cannot instantiate it **A POSTERIORI**. If we cannot instantiate God, then we can never say "God exists".

Confusions to Avoid

The challenges to each argument come as challenges to the **PREMISES**. The first that God is in fact a being than which nothing greater can be conceived and that we accept that definition, and the second, that existence is a **PREDICATE**, as existing in reality is better than in the mind alone. To defeat the argument, scholars attack these premises. NB **PREMISES** contain **ASSUMPTIONS** within them which may be **FALSE**.

Summary - Key Points

1. An a priori deductive argument where the conclusion follows logically from the premises.

2. Anselm's argument refuted by Gauilo's perfect island example.

3. Kant pointed out - existence is not a predicate like yellow in the sentence 'that's a yellow chair'. It is something that must be established a posteriori not assumed a priori.

4. Anyway, if God is truly the greatest imaginable being, why did he create a world with Tsumanis and viruses (an empirical objection)?

Possible Exam Questions (Ontological)

1. 'Anselm's Ontological Argument proves God exists logically.' Discuss.

2. Assess the claim that existence is a predicate.

3. "A priori arguments for God's existence are more persuasive than a posteriori arguments". Discuss

Key Quotes - Ontological Argument

"The ontological argument alone may be classified as an a priori argument, with all other arguments for God's existence being classified as a posteriori arguments". Michael Palmer, A Question of God page 2.

"God is the only being to which the ontological argument can apply because he is the only being whose non-existence is inconceivable". Michael Palmer A Question of God, page 9.

'The fool says in his heart "there is no God".' – Psalm 14:1-3

'There is doubt that there exists a being, than which nothing greater can be conceived, and it exists both in the understanding and in reality.' – Anselm

"We can no more extend our stock of theoretical insight by mere ideas, than a merchant can better his position by adding a few noughts to his cash account". Immanuel Kant

Arguments from Experience

Key Terms

- **ACTUALITY** - When something is in the state of doing something; what a thing is, e.g. fire is actually hot.

- **ANALOGY** - A comparison between two things using one to infer conclusions of the other

- **CONTINGENT** - Something that does not need to exist, it depends on something else to exist

- **NECESSARY** - Something that cannot not be the case

- **POTENTIALITY** - When something has the power to be something else, e.g. wood is potentially hot.

- **TELOS** - (Greek) purpose

The Cosmological Argument

Aquinas' First, Second and Third Way

Thomas **AQUINAS** presented the Cosmological Argument in his first three ways to prove God's existence **A POSTERIORI.**

1. First Way, From Motion

Everything is in a state of motion. This can be observed, e.g. seasons change, planets move in orbit.

Motion is the **CHANGE** from **POTENTIALITY** to **ACTUALITY**. E.g. the wood is cold but has the potential of being hot.

Nothing can move itself. The wood cannot make itself hot; it needs a source of heat, e.g. fire. Motion cannot regress infinitely. If there was no first motion, there would be no subsequent motion and therefore no current motion. But we **OBSERVE MOTION**.

There must be a First Motion that is itself **UNMOVED**. If the first motion were itself moved, then it would not be the first motion. It must be pure **ACTUALITY** and so unmoved.

This is what we call God. Aquinas is arguing that there is a **FIRST MOVER**. He is then stating the God of Christian faith is in fact this First or Prime Mover.

2. Second Way, From Causality

Everything is an **EFFECT** that is caused. We can observe cause and effect in our daily life, e.g. parents cause children to exist etc.

Nothing can cause itself. Everything must be caused by something that is not itself and **PRIOR**.

CAUSATION cannot regress infinitely. If there was no first cause, there would be no subsequent effects and therefore no current effects. But we observe cause and effect now.

So there must be a **FIRST CAUSE** that is itself uncaused. This is what we call God.

3. **Third Way, From Necessity and Contingency**

- All things are **CONTINGENT** (exist because of the way the world happens to be). Everything we observe could potentially not exist; nothing necessarily exists in and of itself.

- All things that exist **CONTINGENTLY** at one point did not exist. Allowing for an infinite amount of time, there could happily be a time when there was nothing in existence at all.

- Nothing comes from nothing. If ever there was nothing, then, since nothing can come from nothing, there would now be nothing at all. But evidently there is something.

- There must be a **NECESSARY EXISTENCE**. In order to account for why there is something at all, we must accept that there is something that cannot not exist, but is necessary.

Aquinas is arguing that there is a **NECESSARY BEING**: God.

Hume's Challenges

1. **We have no experience of universes being created**.

Hume argued that all we can ever know of **MOTION**, and **CAUSE** and **EFFECT** only comes from **EXPERIENCE**. Since we have never experienced the creation of universes, we can never discuss it with any kind of knowledge or certainty. This can be used to challenge the idea that all things need movement or initial cause. Since **INFINITE REGRESSION** is a theoretical possibility, and since we have never experienced the supposed 'initial motion/cause', we can never assume there is one.

2. **Causation cannot be observed**.

Hume argues the principle of causation itself cannot be experienced and so is **ASSUMED**. Hume gives the example of the billiard balls. When we see one ball supposedly hitting the other, we are in fact making an **ASSUMPTION**. We never actually experience the connection and causation between them. In this way we can challenge Aquinas as causation is **IMPLIED**, never observed, and so the second way is undermined.

3. **'Necessary being' has no logical meaning**.

When Aquinas discusses the idea of a **NECESSARY** being that is required if there are **CONTINGENT** things, Hume challenges this as the term 'necessary being' has no meaning in itself. Russell supports this by arguing that the only **NECESSARY** things are **ANALYTIC** propositions (true by definition), like 'triangles have three sides'. Hume supports Kant's claim that all existential propositions are **SYNTHETIC** and so no being can ever be said to exist by **NECESSITY**.

Strengths - Cosmological Argument

1. **AQUINAS'** Cosmological Argument reflects Aristotle's **FOUR CAUSES** and his argument for the **PRIME MOVER**.

- All things are moved from their material cause (**POTENTIALITY**) to their formal cause (**ACTUALITY**). And so if you trace back all movement you must come to a Prime Mover (First Mover).

- All things have an **EFFICIENT** cause (or causes) in order to achieve some **FINAL** cause (**EFFECT**). And so if you trace back all causes you must come to a Prime Mover (**FIRST** Cause).

2. Fr Friedrich **COPLESTONE** supported the cosmological argument by presenting his version of the argument from contingency in a radio debate with Bertrand Russell in 1948.

- Some things in the world are not the explanation for their own existence, e.g. we depend on our parents to exist and the air we breathe to continue existing.

- The world is the real or imagined aggregate of **CONTINGENT** things. There is no world **SEPARATE** from the aggregate of things in the world. And so nothing about the world explains the existence of it.

- We must look for a total explanation for all things. If we find it all well and good, if not we proceed further until we find a total explanation. This links to Gottfried **LEIBNIZ'** argument for sufficient reason.

Weaknesses - Cosmological Argument

1. Immanuel **KANT** argued that the process of cause and effect are subjects of the universe and as such we can never infer that they work beyond this universe. For this reason, we can never postulate what 'causes' this universe.

2. Bertrand **RUSSELL** argued that the terms used in the cosmological argument hold no meaning. Not only does **NECESSARY** being mean nothing, it makes no sense to infer complete chains of causation.

3. The argument produces a distant creator, not an **IMMANENT** sustainer.

The Teleological Argument

Aquinas & Paley

Thomas **AQUINAS** presented his **FIFTH WAY** to prove God's existence a posteriori.

1. **Fifth Way, From the Governance of the World**

Things that lack intelligence act for an **END** or **TELOS**. Things such as natural bodies all act towards some end, e.g. planets orbit stars, plants grow towards the sun and seasons change.

All things act as if **DESIGNED**. Things that lack knowledge are directed by things with **INTELLIGENCE**. The arrow cannot direct itself and so is directed to its mark by the archer.

Since everything in the universe moves towards its **PURPOSE** and cannot direct itself, there must be an intelligence that directs these things and moves all things towards their prescribed goals.

This is what we call God. Aquinas is arguing that there is a **SUPREME INTELLIGENCE**.

2. **Paley**

All things are **FIT FOR PURPOSE**. All natural bodies are suitably designed for their purposes, swans' necks are long enough to reach the bottom of ponds; and the eye is perfectly fit for seeing.

Design needs a **DESIGNER**.

The **ANALOGY** of the watch suggests that if the watch is designed by a watchmaker, then the world which is infinitely more complex than the watch must itself be designed by a world-maker.

Hume's Challenges

David Hume presented his challenges against teleological arguments in general, not against any one particular argument. There are many challenges but these are the most succinct:

1. **Fallacy of Analogy**

ANALOGY can only be used when comparing two similar things. When the world is compared to a **MACHINE** and it is inferred that the world must have a maker as the machine has a maker, this is a false use of **ANALOGY**. He famously said that the world is more like a **CABBAGE** than a machine; not because the world is anything like a cabbage, but because it is evidently nothing like a machine.

2. **Fallacy of Inference**

ORDER is inferred where there is no proof of it. Hume argued apparent order can come from chaos. Since 'order' is self-perpetuating, if all things started in **CHAOS**, when order randomly appears then it maintains itself and we infer an order to it.

3. **Assumption of One God**

Hume used the example of the ship being built by many shipwrights to show that it is very possible that there may be **MANY GODS** who are responsible for the world.

Strengths - Teleological Argument

1. **COMPLEXITY** - The teleological argument includes any observation of nature that leaves us no explanation for its existence other than God. Anthony Flew, following a lifetime of atheism, was finally converted to theism following the reflection of the double helix within DNA. He could no longer deny that the incredible complexity of DNA had no explanation other than God.

2. **BEAUTY** - Paul **DAVIES** argued in The Mind of God that science has allowed us to better understand the world, and in so doing has allowed us to see how we are connected to an intricate universe. This beauty denotes pattern and intention.

Weaknesses - Teleological Argument

1. **MALEVOLENCE** - John Stuart **MILL** argued that if there was a designer of the world, then this designer is either malevolent or stupid to create a world with so much natural evil within it.

2. **BEGS THE QUESTION** - Richard **SWINBURNE** argued that Aquinas' argument committed the **FALLACY** of begging the question. This is a factor in all teleological arguments where the premises infer design.

3. **SCIENTIFICALLY WRONG** - Richard **DAWKINS** - Paley was working with the best knowledge of his time, he was wrong as the appearance of the eye, or the swan's neck can all be accounted for by evolution, not by a designer.

Confusions to Avoid - Cosmological Argument

1. **AQUINAS** was not discussing **MOTION** and causation back in time. He was not saying that the first motion or **FIRST CAUSE** were at the start of the universe. The understanding of fixed point creation and the expansion of time and space was not firmly argued scientifically until the 20th Century. Aquinas was referring to first motion and first cause within the universe now. He was describing the nature of a God that sustains the world now.

2. David **HUME** wrote twenty-three years before William **PALEY**, so his Dialogues Concerning Natural Religion are not a response to Paley's version of the teleological argument. Though it is tempting to see Hume's challenge as saying that the world is not like a watch, and that the world is more like a cabbage than a watch, this is mistaken. Hume was more likely responding to the **NEWTONIAN MODEL** of the universe which saw it like a machine as we cannot experience **CAUSATION** and so we cannot infer this mechanical interpretation of the world.

Possible Exam Questions - Cosmological

1. Assess the claim that the cosmological argument proves that God exists a posteriori.

2. 'The teleological argument proves that the universe is designed.' Discuss.

3. 'Hume's challenges successfully disprove the arguments for God's existence.' Discuss.

4. Assess the claim that God's existence can be proven a posteriori.

Key Quotes - Cosmological Argument

'It is certain, and evident to our senses, that in the world some things are in motion.' – St Thomas Aquinas, Summa Theologica

'This being is either itself the reason for its own existence, or it is not. If it is, well and good. If not, then we must proceed further. But if we proceed to infinity in that sense, then there's no explanation of existence at all.' – Fr Friedrich Copleston,

Key Quotes - Teleological Argument

'Now whatever lacks intelligence cannot move towards an end, unless it be directed by some being endowed with knowledge and intelligence; as the arrow is shot to its mark by the archer.' – St Thomas Aquinas, Summa Theologica

'The inference we think is inevitable is that the watch must have had a maker.' – William Paley, Natural Theology

'Aquinas' statement that all things are directed by some mind towards a purpose, and that mind is God, commits the fallacy of begging the question. Things need a purpose, God gives things a purpose, therefore God must be the purpose.' – Richard Swinburne, The Essence of God

'Paley's argument is made with passionate sincerity and is informed by the best biological scholarship of the day, but it is wrong, gloriously and utterly wrong.' – Richard Dawkins, The Blind Watchmaker

God and the World

Religious Experience - Background

What makes **RELIGIOUS EXPERIENCE** different from any other experience? How do we know that an experience comes from God, and isn't just an illusion (as Freud believed) or a **PROJECTION** of our need for a father-figure? The variety of religious experience people claim to have (from the Bible times onwards) include dreams, voices, visitations, intuitions and the observation of a miraculous event. Does the classification of something as specifically **RELIGIOUS** simply reflect an attitude of **BELIEF**?

Key Terms

- **NUMINOUS** - The apprehension of the wholly other (a sense of wonder)

- **RELIGIOUS EXPERIENCE, DIRECT** - An encounter with God or an experience received from God (voice, vision, miracle etc)

- **RELIGIOUS EXPERIENCE, INDIRECT** - An understanding about God occurring through some temporal experience (birth, sunset, etc)

- **PSYCHOLOGICAL NEUROSIS** - An experience or way of thinking that is explicitly the product of the mind's functions

Structure of Thought

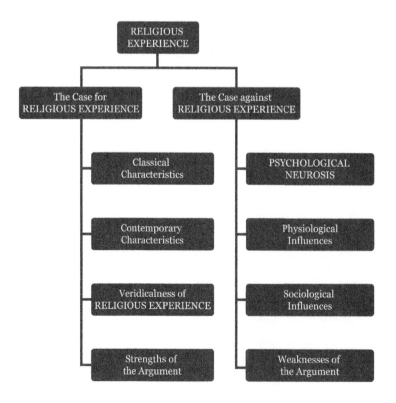

The Case for Religious Experience

Religious experience occurs throughout history and can be particularly identified within biblical and **CATHOLIC** history. These experiences have been explored and investigated to discover what makes an experience 'religious' and what, if anything, can qualify it as genuine.

Classical Characteristics of Religious Experiences

1. Voices

DISEMBODIED Voice: The voice will not come directly from a person, but rather will come from heaven or through some inanimate object, e.g. the voice of God came to **MOSES** disembodied through a burning bush (Exodus 3).

AUTHORITATIVE: The voice will give a command to the recipient and compel him/her into action based on that experience, e.g. St Paul was compelled to go to Damascus and seek out Ananias to be converted based on the direction of Jesus' voice on the road (Acts of the Apostles 9).

NOETIC: The voice will reveal some knowledge or information to the recipient which they would not have gained any other way, e.g. at Jesus' baptism the voice of God revealed that Jesus was in fact God's Son and that God was pleased with Jesus (Mark 1).

2. Visions

CORPOREAL: These visions are of a person in the appearance of flesh and can be interacted with though not everyone will necessarily be about to see them, e.g. St **BERNADETTE** saw Mary appear to her as a beautiful woman.

IMAGINATIVE: These visions appear within dreams and the recipient may receive particular knowledge or prophecy through it, e.g. **JOSEPH** was informed that Mary was pregnant through the power of the Holy Spirit and that he should not be afraid to marry her (**MATTHEW 1**).

INTELLECTUAL: These visions are more awareness of the presence of some being, being seen with the eye of the mind rather than in physical form, e.g. St Teresa of Avila claims she did not so much see Jesus, but was rather aware of him.

Contemporary Characteristics of Religious Experiences

1. William James' Varieties (Acronym PINT)

PASSIVE: All religious experiences must happen to the recipient in order to be religious; they cannot seek them out e.g. Moses was a shepherd in **MIDIAN** with no intention of returning to Egypt where he was wanted for murder, but experienced an encounter with God regardless in which he was directed to return to Egypt (**EXODUS 3**).

INEFFABLE: All religious experiences must either be beyond human powers to describe or must be of such a nature as they go beyond everyday experiences, so are difficult to grasp and explain, e.g. St **TERESA** of Avila used creative language to help her describe what she was experiencing and admitted that aspects could not be explained.

NOETIC: All religious experiences reveal some knowledge that the recipient could not gain by themselves; this may include the identity of the source of the experience, some **THEOLOGICAL** knowledge, or even a deeper understanding of the relationship between God and the recipient, e.g. St Bernadette was told by Mary that she was the **IMMACULATE CONCEPTION**, a revelation that went on to form Catholic dogma about Mary's nature.

TRANSIENT: While the religious experience is a short encounter, the effects of the experience are long lasting and often involve conversion, e.g. St Paul was a staunch Jew persecuting the Christians, but following his encounter with Christ he converted to Christianity and became one of the great Apostles of the early Christian Church.

2. Richard Swinburne's Direct or Indirect Distinction

PUBLIC ORDINARY: The interpretation of an ordinary encounter as something spiritual and meaningful, e.g. seeing the earth from orbit and realising how fragile life is.

PUBLIC EXTRAORDINARY: Being present during a miracle that goes beyond human powers to explain, e.g. witnessing a miraculous healing or one of the biblical miracles.

PRIVATE DESCRIBABLE: A Direct religious experience that can be fully described and understood, e.g. the interpretation of one of **JOSEPH**'s dreams (Genesis 37).

PRIVATE NON-DESCRIBABLE: A Direct religious experience which cannot be fully described or understood, e.g. the experiences of St Teresa of Avila.

PRIVATE NON-SPECIFIC: An **INDIRECT** religious experience where the individual sees the world in a different way to help them come to an understanding of God, e.g. Antony **FLEW**'s reflection of **DNA** as proof of God's involvement in the **DESIGN** of the universe.

3. Veridicalness (provable truthfulness) of Religious Experience

William James

- Religious experiences are **PSYCHOLOGICAL** phenomena; this means that they operate through the psyche. As such all people can have a religious experience; they are not unique to saints.

- Drugs and alcohol can open a recipient up to the divine. In the same way that Indian **YOGI** train their bodies to be more receptive to the divine, drugs and alcohol can lower the inhibitions of the individual to make them more receptive to the divine without instigating the encounter.

- The testimonies of Stephen **BRADLEY** and **S. H. HADLEY**, as well as the biblical experiences and experiences of the Catholic mystics, all share the same **FOUR CHARACTERISTICS** of **religious experience** (acronym **PINT**), which show that they do in fact take place and affect the individuals' lives directly. If they were not genuine they would not have such impact on them to make them change their lives and convert to a new way of life.

Richard Swinburne's Two Principles

- The **PRINCIPLE OF CREDULITY** dictates that we accept the genuineness of the experiences we have unless we have a compelling reason not to, e.g. we do not believe in God for other reasons, we are drunk etc.

- The **PRINCIPLE OF TESTIMONY** dictates that we should accept the genuineness of other people's testimonies about religious experiences as we accept their testimonies about all other things; there is no difference about a religious experience and so we should not discriminate against religious experiences.

Strengths - Argument from Religious Experience

1. **FRIEDRICH SCHLEIERMACHER** argued that we all have a consciousness for the divine. This supports **JAMES'** point that religious experiences are natural to us and that we are the ones who block it off by attaching ourselves to the mundane world.

2. **RUDOLF OTTO** argued that religious experiences were the apprehension of the wholly 'other'. This would respond to Marx' challenge as the wholly other is **INEFFABLE** to us. We would have to translate it into language that we understood and that language would likely be influenced by our societies.

3. **RICHARD SWINBURNE** argued that accounts of religious experiences were evidence in themselves. The **PRINCIPLE OF TESTIMONY** is used within scientific communities as evidence for theories and proofs. We should be able to use it to justify religious experiences as well.

4. **WILLIAM ALSTON** argued that if we accept our senses with regards to ordinary experiences, there is no reason why we should suddenly stop relying on them in terms of religious experiences. This would be a form of **ELITISM**.

The Case against Religious Experience

The case against religious experiences comes from interpreting them as the product of influences on the **PSYCHE**, either due to direct **NEUROSIS** or as a result of physiological or sociological influences.

Psychological Neurosis - the Case Against Religious Experience

SIGMUND FREUD argued that religion was itself a neurosis stemming from childhood neurosis. Belief in God was the **PROJECTION** of the need for an eternal **FATHER FIGURE** and as such had no basis in reality. This being the case, religious experience is nothing more than our need to manifest these neurotic ideas into justifications for our behaviour. This is all supported by Freud's research into the obsessive behaviour of patients at Salpêtriére hospital.

TIMOTHY LEARY presented his findings - when mystical accounts were mixed with the accounts of drug users, the accounts were **INDISTINGUISHABLE**, which suggests that there is nothing distinctive about so-called 'religious' experiences. Rather, they are all products of the psyche.

JL MACKIE argued that if religious experiences were in any way psychological, then those who accept that they have any authority at all are **INSUFFICIENTLY CRITICAL** of them. We should not accept the authority of these experiences if there is any way that they can be accounted for by the psyche itself.

Physiological Influences - the case against Religious Experience

HARLOW described the character of Phineas **GAGE**, a railway foreman, as agreeable and well-liked. Following the accident which resulted in a pole being thrust into his brain, his character changed markedly. This suggests that any physiological changes to the person that affect the brain in any way, will affect his behaviour and experiences. So, 'religious' experiences can be accounted for by **PHYSIOLOGICAL** changes in the person.

LANSBOROUGH argued that St Paul may well have suffered temporal lobe epilepsy, which caused his temporary blindness and the voice he heard.

Many of the Catholic mystics, St **TERESA** of Avila, St Bernadette, St Faustina all suffered severe sicknesses prior to their mystical encounters. It is possible that either the **SICKNESS** itself or any medication they received to combat it instigated the apparent 'religious' experience.

Sociological Influences - the Case Against Religious Experience

KARL MARX argued that a person's society directly affects the kinds of experiences they have. A Christian would encounter Jesus or Mary while a Hindu would encounter Vishnu. This is understandable as their societies dictate what they receive. Marx argued that religion was the **OPIUM** of the people. Much like **FREUD**, he was cynical of the role of religion on people's behaviour and so he rejected it. For **MARX**, the Church was an institution that suppressed the masses so preventing them from flourishing, and so religious experience is part of that institution and propaganda that makes us fall into line. If we believe that God speaks to the leaders of the institution then we are more likely to obey them and do what we are told.

Weaknesses of the Argument from Religious Experience

1. **SEXUAL REPRESSION** - When reading St Teresa of Avila's encounter with the Seraphim from a Freudian perspective, a lot of sexual imagery can be identified. This supports the argument that such experiences are in fact suppressed sexual tension disguised by neurosis and expressed as religious encounters.

2. **OUTDATED VIEW OF MIND** - Modern understanding of the mind has allowed us to probe further into the way we gain knowledge and experiences. This allows us to be more critical about what we experience or think we are experiencing, including 'religious' experiences.

3. **LACK OF RIGOUR** - Anthony O'Hear argued that we should apply checks when considering religious experiences:

   - Checking over **TIME**: Is the experience consistent over a period of time?

   - Checking with other **SENSES**: Do other senses support the initial encounter/experience?

   - Checking with other checkers: Do other **PEOPLE** agree with the genuineness of the initial encounter?

4. If an experience cannot be checked then it is not **SCIENTIFICALLY VERIFIED**. While this does not mean that it is not real or genuine, it does mean that we cannot discuss the experience in the same way that we discuss other experiences.

Confusions to Avoid - Religious Experience

The questions that surround the topic of religious experience all link to one central theme: the **AUTHORITY** of religious experiences over the recipient. If the religious experience is genuine then it has authority over the recipient. If it is not genuine then it should have no authority over them.

All challenges to religious experiences are ultimately challenges to the authority we should grant to the experience. If there is a **PSYCHOLOGICAL** influence then the experience is the product of the mind, not the workings of God. If there is a physiological influence, then the experience is the effect of sickness and so we should treat the patient, not deem their words divine.

We should always look for the line of debate and see how the question of authority of the experience is probed, and the influence the experience has on the recipient.

The **CHARACTERISTICS** of religious experiences do not answer this question by themselves. They should be used in conjunction with the arguments for the genuineness of the experiences and be used to show how religious experiences share characteristics and lead to positive lifestyles and conversions. If the experiences have similar attributes and lead to positive ends, it then supports the genuineness of them as religious experiences.

Possible Exam Questions - Religious Experience

1. Assess the claim that religious experiences prove that God exists.

2. 'Religious experiences are nothing more than forms of psychological neurosis.' Discuss.

3. "Personal testimony can never be reliable evidence for God's existence". Discuss

4. Critically compare corporate religious experiences with individual experiences as a basis for belief in God.

Key Quotes - Religious Experience

'The sway of alcohol over mankind is unquestionably due to its power to stimulate the mystical faculties of human nature.' – William James, Lecture XVI and XVII on Mysticism

'Religion is comparable to a childhood neurosis.' – Sigmund Freud, The Future of an Illusion

'Suppose that drugs can induce experiences that are indistinguishable from religious ones, and that we can respect their reports. Do they shed any light, not (we now ask) on life, but on the nature of the religious life?' – Huston Smith, Do Drugs have Religious Import?

'If it seems to a subject that X is present, then probably X is present; what one seems to perceive is probably so.' – Richard Swinburne, The Existence of God

The Problem of Evil

Key Terms

- **BENEVOLENCE** - The characteristic that God loves us all

- **MORAL EVIL** - The bad things that people do to others to cause suffering

- **NATURAL EVIL** - The bad things that happen in nature that cause suffering

- **OMNIPOTENCE** - The belief that God has all power to do anything

- **OMNISCIENCE** - The belief that God knows all that is happening in the world

Structure of Thought

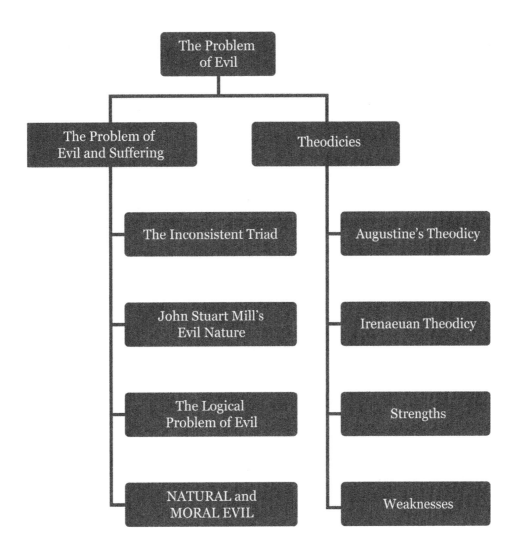

The Problem of Evil and Suffering

The Problem of Evil and Suffering is often called the rock of **ATHEISM**. It challenges the belief in God based on the classical Judaeo-Christian understanding that God is **BENEVOLENT** (all-loving), all-powerful and all-knowing. It considers the revealed nature of God as **INCOMPATIBLE** with the existence of evil and suffering in the world.

The Inconsistent Triad

The inconsistent triad (three characteristics of God) is the **CLASSICAL CHALLENGE** against God's existence based in the existence of evil and suffering. David **HUME** classically presented it.

- Is God able to prevent evil, but not able? Then he is not **OMNIPOTENT**.

- Is God able, but not willing? Then he is **MALEVOLENT**.

- Is he both able and willing? Then where does evil come from?

- Is he neither able nor willing? Then why call him God?

This argument identifies **EVIL** with **SUFFERING** and suggests that if God did exist and were God an all loving, all powerful God as He is presented in classical Christian Theology, then God would both want and be able to **PREVENT SUFFERING** amongst human beings whom he created and supposedly loves. The fact that suffering persists is indication that there is **NOT** a loving God who sustains and watches over the world otherwise He would do something to relieve that suffering.

John Stuart Mill's Evil Nature

MILL argued that the evil and suffering within the natural world is enough to prove that there can be no **BENEVOLENT** designer of the world as no good being would permit such suffering within nature.

Richard **DAWKINS** used the **DIGGER WASP** to develop this point. The wasp paralyses the caterpillar to lay eggs inside it. When the eggs hatch, the caterpillar suffers and dies. This shows evil in nature (if we assume destruction is evil).

J.L. Mackie and H.L. McCloskey's Logical Problem of Evil

MACKIE and **McCLOSKEY** presented a variation of the classical Inconsistent Triad by including God's supposed **OMNISCIENCE** in the equation.

- God is **OMNIPOTENT**. He is able to stop evil.

- God is **OMNISCIENT**. He knows about the suffering that would happen.

- God is **OMNIBENEVOLENT**. He does not want us to suffer.

- Evil exists. People suffer though God knows about it, can and wants to prevent it.

This variation places the **MORAL ACCOUNTABILITY** on God as, not only should God want and be able to prevent suffering, God **INTENTIONALLY** created a world where He knew suffering would take place. God directly and willingly created a world where He knew people would suffer and die. This **PRE-KNOWLEDGE** shows that there cannot be a good and powerful God.

Natural and Moral Evils

Peter **VARDY** identified five types/causes of natural suffering that takes place in the world.

1. **Natural disasters**: earthquakes, tsunamis etc.

2. **Diseases**: cancer, diabetes etc.

3. **Psychological illness**: bipolar, multiple personality, autism etc.

4. **Human frailty**: pain during childbirth, colds and susceptibility to sickness.

5. **Animal suffering**: animals being killed by other animals.

Brian **HEBBLETHWAITE** argued that **MORAL EVIL**, the evils done to others, is received and experienced by our naturally-occurring senses. For this reason, moral evils are in fact naturally suffered and so moral evil is also a type of **NATURAL EVIL**.

The Theodicies

AUGUSTINE's Theodicy (a defence of God's character in the face of objections) stresses **HUMAN RESPONSIBILITY**.

St Augustine argued that evil and suffering were not accountable to God, but rather to **HUMANITY**. His theodicy was an attempt to demonstrate how we are ultimately responsible for the evil and suffering in the world.

Evil as Privation

Augustine said that evil was a **PRIVATION** (a lack of something), not a force of its own. God created all things **PERFECTLY** and evil is only a corruption of that good thing. In the same way that bad teeth are simply good teeth that have not been taken care of, evil in the world is good things that have not been **NURTURED** and cared for, people not doing what they are supposed to be doing. So all that is **EVIL** came from God but when it did, it was still **GOOD**.

The Fall of Adam and Eve

Augustine was not a **CREATIONIST** and so did not believe in the literal interpretation of Genesis 1 and 2, however, he used it to help teach how evil entered the world. It is through human disobedience that evil comes into the world. We disobey God and the ripple effects have consequences throughout creation.

Natural Evil

Augustine's appealing to Adam and Eve and how disobedience causes evil satisfactorily explains **MORAL EVIL**, but not **NATURAL**. For this, Augustine discussed how the Fall of Mankind rippled into the spiritual dimension, and so even **ANGELS** fell from grace, and they cause **NATURAL EVIL** in the world. This is the hierarchy of creation and the consequences of human disobedience.

The Eschatological Question

In the end-times (**ESCHATON**) God will judge us all based on our actions and how much we obeyed or disobeyed God.

Irenaean Theodicy

St **IRANAEUS** presented an alternative theodicy to Augustine, which was easier to fit into the workings of everyday life. It explores evil as a part of God's creation, rather than an **UNWANTED CONSEQUENCE** which would lead to a questioning of God's power to prevent it.

I. **Evil is good**

   Primarily, Irenaeus argued that evil, while bringing suffering, was not in itself a bad thing, but rather a **NECESSARY TOOL** to help us develop as human beings. We need **SUFFERING**, risk and pain in order to make the right choices and develop as people. If we live a life without suffering we will never learn anything and will never value the **GOODNESS OF GOD**.

II. **Adam and Eve**

   While Irenaeus was a **CREATIONIST**, he did not see it **NECESSARY** to read Genesis in that way in order to learn from it.

III. **Image and Likeness**

   Irenaeus' theodicy requires us to re-read the creation story slightly. While God created us in his **IMAGE**, in that we are capable of rational and moral thinking, He did not create us in his **LIKENESS**, but rather we need to live, learn and suffer in order to gain God's likeness.

Hick's Variation of Irenaeus' Theodicy

I. **Soul-Making**

   John **HICK** argued that we are on earth for the purpose of **SOUL-MAKING**. We learn through suffering, and so grow on earth and become more like God.

II. **Epistemic Distance**

We are created at a distance from God, not a geographical distance (e.g. land and sky), but rather an **EPISTEMIC** one (episteme is Greek for knowledge), a **KNOWLEDGE GAP** that cannot be crossed on our terms. Humans are not born with the **INNATE KNOWLEDGE** of God's existence yet have to seek God through faith.

Through our lives we must work on our souls in order to make them more perfect so that we can cross that distance. However, that can never be perfectly done in a lifetime, so **ESCHATOLOGICALLY** (at the end of time) God will cover that distance for us.

This leads to the belief in **UNIVERSAL SALVATION** that in the end all will be saved.

III. **Christ, the New Adam**

Hick argued that Christ was the **NEW ADAM** and did what Adam could not do, resist temptation and ultimately show us how to be perfect. Christ tells us to "be perfect, as your Father in heaven is perfect". This is our call and while we are not perfect on earth we suffer through **NATURAL** and **MORAL EVIL** as Christ suffered before us.

Strengths - Augustinian & Irenaean Theodicy

1. **Augustine**

Brian **DAVIES** supported Augustine's notion that evil is a **PRIVATION** rather than a **SUBSTANCE** in his example of bad deckchairs and sour grapes, all of which were examples of fallen objects. This agrees with **ARISTOTLE**'s notion of goodness as the **FULFILMENT** of our final cause (**EUDAIMONIA** in Greek).

Alvin **PLANTINGA** argued that Augustine was right that **MORAL EVIL** is accountable to human beings and that we cannot blame God - better that God created free agents than obedient robots.

2. **Irenaeus and Hick**

This theodicy avoids the problems of a **PERFECT CREATION** going wrong which Augustine's theodicy faces. Since evil is part of God's creation there is no "problem of evil as such, as evil is part of the plan of God".

This theodicy explains the importance of life on earth as a time of **DEVELOPMENT** and spiritual growth. This is absent in other theodicies and explains why we are here at all.

Gottfried **LEIBNIZ** argued that this must be the best of all possible worlds and the Irenaeus/Hick theodicy follows that model in that this is the only way the world could be. Without **FREEDOM** we would be incapable of **GOODNESS** and without suffering we would be incapable of **GROWTH**.

Weaknesses - Augustinian & Irenaean Theodicy

1. **Augustine**

Friedrich **SCHLEIERMACHER** pointed out the **LOGICAL CONTRADICTION** in the idea that God created a perfect world which went wrong. Augustine did not address this. Grapes can go sour if you leave them out in the sun, but why would God leave nature designed with **IMPERFECTIONS** - surely God's perfect nature would inform him?

Since Augustine did not believe in the **LITERAL INTERPRETATION** of the Creation story or the story of the Fall of Adam, why rely on it to explain **NATURAL EVIL** in the world? The idea that all natural evil comes from the **FALLEN ANGELS** who rebelled following the Fall of Adam seems far-fetched.

The existence of **HELL** suggests that God knew his creation would disobey Him and that things would go 'wrong'.

2. **Irenaeus and Hick**

IRANAEUS' theodicy requires an **UNORTHODOX** reading of creation - we are meant to believe we are not made in God's image and likeness, which the Catholic Church maintains we are. The principle of **UNIVERSAL SALVATION**, which **HICK** argues, is again counter to mainstream Christianity. The belief that we might go to hell if we are bad is a **NECESSITY** if God is good and just and we are free.

This theodicy argues that we have suffering in order to learn and make our **SOULS** complete, but this does not justify the deaths of infants and even the unborn that had no chance to live or learn. The **END** cannot morally justify the **MEANS**. Even if evil and suffering (the **MEANS**) did enable us to forge perfect souls (the **END**, there is so much evil and suffering that surely God would be able to find another way, e.g. a life simulator where people did not suffer.

Confusions to Avoid - Theodicy

St Augustine uses the **FALL** of Adam and Eve to explain human **FREE** WILL and wickedness. In fact, he argued that **ORIGINAL SIN** alone was enough to damn all humanity to hell. However, Augustine was not a Creationist; he did not believe that the Creation stories of Genesis were intended to be literally read. Conversely, St **IRENAEUS'** theodicy teaches it does not matter if Adam and Eve were real, as every time we disobey God we are repeating the sin of Adam and Eve, but he was in fact a **CREATIONIST**.Exam Questions - Theodicy

1. 'There is no solution to the problem of evil and suffering.' Discuss.

2. Assess the success of John Hick's argument for soul-making as a development of Irenaeus' theodicy.

3. Assess which logical or evidential aspects of the problem of evil pose the greatest challenge to belief.

4. Critically assess whether it is possible to defend monotheism in the face of the existence of evil.

Key Quotes - Theodicy

'When a thing is corrupted, its corruption is an evil because it is a privation of the good.' – St Augustine

'Is God willing to prevent evil, but unable to do so? Then he is not omnipotent. Is God able to prevent evil, but is not willing to? Then he is malevolent. – David Hume

'Nearly all the things which men are hanged or imprisoned for doing to one another are nature's everyday performances.' – John Stuart Mill

"Several parts of the essential theological doctrine are inconsistent with one another.' – J.L. Mackie

Nature of God

Background

What is God's nature and character like - and how can we know? God is usually defined by characteristics - positive ones, such as **OMNIPOTENCE** and **BENEVOLENCE** and negative ones such as **IMMORTALITY** and **INVISIBILITY**. The classical descriptions of God's **ATTRIBUTES** have been challenged throughout history, starting with the Greeks; **PLATO** introduced us to **EUTHYPHRO's DILEMMA**, for example. In recent times can a God of **JUSTICE** and **LOVE** really ignore the plight of the starving and the refugee - and theology after the **HOLOCAUST** was never the same again - as **ELIE WIESEL** declared in his book **NIGHT** - "Where is God? There he is hanging on a tree". For evil to exist on such a scale it seemed only possible for Wiesel to believe that God was himself complicit in doing nothing, or did not exist at all. As a **SYNOPTIC** point, **LIBERATION THEOLOGY** (in the Christian Thought paper) invites us to conceive of God as the **REVOLUTIONARY LIBERATOR** on the side of the poor and oppressed. This new attribute of God led theologians of liberation to be initially suppressed and silenced by the Church.

Key Terms

- **BENEVOLENT** – The belief that God is all loving.

- **ETERNAL** – The belief that God exists not inside time, but outside it. God is a-temporal.

- **EVERLASTING** – On-going within the universe.

- **PREDESTINATION** – the belief that God has already decided what will happen to you.

- **OMNIPOTENCE** – The belief that God is all-powerful

- **OMNISCIENCE** – The belief that God is all-knowing.

- **THEOPHANY** – An event revealing the nature of God

- **TIMELESS** – The belief that God is outside of time.

Omnipotence

Biblical Revelation

GENESIS suggests that God is **OMNIPOTENT**, in various examples of **THEOPHANY**, e.g. the Creation story, the Flood and the miracles God performs. The Creation story lends to the Judeo-Christian tradition belief that God created the world **EX NIHILO** –from nothing. With only the power of his commands, all things come to be, as in **DIVINE COMMAND THEORY** in Ethics. The story of the Flood shows the consequences when God chooses to remove his sustaining hand. Finally, in the various examples of miracles within the Bible, not least when He stops the sun in the sky to give **JOSHUA** time to defeat the Amorites in the Book of Joshua, show that God can act in the world and does so with great and limitless power.

Greek Philosophical Thought

The Essential **FORM** of Goodness, theorised by **PLATO** in his Republic, was later identified with Plotinus' The One, the God that is responsible for all things. In this way, God can be identified with the Essential **FORM** of Goodness which gives life to all things, so God is all powerful as He is the source of all that is. Further, in **ARISTOTLE**'s Metaphysics, we see the nature of the **PRIME MOVER**, that which draws all things to itself, the **TELOS** of the world; the first motion that moves all other things in the universe. Such is the power of God.

Interpretations of Omnipotence

OMNIPOTENCE is the belief that God is all-powerful. This can mean one of three possible things:

1. God's ability to do anything including the **LOGICALLY IMPOSSIBLE**.

The attitude that God can do the **LOGICALLY POSSIBLE** and **IMPOSSIBLE** appears in the work of the French mathematician Rene **DESCARTES**. God created the universe and so all apparent logic within it is part of that creation including the **AXIOMS** which are the foundation of all rational knowledge. Since it is all part of God's creation, God is above maths and logic and so God cannot be bound by or subject to it. Therefore, if he wished to change it, He has the power to do so. God is not limited by our understanding of what is logically possible.

2. God's ability to do what is **LOGICALLY POSSIBLE** for God to do.

This attitude is notably held by St Thomas **AQUINAS**. Certain limitations can be placed upon what God can do, including: changing history, sinning, being caught in logical traps, e.g. creating square circles etc. Aquinas's notion of God's omnipotence only took into account what **LOGIC** would permit. Anything that **CONTRADICTS** itself cannot be considered part of God's **OMNIPOTENCE**, e.g. if by square we mean four-sided shape, it is logically contradictory to expect God to create a one-sided four-sided shape. That is a limitation of our own understanding, not of God. If we accept history as events that have happened, we cannot logically expect God to make events that have happened not have happened. That is a limitation on our **UNDERSTANDING**, not God's **POWER**.

3. Omnipotence is a general statement of the Power of God with two possible meanings (**PROPOSITIONAL** & **NON-PROPOSITIONAL**)

Taking the Bible as the primary source of our understanding of God of Judeo-Christian tradition as **OMNIPOTENT**, we can read revelation about omnipotence in one of two ways: **PROPOSITIONALLY** and **NON-PROPOSITIONALLY**. If we read the Bible propositionally we must accept all propositions about God's power as statements of **FACT**. The problem is that statements like 'God held the sun in the sky' give us varied and inexplicable gauges for God's power. If we read the Bible non-propositionally, then statements like 'God made the world in six days' have a **SYMBOLIC** meaning and are reflections of people's understanding about God, not qualifications of what God's **OMNIPOTENCE** means. The problem is that we do not accurately know what it means to call God omnipotent at all.

Benevolence & Human Suffering

Challenge: Why would an all loving God allow human suffering?

Answer: The answer to this is that our suffering does not make God bad. This can be explained through a number of **THEODICIES**, most notably the Augustinian theodicy showing that suffering is a consequence of human **FREE WILL** rather than God's malign will, and **IRENAEUS**' theodicy where human suffering is a part of God's ultimate **PLAN** to help us become more like God, as reflected, for example in the book of **JOB**. However, there is one other way of seeing the existence of suffering by identifying a **NATURALISTIC FALLACY**. Just because something is a certain way, does not make it good or evil. For example, the eighteenth century utilitarian Jeremy **BENTHAM** thought that goodness is tantamount to pleasure and evil to suffering, and could be calculated **EMPIRICALLY** by the Hedonic Calculus. But the description 'I feel pleasure' doesn't entail the conclusion 'pleasure is good'. Therefore, the notion that there is a problem of evil on account of suffering in the world and that this challenges the nature of God as **BENEVOLENT** is a category error. 'God is bad' doesn't follow from 'there is suffering'. Just because people suffer, does not mean God is evil for allowing it.

The Existence of Hell

Challenge: How can a **BENEVOLENT** God allow anyone to go to hell?

Answer: The **ROMAN CATHOLIC** Church encourages the acceptance of belief in Saints who are in heaven, but has never committed itself to stating that anyone is in hell, as only God can judge the **HEART**. Ultimately, God does not want people to go to hell, however, if God is love and if humans have free will, then that love must be all-encompassing, and any human freedom that seeks to reject it must lovingly be accepted. Therefore, God is bound by his own **NATURE** to allow for hell, the place where people send themselves through their own rejection of God's love. Another way of thinking about hell is as C. S. **LEWIS** said: 'the door to hell is locked from the inside'. This means that it is we who **CHOOSE** to condemn ourselves, not God who wishes to condemn us.

SYNOPTIC point - in the Christian Thought paper we consider Calvin's view of evil and hell, which entails PREDESTINATION of the saints to heaven and the sinners to hell. Only certain strands of PROTESTANTISM believe this: most hold that human FREE WILL determines our fate.

The Existence of Miracles

Challenge: How can a **BENEVOLENT** God perform miracles for some and not others?

Answer: This challenge was put forward by Maurice **WILES** who argued that God cannot possibly act in the world as it would be **UNJUST** for God to intercede for the Hebrews in Egypt, but not in Auschwitz.

A response to this requires that we re-evaluate how we readB **REVELATION.** If we read it **PROPOSITIONALLY**, then in fact it appears as though God takes sides and favours some over others and must trust that God knows what He is doing. However, if we read revelation **NON-PROPOSITIONALLY**, then we are more at liberty to interpret miracle events as miraculum or **WONDROUS EVENTS** which may or may not have supernatural explanations even if they do lead to belief in God.

Morality

Challenge: Is God the source of morality?

EUTHYPHRO's dilemma: 'Is the pious pious because the gods love it or do they love it because they are pious?' can be stated more simply as 'is something good because God commands it, or does God command it because it is good?'.

Analysis of the problem: There is a problem with **BOTH** forks of Euthyphro's dilemma:

1. Things are good because God says so: we see this when God issues the **TEN COMMANDMENTS**, when he determines the law that should be obeyed and when he punishes people for disobeying Him. This causes a problem as it shows God to be a moral dictator who, in theory, could change his mind and make something else good. The **ARBITRARINESS** problem exists because some commands in the Bible appear to be **EVIL** eg Joshua is commanded by the Lord to kill every living thing including children in the cities of **AI** and **JERICHO**.

2. God says things are good because they are: this is evident if we think about how the commands of God fit with our understanding of morality through **REASON** and universalisation. This causes a problem as it shows that God merely upholds what is **OBJECTIVELY GOOD** already, therefore, God is not the **SOURCE** of moral goodness, but only an enforcer of goodness.

Answer: Goodness must be a reflection of God's **NATURE**, so God commands what is good because it is his nature and the commandments reflect that nature. If God is pure **ACTUALITY**, as Aristotle suggests, then goodness is fulfilling our **PURPOSE** which is ordained by God. If God is the essence of goodness, as Plato implies, then all our laws and commands that appear in revelation are **SHADOWS** of that nature. They are commanded because they resemble God's nature of goodness.

Omniscience

Definition of Omniscience

God's knowledge can be explained as being either:

- Limited knowledge

- Unlimited knowledge

Limited Knowledge

This position was presented most notably by Richard **SWINBURNE** and means that God is limited as to what He can **LOGICALLY** know. This form of limitation is impacted by the way we define God's **ETERNITY**, but simply put means that God gains knowledge as we gain knowledge. This responds to the problem of **SUFFERING** as God has no **FUTURE KNOWLEDGE** but rather learns as we learn. The difference is that God knows everything we have done, and does not forget. We see evidence of this in **GENESIS** and in **1 SAMUEL** where God learns that Adam and Eve have disobeyed Him, and where God is displeased with David's decisions after they have all taken place. (such as David ensuring **URIAH** husband of **BATHSHEBA** died in battle so that he could marry her).

Unlimited knowledge

This position is the most commonly accepted notion of omniscience and St **AUGUSTINE** and St Thomas **AQUINAS** both hold this position. This is the belief that God has all knowledge, past, present and future. It means that there is nothing that God's **PROVIDENCE** (foreknowledge) cannot know. Any decision is known to God and nothing can fool Him. For **AUGUSTINE**, this position rests on the idea that God is **OUTSIDE** the universe and so his knowledge comes from an **ETERNAL** perspective. For Aquinas this may well rest on his **ARISTOTELEAN** influences. He argues that, since God is not physical and neither is knowledge, God can possess all knowledge, whereas we must learn it.

Free Will

The problem of human free will occurs when we consider God's **OMNISCIENCE**. If God is unlimited in his knowledge, and can never be wrong, then He knows all our future actions, making our actions fixed (predetermined) and humans not free. **AUGUSTINE** discusses this when dealing with **PREDESTINATION**; we are predestined in so far as God knows our actions but does not force us to do them. Instead, he pre-ordains our actions, and then watches what we do, and knows the results of our actions. Augustine takes it as a given that God does not fix our actions, but does not fully explain the apparent paradox.

SCHLEIERMACHER attempts to resolve the problem by suggesting that God's knowledge is like that of friends, intimate and accurate but not **CONTROLLING**. Luis of **MOLINA** attempted to explain it by suggesting that God knows all possible futures, but Elizabeth **ANSCOMBE** argued that such knowledge would be no knowledge at all. Additionally, Gottfried **LEIBNIZ** argued that this was the best of all possible worlds, so there would be no alternative futures for God to know.

Eternity as Timelessness

BOETHIUS addressed the issue of human free will in book five of his **CONSOLATIONS** of Philosophy as a conversation with **LADY PHILOSOPHY**. He presented the problem that if God knows all future actions and can never be wrong then we cannot have free will. He gives the example of the man watching another man sitting. One places a **NECESSITY** on the other. 'A' must be sitting if 'B' sees 'A' sitting. And 'B' must be watching 'A' sitting if 'A' is actually sitting. So if God sees beforehand what I do, then He necessitates it. Lady Philosophy resolves this problem by identifying God's perspective as one of an **ETERNAL** God outside of time (hence **TIMELESS**).

Lady Philosophy suggested the problem lies in human understanding of **ETERNITY**, rather than the problem of God's **KNOWLEDGE**. Knowledge is dependent not on the subject, but the **KNOWER**. In the same way that an adult can know a phone in a more sophisticated way to a baby, God can know us in a more sophisticated way than we know each other. She presented four spheres of knowledge.

1. Sensory

2. Imaginative

3. Rational

4. Pure Intellectual

A knower of one sphere can know the previous but never the next so we can never know subjects as God knows them. Additionally, Lady Philosophy suggested that God's **ETERNAL** perspective means that He sees every event in history in a **PERFECT PRESENT**, not in temporal sequence but in an **A-TEMPORAL** present. So time does not pass for God, it is static. We experience time, God does not. In this way, God can know all things without influencing them for human beings.

AUGUSTINE discusses the problem of considering a 'time' before God since it was God who created time. Augustine sees God as **TRANSCENDENT**, that is a-temporal and outside of space itself. So God's **ETERNITY** means that God is **TIMELESS**. All questions of God's nature must be considered from a non-spatiotemporal perspective. If God is outside of time, then God cannot change as change requires time. God is **IMMUTABLE** (God does not change), which suggests that God wills from **ETERNITY**. There was never a time when God changed what he wills. E.g. God must have willed the universe eternally.

This position was later reaffirmed by St Thomas **AQUINAS** who was heavily influenced by **BOETHIUS** and Augustine. He repeats Boethius' notion that God sees everything in an **ETERNAL** simultaneous present. Aquinas sees God as the **UNMOVED MOVER**, or uncaused cause. This can only make sense if God is an **ETERNAL TRANSCENDENT** being. From this position, God is timeless.

Anthony **KENNY** criticises Aquinas with his challenge that if his own writings are simultaneous with **ETERNITY** as is Rome's burning under **NERO**, then the writing of Kenny's paper takes place simultaneously as Nero's actions. However, Kenny's is a misunderstanding. God sees all simultaneously, this does not mean that two temporal events are simultaneous with each other. All temporal events follow the course of time, but God observes them simultaneously because of the **UNIQUE NATURE** of God being **TIMELESS** - God 'sees' everything outside of time.

Eternity as Everlasting

This position is presented by Richard **SWINBURNE** as part of his attempt to reconcile God's **OMNISCIENCE** with the problem of evil and suffering and free will. Within the Bible, God is revealed to learn along the same timeline as we do. God learns as we learn. This can only make sense if God is **EVERLASTING** within the universe rather than outside of it. Swinburne argued that for God to know what it is to be in the world in 1995, He needed to be in the world in 1995. This perspective also makes sense in terms of how we build a relationship with God. If God is within the world, then we can pray to God and He can answer. God can perform miracles and take an interest in our lives. If God is **ETERNAL**, then, as **BOETHIUS** suggests, prayers are in vain.

Swinburne's position does have weaknesses. As **AUGUSTINE** suggested, if God created all things then time is one of those things, and God cannot be subject to time. Additionally, this **LIMITS** God considerably as God is now subject to time. It raises questions about how God could create the world if God is within the boundaries of the world and time.

Confusions to Avoid - Nature of God

I. The Problem of Evil and Suffering is not identical with the issues surrounding the character of God. The problem of evil is indeed a problem raised by each of the characteristics of God: **OMNIPOTENCE, BENEVOLENCE, OMNISCIENCE** and God's **ETERNAL** existence. However, any questions in this section will not be expecting a Problem of Evil essay. Rather, the problems can be raised but should be raised directly with regard to the nature of that characteristic, and solutions should be presented that are in line with addressing that characteristic.

II. A failure to separate and then link Greek and Christian thinkers. The influence of the **GREEKS** (**PLATO** & **ARISTOTLE**) can never be understated. They are the foundation of so much philosophy, however, when addressing the nature of God, we need to make it clear we know that the Greeks are discussing God in a more abstract sense, the Essential **FORM** of Goodness, the **PRIME MOVER** whereas Boethius, Augustine and Aquinas are referring specifically to the God of Christianity. So we should never interpret Plato and Aristotle as discussing the nature of the Christian God. They are not. Their concept of God is closer to **DEISM**. We can borrow their ideas to help us, but we are not talking about the same things, and therefore we need to distinguish clearly between them.

Possible Future Exam Questions

1. Critically assess the philosophical problems raised by believing in an omnibenevolent God.

2. Evaluate the philosophical problems raised by the belief that God is eternal.

3. Assess the claim that the universe shows no evidence of the existence of a benevolent God.

4. "Boethius was successful in his argument that God rewards and punishes justly". Discuss.

Key Quotes - Character of God

'God said: "Let there be light", and there was light.' – Genesis 1:4

"With God, all things are possible." – Mark 10:27

'Without Him, nothing was made that is made.' – John 1:3

'For God to sin would mean losing control of his actions which is illogical as it would mean he is not omnipotent.' – St Anselm

'God's power can do anything.' – St Thomas Aquinas

'God can do anything, including what might seem impossible.' – Rene Descartes

'A being is Omnipotent if it has every power which is logically possible to possess.' – Anthony Kenny

Classical Religious Language

Background

How can we talk about God without reducing God to a slightly larger-sized human being (**ANTHROPOMORPHISM**)? How can we describe in words an entity that is both invisible and eternal? How can we do justice to the breadth of language used in the BIble for God - **PARABLE, METAPHOR, POETRY, HISTORY, PROVERB**? Is God-talk a special type of speech-act, and if so, what? In this section we range across medieval ideas of **ANALOGY** as posited by **AQUINAS**, and modern theories of language based on **SYMBOL** proposed by **TILLICH**. All of them are about making God-talk meaningful as a special type of language. As a **SYNOPTIC** point, in the Christian Thought paper we meet the **FEMINIST** challenge that the presentation of God is **PATRIARCHAL** - produced by men reinforcing male imagery to justify a relationship of **POWER** over women. How many times in this guide is God described as **HE** or **FATHER**? Is the whole debate set up in masculine terms (eg about the power of God, or God's **TRANSCENDENCE**, rather than **NURTURE** and **IMMANENCE**)?

Key Terms

- **ANALOGY** – Comparing two things, by knowing the one we can understand the other.

- **APOPHATIC WAY** – The Via Negativa.

- **ATTRIBUTION** – The attributes of one reveal the attributes of the other.

- **CATAPHATIC WAY** – The Via Positiva.

- **EQUIVOCAL** – The same word has a different meaning when applied to two things.

- **SIGN** –Arbitrary indicator of something else. Useful as long as we agree on what it means.

- **SYMBOL** – When a term is linked to the subject to which it refers.

- **UNIVOCAL** – A word has the same literal meaning when applied to two things.

- **VIA NEGATIVA** – The belief that the only way to talk about God is with negative language about what God is not.

- **VIA POSITIVA** – The belief that you can talk meaningfully about God with positive language.

Structure of Thought

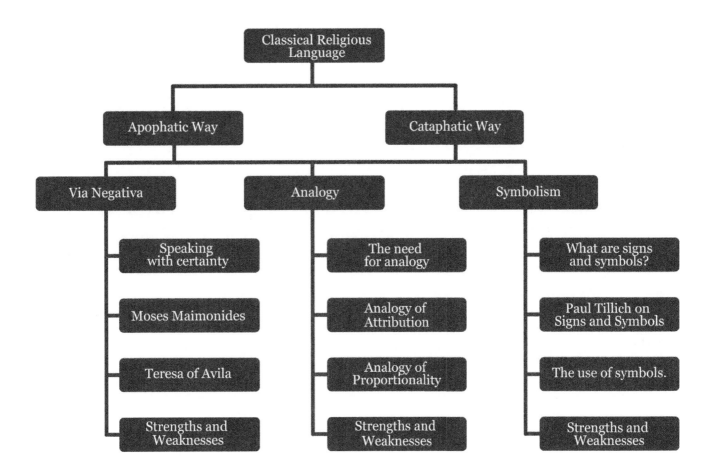

The Apophatic Way

It is impossible to say anything with certainty about God.

The **Apophatic Way** is an approach to Religious Language that suggests we can only talk about God using **NEGATIVE** language. Without realising it, we use **VIA NEGATIVA** all the time when discussing God. Terms like immortal (**NOT** mortal), immaterial, immutable, immanent etc. are all **VIA NEGATIVA** terms which emphasise that God is apart from this universe, beyond all human comprehension and understanding.

Plato's Essential **FORM** of Goodness was an **ABSTRACT** notion, not in time or space. And so it is impossible to say anything about it other than that it gives life to all things and is the **SOURCE** of all goodness. But there is nothing to say about it directly. **PLOTINUS**, the Neo Plotinus, identified the Essential **FORM** of Goodness with God, and so God takes on that abstraction.

BOETHIUS, St **AUGUSTINE** and St Thomas **AQUINAS** all argued that God existed in a **TIMELESS** eternity. This being the case, we cannot deny that He exists, as John **HICK** terms it, an **EPISTEMIC** distance from us (a gulf of knowledge and understanding). As shown in the study of Religious Experience, any direct revelation of God is **INEFFABLE** to us. Since our language is rooted in our human experiences and God is beyond all human experiences, no language can adequately describe any aspect of God's nature. Therefore, we cannot ever speak with any certainty about God.

Moses Maimonides

In his work, Guide to the Perplexed, Moses **MAIMONIDES** reminded them that there was no need to ever use **POSITIVE LANGUAGE** to try to glorify God. He argued that two important points:

1. God can better be understood through **NEGATION**.

Moses **MAIMONIDES** gave an interesting example of how negation can accurately lead one to understanding a subject without any recourse to **POSITIVE LANGUAGE**. The example was of a ship and the method of emphasising the superiority of the **VIA NEGATIVA** was to play a form of twenty questions game, where, by process of elimination, a group of enquirers would eventually come to understand that the subject in question – a ship – as it was not a mineral, a solid, a sphere etc.

However, this example is very limited in its use as Brian **DAVIES** commented that the subject could quite easily be a wardrobe as a ship, such was the limited power of the process of elimination. Further, unless the subject is already in the understanding of the audience, the process of elimination will never result in reaching the subject. If God is **OUTSIDE** human experience and all I have to go on is my experience; I will never reach the understanding of God.

2. Any attempt to use positive language would ultimately lead to a loss of **FAITH**.

MAIMONIDES' second point has some merit to it. Consider the notions of Sigmund **FREUD** (700 years after Maimonides), that we project our **DESIRE** for an eternal father figure to create the idea of God. By using **POSITIVE LANGUAGE** to describe God, we are using the language of human experience, and in doing so, we are **PROJECTING** our human desires onto an external father-figure. Indirectly, we are reducing God to a human construct and assigning **ANTHROPOMORPHIC** (human-like) characteristics to Him. These characteristics would then be **CONTRADICTORY**. Take for example the quality of **OMNIPOTENCE**. As previously shown, by seeing God's omnipotence as the ability to do anything as we understand it, we fall into problems: what it means, how we deal with suffering etc. In this way, we find ourselves doubting God's existence, all because we used **POSITIVE** language.

Teresa of Avila

TERESA of Avila was a 16th Century Spanish mystic who received many religious experiences and recorded them. In her writings she clearly shows the **INEFFABILITY** of God as revealed to her. Ineffability literally means that something cannot be explained or defined. While not all Teresa of Avila's writings are in the form of **VIA NEGATIVA** (e.g. the description of the angel with the golden lance), we can interpret that she used **FIGURATIVE** language to account for experiences which were in themselves beyond ordinary human experience (e.g. 'he left me aflame with love for God').

Teresa of Avila often describes the ineffability of her experience when she states that she does not in fact see Christ, 'I told him that I did not know how I knew it was the Christ, but that I could not help realising that He was beside me.' This clear lack of clarity in her description shows that the experience is not a **CORPOREAL** or imaginative experience but rather an intellectual one. This denotes that the experience is not ordinary, and that Teresa of Avila has borrowed language from human experience to help mediate its meaning.

The **VIA NEGATIVE** emphasises the ineffability of God's nature. He goes beyond all human powers to understand and describe. The fact that we must resort to **NEGATIVE LANGUAGE** shows that God's nature goes beyond all comprehension.

Strengths - Via Negativa

1. The Via Negativa identifies that God's nature goes beyond the experiences of everyday life. This can be linked back to Plato's description of the Essential **FORM** of Goodness.

2. Since God is at an **EPISTEMIC** distance from us (a gulf of knowledge and understanding), any positive human language fails to accurately describe God.

3. God is essentially other, as Pseudo-**DIONYSIUS** describes.

4. In attempting to positively describe God we will ultimately lose our **FAITH** in God as we reduce Him to a human construct - Moses **MAIMONIDES'** second argument.

Weaknesses - Via Negativa

1. As Moses **MAIMONIDES'** example of the ship ironically shows, if God is beyond our understanding, no process of elimination will ever reach Him and so we can learn nothing about God using the Via Negativa.

2. By describing God through **NEGATION**, we are in fact doing little more than refuting any qualities and refusing to qualify anything to Him. This causes the un-falsifiability problems raised by Anthony **FLEW**.

3. We see **POSITIVE LANGUAGE** used to describe God in scripture and within communities of the faithful. In Christianity, God is described as Father. This is a positive description. God is described also as Love and as **SAVIOUR** and **LIBERATOR** from slavery - **SYNOPTIC** point, in the Christian Thought paper we study **LIBERATION THEOLOGY** which adapts the historical events of the **EXODUS**.

4. When we speak about God, we are saying actual things about Him, and building a relationship. We experience this relationship in **PRAYER** and by **EXPERIENCES** of the **NUMINOUS** (events that inspire awe and wonder).

The Cataphatic Way 1 – Analogy

The Need for Analogy

St Thomas **AQUINAS** considered how religious language is actually used by believers as a means to communicate about God and build a relationship with Him. While he began his career as a user of **VIA NEGATIVA**, he finally rejected it famously describing how calling God 'the Living God' we are saying more than 'God is not dead'.

Typically, language is either **UNIVOCAL** or **EQUIVOCAL**. **UNIVOCAL** language is when a term is used in the same way in two different situations: where I say 'the oven is hot' and 'the desert is hot', I mean 'hot' in the same way. Whereas, **EQUIVOCAL** language is the use of the same word but meaning different things, for example, 'I am scared of bats' and 'cricket uses bats'; we mean two different things here. **AQUINAS** suggested that **ANALOGY** was an alternative approach to language where we can use language properly but mean different things due to the nature of that which we are discussing.

Analogy of Attribution

Aquinas said that the relationship between two things was the basis for an **ANALOGY**. He gave the example of the urine and the medicine. If a **DOCTOR** were to prescribe medicine and following its use the patient's urine were to improve, this would indicate that the medicine was working. The qualities of the first (the medicine) lead to the qualities of the second (the urine). In this way, we can attribute the qualities of the second to the first and so we can learn about the first from the second.

This example was supported by Brian **DAVIES** who gave his own example, that of the **BAKER** and the **BREAD**. Where a loaf of bread is tasty, soft and crispy on the outside, we can know that the baker who baked the bread is skilled and proficient. The qualities of the two are different and so when we say 'the bread and the baker are both good' we know that we mean **GOOD** in different ways. However, we know that the good qualities of the bread are one thing and that good qualities of the baker are another. They are linked but quite different.

We can see **ARISTOTLE**'s Influence here where he described how everything has **FOUR CAUSES**, and so if the **TELOS** (purpose) of one is a certain way, it reveals something of the nature of the **EFFICIENT** cause (that which brings about the final purpose).

Analogy of Proper Proportion

AQUINAS said that all things can be good to their own level. A person is good or bad based on their **CHARITY** and kindness while a dog is good based on his ability to follow instructions. The expectations are different as their **TELOS'** are different. A dog can be good if it does not urinate on your sofa, a husband is good if he does not forget an anniversary. Both are good but to their own degrees. In the same way, when we call a man **JUST** it is because he is fair and deals with people in an **APPROPRIATE** way, but to call God just we mean so much more. We know we cannot limit God to our sense of fairness, and so God may not be fair as we see fairness, but we know that in His **INFINITE** way, God must be just. God is infinitely greater than us, but we can still speak of the areas in which God is good: God's **JUSTICE** and **LOVE**.

We see this emulated in Ian **RAMSEY**'s use of models and qualifiers. We identify the **MODELS** in this world and through our experiences: goodness, justice, love etc. But we accept that the extent to which they qualify differ dramatically. Our goodness is limited to what humans can possibly do, but God's goodness is infinite and so is immeasurable. We know what we are talking about and we accept the limitation of human understanding. But that does not mean that we do not know what are describing.

Again, we see an **ARISTOTELEAN** influence here. The **FINAL CAUSE** (true purpose) of each thing is determined by its nature and so can only be good in its own way. God is infinite with a **TELOS** (purpose) well beyond ours. We can use our language without being able to express the fullness of God's telos.

Strengths - Analogy

1. Analogy allows the use of **POSITIVE LANGUAGE** to make meaningful statements about God.

2. Analogy allows members of religious groups to use religious language to build an understanding of God and build a **RELATIONSHIP** with God.

3. Analogy is used by religious believers and exists within revelation and scripture. For example, **PARABLES** act like analogies: in the parable of the Good Samaritan, the **SAMARITAN** is Jesus, the generous **SAVIOUR**, and in the **PRODIGAL SON**, the Father is like God - mercifully welcoming the errant son. who has wasted his life

Weaknesses - Analogy

1. William **BLACKSTONE** argued that any analogy must always be translated into **UNIVOCAL** language to make any literal sense. This is an echo of David Hume's challenge to the **TELEOLOGICAL** argument where he challenged the use of analogy, as you can only compare two things that are similar: the world is more like a cabbage than a machine.

2. Stephen **EVANS** argued that there was nothing wrong with accepting that knowledge of God is limited. God is a **MYSTERY**, all we need know is enough so that we can worship him.

3. Rudolph **OTTO** - religious language needs only show the *mysterium tremendum et fascinans* (**AWESOME MYSTERY** of God).

The Cataphatic Way 2 – Symbolism

What are signs and symbols?

SYMBOLS can be linguistic, pictorial or gestural. Pictorial symbols may be images of the crucifix or a crescent moon; gestural **SYMBOLS** may be kneeling in front of a tabernacle or ritual washing etc. **LINGUISTIC SYMBOLS** are no less common, and in fact they appear throughout language. John **MACQUARRIE** who discusses arbitrary and conventional symbols, where the prior is arbitrarily selected and the latter is involved in an intimate and significant way with the event.

We can see this in religious **SYMBOLS** as a **CROSS** is more than an arbitrarily selected picture; it **PARTICIPATES** in the event of being Christian as Christians are followers of Jesus of Nazareth who was crucified on a cross. Therefore, the wearing of a cross connects the wearer to the **EVENT** of Jesus' crucifixion naming the wearer as a member of that group of believers and holding all the beliefs they share – so the Cross is a **CONVENTIONAL SYMBOL**. However, if a Christian were to become a nun, the wearing of a black and white habit is arbitrary; she could easily wear a blue and red habit.

Paul Tillich on Signs and Symbols

According to Paul **TILLICH**, a **SIGN** is arbitrarily chosen to point to something other than itself. There is some debate here as heavy clouds are a sign of rain. The heavy clouds are not arbitrary, but they are also not selected by humans and so we can accept this as an exception to Tillich's point. A **SYMBOL** is greater than a sign, not only does it point to something else; it indicates that something special is happening. A candle at a tabernacle symbolises the **ETERNAL PRESENCE**, something is happening and we should take notice.

Paul Tillich argued that religious language is **SYMBOLIC** language in the sense that it communicates significant meanings and understanding about God. He described God as "The **GROUND** of Our Being". This means that God was the basis of all that existed and the reason for all that exists; nothing else was of importance - material possessions and ideas cannot replace God. However, since it is impossible for us to comprehend the ground of our being **DIRECTLY** and personally, we do so through **SYMBOLS**. Ideas such as **ATONEMENT**, eternal life and sacrifice and even the life and work of Jesus become **SYMBOLS** to reveal to us this ultimate truth of God.

TILLICH argued that society is what gives and what can take away the meaning of **SYMBOLS**. However, symbols cannot be destroyed; attempts to destroy symbols in a society often have the **OPPOSITE** effect of it becoming more powerful, e.g. the Christian **ICTHUS** was used by Christians in the Roman times. Tillich insisted that the greatest strength of a symbol was that it not only indicated a greater event, it **PARTICIPATED** in the event to which it pointed. Wearing a cross is not just a symbol of the crucifixion; it is a **PARTICIPATION** in the event and an acknowledgement that it was a necessary action. While non-users may recognise the symbol, e.g. the **ICTHUS**, only users will understand them.

The use of Symbols in Scripture and Religious Language

We see symbolic language used throughout scripture and religious tradition:

Genesis

The Creation Stories that appear in **GENESIS 1 & 2** are taken by most Christian traditions, including the Catholic Church, as being **SYMBOLIC**. This is not to mean they are not 'true', but they contain 'symbolic truth'. In **GENESIS 1**, God creates the world in six days. This is symbolic as it gave the Hebrews the seven day week structure against which they built their lives, and enshrined the principle of one rest-day. In **GENESIS 2**, God creates woman from man; this is symbolic as it shows the intimate **DEPENDENCE** of man and woman on each other: God said, 'it is not good for man to be alone" (Genesis 2:18). In fact, the same chapter is the foundation of the belief about the importance of marriage, and how man and woman become "**ONE FLESH**".

Psalms

The Psalms are 'songs of praise' filled with **SYMBOLIC IMAGERY** for God. In **PSALM 23**, The Lord is called "my **SHEPHERD**". This is not to say that we should look at God as a man who stands in a field following sheep around. But as a **SYMBOLIC** phrase, it means that we should depend on God in the way that sheep depend on the shepherd as **PROVIDER** and **PROTECTOR. JEHOVAH-JIRAH** is the Hebrew name for God the **PROVIDER**. The symbol calls us to view the words in a different way. They say that we understand the word **SHEPHERD** to mean what we cannot possibly know first-hand.

Symbols within Christian Tradition

Lamb of God

One of Jesus Christ's titles is **LAMB OF GOD**. In ancient Jewish culture, men and women would sacrifice animals at the Temple in order to **ATONE** for their sins. Through the spilling of the **BLOOD** of the lamb, the sins would be washed away. The penitent would be cleansed by the blood of the sacrifice. When Jesus Christ was crucified on the cross, Christians believe Jesus paid for their sins. In this way, Jesus was the sacrificial lamb whose blood washes away sins. So we **SYMBOLICALLY** call Jesus the Lamb of God. As John the Baptist observed 'Behold the Lamb of God who takes away the sins of the world" (**JOHN 1:29**), echoing **ISAIAH 53:7-8** "All we like sheep have gone astray...The Lord has laid on him the sin of us all".

Icthus

In Greek, the word for **FISH** is **ICTHUS**. This word is an acronym for the Greek words: Iesous, Christos, Theou, (H)yios and Soter, meaning in English: Jesus Christ, Son of God and Saviour. In early Christian times when Christians were persecuted, it was not safe to announce one's religion, and so drawing the simple image of a **FISH** was a symbol that one believed in Jesus Christ, Son of God and Saviour, identifying them as a Christian to whoever understood that symbol, but protecting them against anyone who did not.

Strengths - Symbol

1. Symbols go beyond language and culture. If pictorial or gestural, they do not need language at all. If they are linguistic, they last beyond the language themselves, as ideas in our **CULTURE**.

2. Symbols convey ideas about God that cannot be literally expressed. They give rise to **ANALOGICAL** beliefs and present them in linguistic ways that users can understand.

3. Symbols **PARTICIPATE** in what they are referring to and so several ideas and beliefs can be carried by a simple word or phrase.

Weaknesses - Symbol

1. Symbols can be bastardised into something else, e.g. the **SWASTIKA**. This means that they are not pure in their use. The **UNION JACK** has become at times a symbol of right-wing racists.

2. Symbols can have various meanings and are often the product of a time and place. Therefore, their original meaning may be **LOST** and their value may be reduced. The symbol of God as a **SHEPHERD** (protector and provider) does not have the same value in 21st Century England as it did in 1st Century BC in Israel where it emerged.

3. Symbols are human creations and still do not bridge the **EPISTEMIC DISTANCE** (understanding gap) between

God and man.

Confusions to Avoid - Religious Language

A question on Classical Religious Language may either ask for an **ANALYSIS** of one particular type of religious language or be OPEN and ask for **COMPARISONS** between different types of religious language. In both cases, students are expected to analyse the named form of religious language and make comparisons with other forms of religious language. However, it is very important to note that student are not supposed to write three separate essays. The primary focus should be on the **FORM** of language specified in the question (eg **ANALOGICAL** or **SYMBOLIC**), and then comparisons should be drawn with the other forms of religious language.

For example, if the question is about **ANALOGY**, (God is like…) students should fully analyse analogy with its strengths and weaknesses, and then compare it with **VIA NEGATIVA**, (God is not mortal…) showing how Via Negativa resolves the problem that analogy has in anthropomorphising God. Conversely, show how **AQUINAS** moved away from Via Negativa as religious language means more than **NEGATION**. The comparisons should be direct. It is a common and avoidable error to write about one type of religious language and then in the next paragraph write about another form utterly independently of the previous paragraphs - showing no connection between the paragraphs and with no link back to the question.

Possible Exam Questions - Religious Language

1. To what extent is the Via Negativa the only way to talk about God?

2. Evaluate the claim that analogy can successfully be used to express the human understanding of God.

3. Critically assess the views of Paul Tillich on religious language.

Key Quotes - Religious Language

'In regard to what they express, these words apply literally to God… But as regards the way they express it, they don't apply literally to God; for their manner of expression is appropriate only to creatures.' – St Thomas Aquinas, Selected writings.

'I went at once to my confessor, to tell him about my vision. He asked me in what form I had seen Him. I told him that I had not seen Him at all. Then he asked me how I knew it was Christ. I told him that I did not know how, but that I could not help realising that He was beside me.' – Teresa of Avila

"God is beyond assertion since he is 'the perfect and unique cause of all things'. – Brian Davies

'A sign points to something by arbitrary convention, but a symbol participates in that to which it points.' – Paul Tillich, Dynamics of Faith

Religious Language - 20th Century Challenges

Background

Part of the **ENLIGHTENMENT** project was to eliminate the need for **METAPHYSICS,** and for a reliance on belief in God as the source of **CREATION**, and **MORALITY**. At the same time thinkers like **KANT** and **MILL** were challenging **NATURAL LAW** theory as it suggested that morality was part of the **DESIGN** of the world, rather than a product of human **REASON**. Philosophers such as David **HUME** surprised his contemporaries by dying a happy **ATHEIST**. He also sowed the seeds for challenging religious language as **MEANINGLESS**, which was picked up aggressively by the **LOGICAL POSITIVISTS** of the twentieth century. The issue remained - is God-talk meaningful, and if so, how?

Key Terms

- **BLIK** – A statement made from a personal or shared paradigm where only the claimant can decides what is evidence against the assertion.

- **FALSIFICATION** – The truth of falseness of a statement can be tested by empirical observation.

- **GOD-TALK** – Any statements made pertaining to the existence of God.

- **LANGUAGE-GAME** – The belief that language only makes sense within a given context.

- **LOGICAL POSITIVISM** – The belief in Verificationism that truth must have an empirical (factual) foundation.

- **VERIFICATION** - Proving something to be true.

Structure of Thought

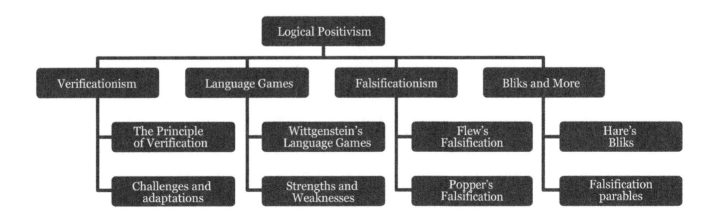

Logical Positivism & Verificationism

The Principle of Verification

David **HUME** argued that there were two areas of human study:

1. Relations of Ideas – **ANALYTIC** statements which are rationally known

2. Matters of fact – **SYNTHETIC** statements which are empirically shown to be either true or false (they have 'truth content')

The 1920's **LOGICAL POSITIVIST** movement of the **VIENNA** Circle, chaired by Moritz **SCHLICK** postulated that the only statements that have **FACTUAL** meaning are those which can be observed by the senses, or tautologies - **SYNTHETIC** (with **EMPIRICAL** truth value) and **ANALYTIC** statements (true by **DEFINITION**) - an argument originating from **HUME**. All statements which are not synthetic or analytic are deemed to be factually **MEANINGLESS**. These include statements about **ART**, **MORALITY** and **RELIGION** and any form of **GOD-TALK**. But many statements of science also such as 'the world began with a **BIG BANG**').

But if the only meaningful statements are sense **OBSERVABLE** or **TAUTOLOGIES**, then the Verification Principle is neither sense-observable, nor is it a tautology. Additionally, Richard **SWINBURNE** pointed out that very few statements, even within the world of **SCIENCE**, could be sense-observed. For example, to state 'water boils at 100 degrees Celsius' would require all water in the universe to be boiled. Swinburne used Carl **HEMPLE**'s example 'Ravens are black' requires **EVERY** raven to be observed - impossible and impractical. **A.J. AYER** adapted and made sense of the Principle of **VERIFICATION**, however, he found himself repeatedly challenged, which show the principle largely unsustainable.

Challenges and Adaptations of Verificationism

AYER presented three versions of his Principle of **VERIFICATION.**

Strong and Weak Verification

STRONG VERIFICATION is verification of something using sense observation here and now. There is clear evidence for it and it can be stated conclusively.

WEAK VERIFICATION is verification though **INDUCTIVE** reasoning. 'It is probably the case based on past **EVIDENCE** and verification'. Most knowledge is **WEAKLY** verified, e.g. that water boils at 100 degrees, that humans are mortal etc.

This form of verification still found criticism and challenge. Richard **SWINBURNE** argued that **HISTORICAL FACTS** cannot be verified even weakly that are meaningful to discuss. Nor can theoretical physics, quantum physics etc.

Verification in Practice and Principle

Verification in practice is like **STRONG** verification where it can be verified in the here and now and can be seen as conclusive.

Verification in **PRINCIPLE** is the verification where we accept the limitation of what we can practically verify, however, since we know how we would verify something that cannot be weakly verified, we are able to discuss it. For example, even though I cannot see a **QUARK** or quantum strings, I know the theory of how I would be able to verify them and so it is meaningful to discuss it. Furthermore, even though we have no proof of aliens, we know how we would verify them, by visiting all planets etc. Even though it is not practical, it is in principle **POSSIBLE** and so it is verifiable.

HICK's argued God is verifiable in **PRINCIPLE**. He gave the parable of the two travellers walking on a road. One is convinced that there is a **CELESTIAL CITY** at the end and argues that eventually they will either arrive at a city or not, at which point they will be able to **VERIFY** or **FALSIFY** the city's existence. In the same way, **ESCHATOLOGICALLY** (at the end of time, eschaton = the last days) we will be able to verify or falsify God's existence. Additionally, I know how I would prove God's existence, with a miracle or a vision etc.; so **GOD-TALK** is meaningful as God can be **VERIFIED** in **PRINCIPLE.**

Direct and Indirect Verification

DIRECT verification considers meaningful any statement that is "itself an **OBSERVATION**-statement, or is such that in conjunction with one or more observation-statements it entails at least one observation-statement." The example Ayer gave was that of **TORRICELLI**'s endeavour to prove the changes in atmospheric pressure by taking a barometer to the top of a mountain and directly verifying that mercury rose.

INDIRECT Verification considers meaningful any statement that, while not being directly verifiable, "in conjunction with certain other premises it entails one or more directly verifiable statements which are not deducible from these other premises alone." Ayer's example was that of **GALILEO**, who proved the changes in atmospheric pressure indirectly by dropping two objects of different weights at a height and showing they landed at the same time. While this did not prove atmospheric pressure directly, it was evidence that reveals it **INDIRECTLY**. The focus here is on evidence. If there is evidence for something, you do not need to verify it directly. There is evidence to suggest it, so it is meaningful to discuss it.

Language Games

Ludwig **WITTGENSTEIN** began his career as a **LOGICAL POSITIVIST** writing in his Tractatus "whereof one cannot speak, thereof one must remain silent", but then changed his way of thinking by the time he wrote his **PHILOSOPHICAL INVESTIGATIONS** having revised his entire approach to philosophy.

Wittgenstein argued that language is not a **RIGID** set of terms or formulae, but rather it **ADAPTS** and grows. It is unique to the people engaging in the language and is meaningful to them. He developed a theory that language was ever growing and adapting and it only makes sense in very specific contexts and as such could not be subject to verification. He gave the example of builders working on a site where they use terms such as 'plank' and 'block'. When the foreman calls the term the workers know what he wants and brings it to him. This dialogue, Wittgenstein argued, was an example of a **PRIMITIVE** language which is unique to builders.

In the same way that chess has its own language and uses of terms, so does football and the two are distinct, therefore, to be 'check-mated' is utterly meaningless in football, as much as being 'off-side' means nothing in chess. The terms are meaningless as meaning is found within **CONTEXT**.

Wittgenstein called the business of using language in its context a **LANGUAGE-GAME**. He argued that the use of language was not private but **PUBLIC** within a community, and each language using community is different, e.g. the community of English speakers, the community of chess players, the community of mathematicians. Language can only make sense when it is used with other members of that language using community, what he called the **FORM** of **LIFE**. In the community of theism, statements such as "God is good" make sense, but statements like "F=MA" mean nothing.Strengths - Verificationism

1. Language Games directly respond to and undermine the challenges of **VERIFICATIONISM**. **LOGICAL POSITIVIST** arguments that meaningful statements must be **VERIFIED** make perfect sense within the context and **LANGUAGE GAME** of scientific **EXPERIMENTS** and maths, but not in the language game of God-talk (a **METAPHYSICAL** language-game).

2. Many forms of language, God-talk, morality, history, art, music, poetry etc. are language games of their own. We all speak **MULTIPLE** language games depending on where we are and what we are doing. We adapt our language to our audiences and one use of language, e.g. Italian, sport, Star Wars terminology, would have no meaning in another, e.g. on a driving test you would not say "the Force is with you", and in an English exam you would not write in Italian. Language is always **CONTEXTUAL**.

Weaknesses - Verificationism

1. In separating different types of talk as different language games the theory removes the link between **GOD-TALK** and what we would consider to be **EMPIRICAL** evidence, where believers do make statements that they mean scientifically, e.g. God created the world, Jesus Christ rose from the dead. In this way, God-Talk is **ONLY PARTLY** redeemed by calling it a different language-game, as believers would argue that some religious statements are empirical and historical and literal, not contextual **ALONE**. If I can have a **FACT** that something causes me pleasure, can't I also have a **FACT** that I have just had a numinous experience of God?

Falsification - Anthony Flew and Karl Popper

Flew's Falsification

Anthony **FLEW** argued that God-talk was meaningless because it was **UNFALSIFIABLE**. By this, he meant that believers make their claims about God but do not accept any basis by which their claims might be **REFUTED**. By not accepting such refutations, believers make their claims unfalsifiable and so **MEANINGLESS**.

Flew argued that when we make assertions we unconsciously refute the **NEGATION** of that assertion, so if I assert 'my pen is black' I am unconsciously asserting 'my pen is **NOT** red, blue, green or any other colour than black'. This way, I am allowing that if it could be shown that my pen is green, it would **REFUTE** my original assertion. If we do not allow any conditions for the negation, then we are unconsciously omitting any conditions for the assertion itself. If I do not allow that my pen is categorically **NOT** green, then should my pen be revealed to be green, I might deny that my original assertion was false by modifying it to say: 'my pen is black, or green.' Thus my original assertion means nothing.

Flew used John **WISDOM's** parable of the **EXPLORERS** (and the **GARDENER**) to emphasise his point; when two explorers happen on a garden in a forest, one asserts "there is a gardener", but the second shows all evidence to the contrary. However, no evidence will shake the first's resolve and he maintains "there is an intangible, invisible, inaudible gardener". The second declares: "what remains of your original assertion?" Flew maintained that when believers are faced with evidence that **CONTRADICTS** their assertions, like "God loves me", of "God has a plan", they are so vague and void of any refutations of negations, that the assertion "dies a death of a **THOUSAND QUALIFICATIONS**" and becomes "factually **MEANINGLESS**".

Popper's Falsification

The principle of **FALSIFICATION** was first brought to light by Karl **POPPER** in Conjectures and Refutations, where he is responding to what he called **PSEUDO-SCIENCE**, that is astrology and Freudian **PSYCHOLOGY**. He argued that such disciplines masquerade as science but are themselves not actual science as they fail the test of falsification and have no actual scientific basis. As a **SYNOPTIC POINT** - **FREUD'S** theory of **CONSCIENCE** (Ethics paper) makes assertions which are just hypotheses of the existence in the mind of **EGO**, **ID** and **SUPEREGO**.

POPPER argued that if any claim was to be considered scientific, it must be **IN PRINCIPLE** falsifiable. For example, if one were to claim 'water boils at 100 degrees Celsius', they are claiming that it does not boil at 98, 99, 101, 102 etc. Should it be shown that water boils at 101 degrees Celsius, then it shows the original assertion false, but still scientific as it was subject to **FALSIFICATION**. Science is the process of attempting to disprove assertions. If an assertion has no principle basis for falsification, then it is not scientific. For example: 'your fortune will grow as Mars moves into Pisces' or 'men want to kill their fathers and marry their mothers' (**FREUD**). Such assertions are not scientific as there is no '**IN PRINCIPLE**' basis for falsification.

Popper called this the principle of **DEMARCATION** between what is science and what is pseudo-science. Flew takes this principle and assumes that it demarcates between what is **MEANINGFUL** and meaningless. But this is not present in Popper's original thesis. To assume that **FALSIFICATIONISM** can demarcate between meaningful and meaningless language is to change Popper's original thesis.

Bliks and Philosophical Parables

Hare's Bliks

R. M. HARE responded to **FLEW**'s challenge of **FALSIFICATION** by presenting the concept of **BLIKS**, claims that may well be unfalsifiable but are nonetheless **MEANINGFUL** to us as they influence the way we see the world and live our lives. Hare presented the parable of the **LUNATIC** student who is convinced that his dons (tutors) are out to kill him. Despite how many mild-mannered dons are presented to him by his friends, he maintains that it is a ruse and that they want him dead. Hare admits that the student is a lunatic and that his assertion is indeed **UNFALSIFIABLE**. However, he maintains that it is still meaningful to him. It affects his life, and he alone can control what counts as **EVIDENCE**.

Hare discussed what people really believe and think about things. He gives his own example of being utterly convinced that the steering column in his car works. If he did not believe it, he would not drive. His **BLIK** (unverifiable belief) that the steering column works affects his life as he drives his car. Were he to have any reason to believe that it did not work, he would not drive! Hare argues that we all have **BLIKS** about everything whether or not we have thought about it and we alone are in control of what counts as evidence for or against it. Just as the friends of the student are convinced by the dons' mild manner, the lunatic is not and he alone controls the evidence that may convince him one day.

What we really believe is what forms our **BLIKS**. Bliks determine what evidence you accept. They are shared and life-changing. For Hare, religious language is **MEANINGFUL** as it is about what people believe. In this way, Flew's **FALSIFICATION** does not threaten religious language because unfalsifiable statements can still hold meaning for users and can still be **BLIKS**. As a **SYNOPTIC** point - we can link this to **KANT**'s idea that **CATEGORIES** of the mind determine how we perceive the **PHENOMENAL** world of cause and effect - something we encounter in the Ethics paper.. These **CATEGORIES** filter experience, so that when we hear a bang, for example, we assume something caused it.

Falsification Parables

Parable of the Explorers

John **WISDOM**, who originally wrote the Parable of the Explorers (and the gardener) as a dialectic about the way different people see evidence for God, argued that God cannot be **VERIFIED** or **FALSIFIED** as He is not part of what we traditionally consider scientific.

The Parable of the Partisan and the Stranger

Basil **MITCHELL** wrote the parable of the **PARTISAN** (freedom fighter) in a country occupied by an enemy. He meets a stranger who impresses him greatly and is convinced that the stranger is an ally. When the stranger is seen helping friends the partisan declares "see, he is on our side", and when he is seen helping the enemy, the partisan declares "he must have a reason to behave that way". This is a reflection of how believers **INTERPRET** good and bad events as though God is still good.

Mitchell warned that believers should not allow religious beliefs to be vacuous formulae, but that experience should in fact make a **DIFFERENCE**. For example, if I believe "Thor makes the lightning", what of all the evidence that shows that lightning is a natural phenomenon? Will I deny the evidence to maintain my blind faith? Mitchell argues that we should not do that. In this way, falsification does help to **DEMARCATE** between what is meaningful and what is meaningless, though not to the extent that **FLEW** does.

Toys in the Cupboard

Richard **SWINBURNE** presents the idea that we can talk meaningfully about toys in a cupboard that come alive when no-one is watching. While this is not **FALSIFIABLE**, it does not change that it is still meaningful to discuss it. It may be **UNSCIENTIFIC**, but it is not meaningless.

Confusions to Avoid - Religious Language

1. Religious Language is about God-talk, not about the **EXISTENCE** of God. It would be a mistake to assume that **AYER** and **SCHLICK** are making direct assaults on the existence of God. That said, it could be argued that their attacks on **GOD-TALK** are camouflaged attacks on religion, as without language one cannot have a functioning religion. Also they argue that we should be **SILENT** about things we cannot verify or establish as **ANALYTIC** truth.

   George Orwell's 1984 has **NEWSPEAK** created with the purpose of diminishing the scope of human thinking in order to control the populace.. As a **SYNOPTIC** point - this section can be studied together with **META-ETHICS** where **AYER** also features for his attack on **NATURALISM** and **MORAL FACTS** in Ethics. In Christian Thought, the rise of **SECULARISM** is partly about the attempt to exclude **GOD-TALK** from public discussion and force religion into the **PRIVATE** realm. In a **PLURALIST**, multicultural society there are many competing truth-claims in religion and the consensus seems to be to outlaw direct public attacks on religious beliefs.

2. Falsificationism is not primarily a discussion on meaningfulness and meaninglessness of religious language. There is a divide as to whether it can be used at all in a question on whether or not **GOD-TALK** is meaningful. When asked, this question does refer to **VERIFICATIONISM**; however, the reality is that Anthony **FLEW** specifically stated: "Believers will allow nothing to falsify their belief claims. Therefore, God-Talk is meaningless as it is unfalsifiable." So it is clear that he considered religious language to be meaningless on the basis of its inability to be **FALSIFIED**. However, students should be wary that this may not be what the examiner wants to see.

   If falsification is going to be used on a question about meaningfulness, it should be done with care, referring to Flew's quote and Popper's original use of the principle of **DEMARCATION**.

Possible Exam Questions

1. Critically assess Wittgenstein's belief that language games allow religious statements to have meaning.

2. The Falsification Principle presents no real challenge to religious belief. Discuss

3. Critically assess the claim that religious language is meaningless.

Key Quotes - Verificationism

'If relentlessly pursued, the theologian will have to resort to the avoiding action of qualification. And there lies that death by a thousand qualifications, which would, I agree, constitute a failure in faith as well as in logic.' – Anthony Flew

'Believers will allow nothing to falsify their belief claims. – Anthony Flew

'Unfalsifiable statements can be meaningful to the claimant. If an unfalsifiable statement affects the way a person lives and interacts with people, then that statement is not simply meaningless. It can be called a Blik.' – R. M. Hare

'At the end of the day, if God does exist, then the verification of his existence is verifiable in principle, but if God does not exist, then his existence is not falsifiable.' – John Hick

The Ethics Paper H573/2

The OCR Ethics Course seeks to connect **NORMATIVE THEORIES** to **APPLIED** topics, two in year 1 - euthanasia and business ethics, and one in Year 2 (sexual ethics) Norms (values of goodness) are produced by the key moral theories of Utilitarianism, Situation Ethics, Kantian ethics & Natural Law. We are required to apply Natural Law and Situation Ethics to issues surrounding euthanasia, and Kant and Utilitarianism to business ethics. All theories must be used in the consideration of **SEXUAL ETHICS**. Then we ask (in Year 2) what is the foundation of ethics (**META-ETHICS**) and how does **CONSCIENCE** guide us, and where does it come from?

- **CASE STUDIES** are an excellent way of thinking through issues surrounding applied ethics - such as Diane Pretty in 2002 (euthanasia) or Enron in 2003 (business ethics). You will find these on the website www.peped.org

- **MAPPING THE THEORIES** gives a sequence of thought which goes from a starting point (such as **SYNDERESIS** for Natural Law) to a finishing point (**EUDAIMONIA** for Natural Law) and then links the concepts together to form an analysis.

- **TEXTBOOKS** may have their place, but you are examined on the syllabus alone, so study it carefully. There are many ways of doing and thinking about ethics. Wilcockson and Wilkinson (2016) frequently take a Roman Catholic perspective (eg quotes from encyclicals and the Catholic Catechism). But you could just as well quote from the Church of England, the United Reformed Church or the Baptist or Orthodox churches to gain a Christian perspective. Or line up a humanist or atheist perspective against it. Textbooks also include extra material which is not strictly necessary to be an A grade candidate.

- Finally we need to concentrate on the skills of **ANALYSIS** and **EVALUATION**. The specification **OCR H573/2** is quite brief and relatively few authors are named. For example, the specification does not mention the theory of **CONSCIENCE** (section 5) of **BUTLER**, but I have retained them to aid analysis and evaluation of **AQUINAS** and **FREUD**. The meta-ethical theory of **PRESCRIPTIVISM** is included here in order to evaluate **EMOTIVISM** properly (which is named) - we need to consider **PRESCRIPTIVISM** as a more complete theory of how moral language functions.

Introduction to Ethics

Key Terms

- **NORMATIVE ETHICS** - how norms (values of good and bad) are derived and then applied to the real world.

- **META-ETHICS** - the meaning and function of ethical language.

- **OBJECTIVE TRUTH -** the view that truth is testable by observation and experience.

- **RELATIVISM** - the view that all values (norms) are simply expressions of culture and there are no universal, unchanging values of 'good'.

- **SUBJECTIVE TRUTH** - the view that truth is something that depends on an individual perception or belief system and cannot be shared objectively.

- **SITUATION ETHICS** - what is good or bad needs to be assessed according to what maximises love in any situation.

- **TELEOLOGICAL ETHICS** - focuses on the end or telos of an action, for example, Situation Ethics focuses on love.

- **DEONTOLOGICAL** - ethics that focuses on the duty (deon) or rule.

Structure of Thought

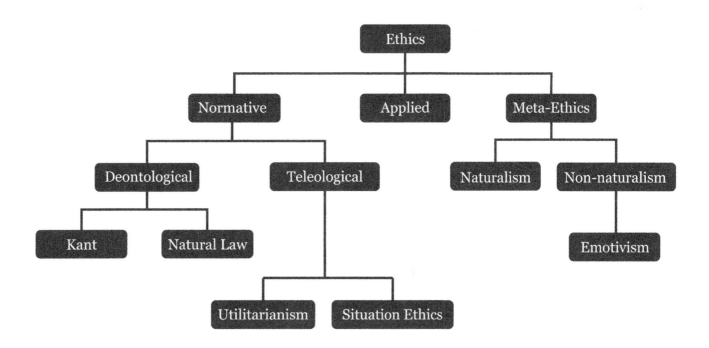

Normative Ethics

Asks the question "how should I act, morally speaking?" or "what ought I to do?"

A **NORM** is a "value" i.e. something I think of as good. The normative theories we study at AS or Year 1 (OCR) are: Natural Law, Kantian ethics, Utilitarianism and Situation Ethics. Each theory derives the idea of goodness a different way: **NATURAL LAW** with reference to the true rational purpose of human beings; **UTILITARIANISM**, with reference to the one assumed norm of happiness and its maximisation; **KANTIAN ETHICS,** by an a priori method of taking an imaginative step backwards and universalising our action; and **SITUATION ETHICS** by maximising the one norm of love in a given situation.

Meta-ethics

META-ETHICS studies the foundations of ethics and meaning of ethical terms (what does it mean to say something is good?). It particularly focuses on ethical language. Key meta-ethical questions include:

- "Is morality absolute – applying everywhere and for all time, or is it relative, specific to a time and place – a culture, situation or viewpoint?"

- "Is there such a thing as a moral fact?"

- "What do different ethical theorists mean by 'good'?"

- "Is goodness a natural feature of the world to be accessed and measured (a bit like science)?"

Applied Ethics

Applies ethical theories to real world situations. The applied issues at AS or Year 1 (OCR) are:

- Euthanasia applied to Natural Law and Situation Ethics

- Business Ethics applied to Utilitarianism and Kantian ethics.

- Sexual ethics is studied in Year 2 and all Year 1 normative theories are required.

A key question in applied ethics is: how do I apply the norm derived by any one ethical theory to the issues surrounding euthanasia and business ethics? The syllabus helps us identify these issues: sanctity of human life, quality of life and autonomy for euthanasia, and globalisation, whistle-blowing, and the interests of stakeholders for business ethics. We could also add our own, such as **SLIPPERY SLOPE** arguments in euthanasia and environmental responsibility for business.

Moreover, we can ask the question generally: is there any difference between an **ACT** (doing something deliberately) and an **OMISSION** (failing to do something)? For example, in cases of euthanasia is failing to offer life support the same ethically as deliberately administering a drug that will kill?

Deontological

Acts are right or wrong in themselves (intrinsically) – it is not about consequences. Often stresses the rules or duty (Kantian ethics is pure deontology and Natural Law has both teleological and deontological aspects). **DEON** is Greek for duty.

Teleological

Teleological theories (**TELOS** = end in Greek) focuses on the purpose and consequences of actions. An action is good only if it brings about beneficial consequences and so fulfils the good purpose (it is instrumentally good, not intrinsically because actions are **MEANS** to some other **END** like happiness or pleasure), for example, Utilitarianism (good purpose is maximising happiness) and Situation Ethics (good purpose is maximising agape love). Joseph Fletcher declares: "the end justifies the means, nothing else".

Four Questions to Ask of Ethical Theories

- **Derivation**: How does the moral theory derive (produce) the idea of goodness?

- **Application**: How can we apply the "good" to choices we make, such as Natural Law to euthanasia or Kantian ethics to business?

- **Realism**: How realistic is the theory with reference to human psychology and our own experience?

- **Motivation**: Why should I be moral? How does this ethical theory suggest I should be motivated to save a stranger in need? What stops me living my life as an ethical egoist, just putting my self-interest first?

These questions will be answered for all moral theories in the final chapter.

Key Quotes - Norms

"There are no absolute universal moral standards binding on all men at all times". John Ladd

"All men are created equal…they are endowed with certain unalienable rights". US Declaration of Independence

"Values are merely culturally approved habits". Ruth Benedict

"The end justifies the means, nothing else". Joseph Fletcher

"There is no objective truth". J.L.Mackie

"We are in danger of falling into a tyranny of relativism". Pope Benedict

Natural Law

NATURAL LAW is a normative **DEONTOLOGICAL** theory coming from a **TELEOLOGICAL** worldview, as Aristotle argues that the good is defined by the **RATIONAL ENDS** (telos = end) or **FINAL CAUSES** which people by nature pursue.

"Natural Law is the sharing in the eternal law by intelligent creatures" argues **AQUINAS** and calls these rational ends **OBJECTS OF THE WILL**. Key assumptions are that we have a fixed human nature, there is an eternal law in God himself, and the **SYNDERESIS** principle – that all human beings naturally share a conscience that guides us to "do good and avoid evil". Aquinas calls synderesis "the **FIRST PRINCIPLE** of the natural law" and it is one of two words he uses for conscience.

Key Terms

- **NATURAL LAW** - "right reason in agreement with nature", (Cicero). "The sharing in the eternal law by rational creatures', (Aquinas).

- **SYNDERESIS** - the first principle that we by nature seek to do good and avoid evil – or have an innate knowledge of first principles (the primary precepts). This makes the theory universal in application (it applies to a Christian believer and a non-believer or believer of another religion).

- **PRIMARY PRECEPTS** - principles known innately which define the rational ends or goods of human existence and define the good goals we pursue - these are general and do not change.

- **SECONDARY PRECEPTS** - applications of the primary precepts using human reason, which are not absolute and so may change. For example, the Catholic church may revise its absolute ban on contraception as a violation of the precept of reproduction.

- **APPARENT GOODS** - acts done from reason which do not correspond to the natural law.

- **REAL GOODS** - acts done from human reason which correspond to the natural law.

- **NATURAL RIGHTS** - rights given to human beings because of their very nature as human. These are enshrined in the US Declaration of Independence which starts: 'we hold these rights to be inalienable'.

- **ETERNAL LAW** - the law as conceived by God and existing as an ideal of all law and projected in the design of the Universe.

- **DIVINE LAW** - the law revealed to humankind in the Bible, such as the ten commandments in the book of Exodus or the beatitudes in Matthew.

- **HUMAN LAW** - the laws we establish by human reason as our social laws.

Structure of Thought

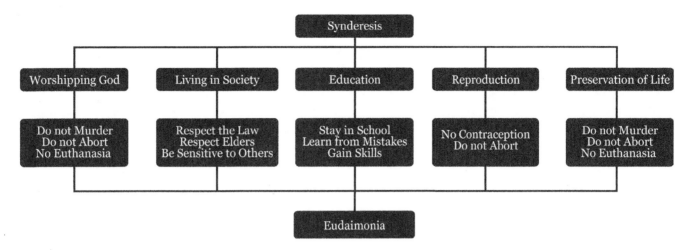

Self-test: one of the secondary precepts boxes (second row down) is wrong. Cam you spot which and correct it?

Aquinas' Argument

AQUINAS sought to reconcile Christian thought with Greek thinking (**ARISTOTLE**'s works) discovered in Islamic libraries at the **FALL OF TOLEDO** (1085), when Christian armies reconquered Spain.

He sees goodness in the **DIVINE ESSENCE** (nature of God) which has a purpose – the **ETERNAL LAW** – reflected in our **HUMAN NATURE** and the ends we rationally pursue. A key assumption Aquinas makes is called the **SYNDERESIS**

Synderesis: 'each precious child, born with the desire to do good, and avoid evil'

principle that we naturally "do good and avoid evil" – which is the opposite of the **REFORMATION** assumption that "all have sinned and fall short of God's glory" (Romans 3:23).

We are born with good natures, able to reason and so pursue good ends or objects of the will. The **DIVINE LAW** reflects God's eternal law and is revealed in holy Scripture (eg Ten Commandments of Exodus 20). From these observable God-designed rational ends (goals) we get the **PRIMARY PRECEPTS**.

Primary Precepts

There are five observable "goods" or rational ends we pursue. (Acronym **POWER**).

- **P**reservation of life

- **O**rdered society

- **W**orship of God

- **E**ducation

- **R**eproduction

These reflect the **DIVINE WILL** because God designed us with a rational nature in His image. Notice that **VERITATIS SPLENDOR** (1995 Papal document) has changed the emphasis – Worship of God becomes **APPRECIATION OF BEAUTY** (to fit with our agnostic age), and it adds concern for the environment to reflect the new emphasis on stewardship rather than **DOMINION** (Genesis 1:24 "and let man have dominion over the earth"). Note that the commitment to environmental value is weak in Veritatis Splendor: "to preserve and cultivate the riches of the natural world'. These subtle changes may indicate that Natural Law is not as **ABSOLUTE** as we sometimes think. The fourth type of law is **HUMAN LAW**.

For society to flourish (Greek telos (purpose) of **EUDAIMONIA** sees happiness as personal and social flourishing) we need to bring our human law in line with the **ETERNAL LAW** of God, or put another way, make it appropriate for rational human beings to fulfil their Godly destiny – being with God forever, and being Christlike.

The Four Laws

Natural Law can be mapped in two ways. The first way is **TELEOLOGICAL** because it focuses on the end or telos of human behaviour - to achieve a flourishing or fulfilled life, **EUDAIMONIA** (see mind map). Aristotle begins Nichomachean Ethics by arguing 'the intrinsic good is that at which all things aim' - a broad and general goal.

The second way is by focusing on duties created by the four laws.

- **ETERNAL LAW** - a blueprint in the mind of God of the principles by which God made and controls the universe, which we discover by observation **A POSTERIORI** - through scientific experiments for example, or **A PRIORI** by pure reason as in Mathematics.

- **NATURAL LAW** - the moral law inherent in human beings, discoverable by reason, and expressed in the rational goals which humans by nature pursue.

- **DIVINE LAW** - expressed in the Bible (eg the Ten Commandments or Sermon on the Mount) and then interpreted and applied by human reason.

- **HUMAN LAW** - formulated as codes that create the common good and the precept of an ordered society, and should reflect the eternal law in order to be seen to be good and just. If a ruler ordered that we kill all female babies this would be bad for human flourishing and contrary to the **PRMARY PRECEPT** of preservation of life. and so an unjust and 'bad' law.

These can be represented as a diamond with eternal law at the top. Note that we 'are only required to obey secular rulers to the extent that justice requires' (Aquinas). Evil laws should be resisted and disobeyed.Secondary Precepts

These are **APPLICATIONS** of the **PRIMARY PRECEPTS** and may change eg as our society changes, science advances our understanding of the Divine Mind, or a situation demands it (eg Thou shalt not kill gets suspended in times of war).

Aquinas suggests **POLYGAMY** (many wives) may sometimes be justified. We don't necessarily have to accept Roman Catholic applications eg Abortion is tantamount to murder, Euthanasia breaks the **SANCTITY OF LIFE**, contraception goes against the primary natural purpose of sex, which is **REPRODUCTION**, and homosexual behaviour is described as **INTRINSICALLY DISORDERED** (the phrase used in **HUMANAE VITAE**, 1968).

There is another assumption here, that there is one human nature – heterosexual- and so there can't be a gay nature. Modern Psychology (eg Carl **JUNG**) suggests we have male and female aspects to our natures and Chinese philosophy has always talked in terms of **YING** and **YANG** – the two aspects of our nature.

Phronesis

Practical wisdom (**PHRONESIS** in Greek) is important because we need to cultivate right judgment to identify the non-absolute **SECONDARY PRECEPTS**. "Practical wisdom turns the application into action, which is the goal of practical reason" (Aquinas). So Natural Law has a situational aspect - we need to assess and 'the more specific the conditions are, the greater the probability of an exception arising', argues Aquinas (ST I -II q.94 a.4c). **SYNDERESIS** gives us a general orientation towards the good but **PHRONESIS** fills in the details of how to apply any primary precept.

Apparent Goods

We cannot consciously sin because our nature is such that we believe we are "doing good and avoiding evil" – the **SYNDERESIS** principle – even when practising genocide. However, though we rationalise it, this clearly breaks the **ETERNAL LAW** reflected in the **NATURAL LAW** that most rational humans want to **PRESERVE LIFE** (primary precept **P** of **POWER** acronym above). We cannot flourish if we break the Natural Law – in this sense we are being sub-human and irrational (even though we believe otherwise). **AQUINAS** calls these **APPARENT GOODS** – which we mistakenly believe (eg Hitler's genocide) are **REAL GOODS**. We can sin, but not consciously, which is why Evangelical

Christians dislike Natural Law theory – arguing it is unrealistic (our very reason is distorted by sin) and unbiblical (it seems to deny Paul's teaching on **ORIGINAL SIN**, inherited from Adam after the **FALL** in Genesis 3).

Two Goods in Conflict

In business ethics the principles of truthfulness and loyalty to the company come into conflict when a whistleblower discovers evidence of wrongdoing, or with euthanasia, when doctors increase the morphine dose to alleviate pain in the knowledge that they will kill the patient. **DOUBLE EFFECT** argues that if the primary effect results from a good intention (alleviate suffering) then the secondary effect isn't evil (causing a death). Notice you can only make the judgement by considering **CONSEQUENCES** and the end of patient welfare. Aquinas argues: "moral actions take their character from what is intended" and so if I act in self defence and unintentionally kill someone I am not doing wrong as long as the action is **PROPORTIONATE.**

Strengths

AUTONOMOUS AND RATIONAL: Natural law is an autonomous, rational theory and it is wrong to say that you have to believe in God to make sense of it. Aquinas speaks of "the pattern of life lived according to reason". You could be a Darwinian atheist and believe in natural law derived by empirical observation, with the primary precept of survival (Aquinas' preservation of life). Richard **DAWKINS** (The Selfish Gene) goes so far as to argue for a natural genetic tendency to be altruistic: a lust to be nice. "The theory of Natural Law suggests..morality is **AUTONOMOUS**. It has its own questions, its own methods of answering them, and its own standards of truth, and religious considerations are not the point". Rachels (2006:56)

AN EXALTED VIEW OF HUMAN BEINGS: We use reason to work out how to live. So we are not slaves to our passions or our genes. Natural Law has a purpose: a flourishing society and a person fulfilled and happy - **EUDAIMONIA**. It is not ultimately about restricting us by rules, but setting us free to fulfil our proper purpose or **TELOS**, inherent in our design: to rationally assent to personal growth. If we can agree on our purpose we can agree on what morality is for. Moreover, we don't have to accept the fact/value division inherent in Moore or Ayer's philosophy. "The natural world is not to be regarded merely as a realm of facts, devoid of value or purpose. Instead, the world is conceived to be a **RATIONAL ORDER** with value and purpose built into its very nature". Rachels (2006: 50)

FLEXIBLE: Natural Law is not inflexible. The primary precepts may be general and unchanging, but as Aquinas argued, **SECONDARY PRECEPTS** can change depending on circumstances, culture and worldview.   Aquinas calls them 'proximate conclusions of reason'. The Doctrine of **DOUBLE EFFECT** is also a way to escape the moral dilemmas which exist when two rules conflict, (See Louis Pojman 2006: 47-51) – so not as **ABSOLUTE** as textbooks suggest.

Weaknesses

A FIXED HUMAN NATURE: Aquinas believes in one fixed, shared human nature with certain natural properties eg heterosexual. But evidence suggests there are gay genes and so there is no one natural human nature, but many. This is actually a form of the **NATURALISTIC FALLACY**, the movement from an "is" to an "ought". "It may be that sex does produce babies, but it does not follow that sex ought or ought not to be engaged in only for that purpose. Facts are one thing, values are another". Rachels (2006:52)

AN OPTIMISTIC VIEW: Aquinas believes that we **INNATELY** (we are born with) have a "tendency to do good and avoid evil", **SYNDERESIS**. This is in contrast with Augustine who believes that, due to the Fall, we are born into sin, the sin of Adam, or perhaps the view of psychologists like Freud, that natural selfishness becomes moralised by upbringing and socialisation.

IMMORAL OUTCOMES: Natural Law has been interpreted to ban contraception, because this interferes with the natural primary precept of reproduction. But a. it's not clear that sex is exclusively for reproduction, in fact, the function of bonding may be primary and b. the consequence of this policy in Africa has had evil effects of the spread of **AIDS** and the birth of **AIDS** infected children who often become orphans living on the streets.

Confusions - Natural Law

1. "Natural" means "as we see in the natural world". This isn't true because many things we see in the natural world we would argue are **IMMORAL** (eg killing the weak which animals do all the time). "Natural" means something closer to "**APPROPRIATE** for our rational human nature", for example, we may naturally feel lust but it is **IRRATIONAL** and wrong to seek to indulge this lust with a complete stranger.

2. "Natural law is dogmatic and inflexible". This is a wrong reading of Aquinas who himself argues that the **SECONDARY PRECEPTS** are liable to change with circumstances and our developed understanding. It is quite possible to be a Natural Law theorist and argue in favour of contraception on the grounds that it is necessary to save lives and reduce destructive population growth. Roman Catholic interpretations are open to debate.

3. "Natural Law is deontological". This is an overstatement as Natural Law is profoundly **TELEOLOGICAL** in its goal of eudaimonia and follows the Greek teleological worldview. However, it is still law, and is enshrined in principles and rules and codes of law which should reflect the **ETERNAL LAW** of God. The laws have to be **JUST** and subject to right reason.

4. "Natural Law requires God". Aquinas rejects **DIVINE COMMAND THEORY** (the argument that something is good or bad because God commands it). Natural Law therefore does not require God but is knowable by reason alone and observable in nature. Christian Natural Law theory argues that the divine blueprint for the Universe is reflected in its design and discoverable by scientific research, as well as reflection on the proper rational purposes of human beings.

Possible Exam Questions

1. "Natural Law does not present a helpful method for making moral decisions". Discuss

2. "Moral decisions should be based on duty, not purpose". Assess with reference to the theory of Natural Law.

3. "Human beings are born with the tendency to pursue morally good ends". Evaluate in the light of teleological aspects of Natural Law.

4. "Explain and justify the doctrine of double effect with reference to an ethical dilemma of your choice concerning euthanasia".

Key Quotes - Natural Law

"The natural law is the sharing in the eternal law by intelligent creatures". Thomas Aquinas

"The order of the precepts of the natural law is the order of our natural inclinations". Thomas Aquinas

"The natural law is unchangeable in its first principles, but in its secondary principles it may be changed through some special causes hindering the following of the primary precepts". Thomas Aquinas

"The natural law involves universality as it is inscribed in the rational nature of a person. It makes itself felt in every person endowed with reason". Veritatis Splendor (1995)

"Every marital act must of necessity retain its intrinsic relationship to the procreation of human life". Humanae Vitae (1968)

"The world is conceived as a rational order with value and purpose built into its very nature". James Rachels

Kantian Ethics

Background

KANT aimed to produce a **COPERNICAN REVOLUTION** in Ethics, by arguing that moral principles can be derived **A PRIORI** (by abstract reasoning) in contrast with the Utilitarian **A POSTERIORI** (experiential) method. Both are children of the **ENLIGHTENMENT** whose method is 'dare to reason'. David **HUME** awoke Kant from his 'dogmatic slumbers' by showing how a freely thinking philosopher can transform the way we look at things, including morality.

Key Terms

- **AUTONOMY** freedom to reason about the moral law

- **CATEGORICAL** unconditional, absolute, with no 'ifs"

- **HYPOTHETICAL** conditional, relative to circumstances, with 'ifs'

- **SUMMUM BONUM** the greatest good, combining virtue and happiness

- **DUTY** the sole moral motive of pursuing a line of action because it is right, whether or not we feel like it

- **ABSOLUTE** means the moral good cannot change with circumstances (non-consequentialist) and is universal (applies to all people everywhere in any culture).

Structure of Thought

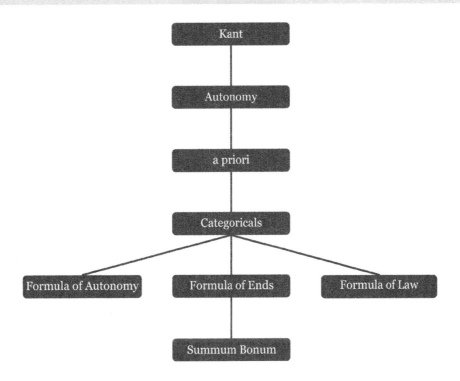

Deontological

A **NORMATIVE** theory (tells you what is right and wrong/what you ought to do), that is **DEONTOLOGICAL** (acts are intrinsically right and wrong in themselves, stressing rules and duties), **ABSOLUTIST** (applies universally in all times, places, situations) and is **A PRIORI** (derived from reason alone, not experience).

Autonomy

The key Kantian assumption is that we are **AUTONOMOUS** moral agents (self-ruled) which have free choice and free reason, rather than **HETERONOMOUS** meaning "ruled by others", where the others could be God, your peer group, or the Church. Kant adopted the **ENLIGHTENMENT** slogan "dare to reason" and was awakened out of his slumbers by reading Jean-Jacques **ROUSSEAU**'s theory of the social contract.

Good Will

Kant argues that the only thing that is morally good without exception is the **GOOD WILL**. A person of good will is someone motivated by **DUTY** alone. They are not motivated by self-interest, happiness or a feeling of sympathy. The good will is an **INTRINSIC** good (it is good in itself and not as a means to something else) and it doesn't matter if it doesn't bring about good consequences. Even if the good will achieved nothing good – even if it were combined with all manner of other evils – "it would shine forth like a jewel, having full value in itself". He contrasts this with other qualities (such as courage) which **CAN** be good but might also be bad depending on the situation (eg a courageous suicide bomber) which are **EXTRINSIC** goods as they depend on the circumstances.

Duty

Kant argues that we must follow our duty. It is not about what we want to do (our **INCLINATIONS**) or what will lead to the best consequences: only the action which springs from duty is a moral action. Doing your duty (eg helping a beggar) may be pleasurable, but this cannot be the reason why you did your duty (the **MOTIVE**). For it to be moral you have to act because it is your duty, and **FOR NO OTHER REASON**.

Categorical Imperative (C.I.)

How do you know what your duty is? Kant argues that this comes from the **CATEGORICAL IMPERATIVE**. It is categorical because it applies to us universally – simply because we have rational wills. By contrast a **HYPOTHETICAL IMPERATIVE** takes the form "If you want X, then you must do Y" (eg if you want to lose weight, then you must stop eating so much). The difference is the categorical imperative applies to us unconditionally, without any reference to a goal we might have (it is simply the form "You must do Y").

C.I. 1 The Formula of Law

"So act that the maxim of your action may be willed as a universal law for all humanity". For any action to be moral, you must be able to **CONSISTENTLY UNIVERSALISE** it. For example, if you decide not to keep a promise, then you must be able to consistently imagine a world where **EVERYONE** doesn't keep their promises – something Kant thought was impossible (because then no-one would believe a promise and so promise-keeping would vanish). He calls this a **CONTRADICTION IN NATURE** because the very nature of the thing – promising – is destroyed and so the action becomes self-contradictory.

C.I. 2 Formula of Ends

"Never treat people simply as a means to an end but always also as an end in themselves". People are **RATIONAL** and **AUTONOMOUS** (self-legislators) and so are worthy of respect. We cannot ONLY use them as a means for getting something else, but always as rational beings with dignity. We universalise our common humanity – which means we treat others as equals, with rights.

C.I. 3 Formula of Autonomy

Kant imagines a community of purely rational agents, each of whom is a **LEGISLATOR** (someone who decides laws) and a **SUBJECT** (someone who has to follow those laws) in what he calls a **KINGDOM OF ENDS**. We can only act on moral laws that would be accepted by this fully rational community – we belong to a moral parliament where we are free participators in the law-making process. This introduces an important **SOCIAL** aspect to Kantian ethics. "Kantian ethics is the ethics of democracy", (James Rachels)

Summum Bonum

The **SUMMUM BONUM** or "supreme good" is **VIRTUE** (a person of 'good will' who follows their duty by applying the Categorical Imperative) combined with **HAPPINESS**. We should not act in order to get happiness (because moral action should only involve doing our duty for duty's sake), but the ideal is that we should be happy to the degree that we **DESERVE** to be happy. This is obviously not something that can be found in this life – we see bad people living happy lives and good people living unhappy lives – therefore the Summum Bonum must be able to be achieved in the **AFTERLIFE**.

Three Postulates

Kant argued there are three necessary **POSTULATES** (or propositions which we **ASSUME** rather than **PROVE**) for morality:

1. **FREEDOM** (we must be free to make moral decisions)

2. **IMMORTALITY** (there must be an afterlife in order to achieve the summum bonum).

3. **GOD** (necessary to guarantee the moral law and to judge fairly and reward or punish).

Strengths

It's **REASONABLE** – pretty much what most people consider morality to be about (ie universalising your behaviour). The various formulations of the Categorical Imperative take the **DIGNITY** and **EQUALITY** of human beings very seriously. The innocent are protected by the universal equality given to all human beings.

Weaknesses

It is **INFLEXIBLE** as absolutes have to be applied in all situations irrespective of what we consider to be the wisest choice. Kant also seems to make a clear distinction between our **EMOTIONS** and the ethical choice done from duty alone - but is it really morally doubtful if I act out of emotion like compassion and not just from **DUTY** alone? Also, what happens when two duties **CONFLICT** (eg I need to lie to a crazy knifeman who is enquiring if my friend is in the house - Kant's own example where he insists we tell the truth whatever happens). Surely **CONSEQUENCES** do matter, and arguably there has to be a consequential element to Kant when we imagine universalising an imperative.

Notice that the weaknesses may also be **STRENGTHS** in certain circumstances - such as a difficult choice which may affect human lives whichever way we choose.

Confusions - Kant

1. "Duty means blind obedience". This is what Adolf Eichmann implied in his trial in 1962 - but it's not Kant's view of duty which involves reasoning through the **UNIVERSALISABILITY** of your action and treating all human beings with equal respect.

2. "Duty means ignoring emotion". This is a possible reading of Kant, but not the only one. Another reading is to say that Kant saw **DUTY** as the primary motive and so long as emotions don't conflict with duty then having moral emotions is fine - just don't base your reason on emotion as it is unreliable.

3. 'Kantian ethics is deontological". William Frankena classified Kant as deontological and it is true Kant argues for unconditional commands (categoricals). But when we universalise we can't help thinking about consequences - there is a consequential dimension to Kant. Whether we have done our duty from the right motive is deontological - but determining the right duty needs a **TELEOLOGICAL** approach.

Possible Exam Questions

1. "Kantian ethics is not helpful in providing practical guidelines for making moral decisions". Discuss

2. Evaluate to what extent duty can be the sole basis for a moral action.

3. "Kantian ethics is too abstract to be useful in practical ethical decision-making'. Discuss

4. "In neglecting the role of emotions in favour of pure reason, Kantian ethics fails to give a realistic account for our human nature". Discuss

Key Essay Ideas

1. Kant's theory is a priori using logical education - like the ontological argument (Paper 1).

2. Kant's theory is absolute because the categorical imperative doesn't change with circumstances.

3. The first formula is close to Jesus' Golden Rule of Matthew 5.

4. The second formula asks us to imagine what it's like to be the other person.

5. Kant has a problem what to do when two duties conflict, and one must be overridden.

Key Quotes - Kant

"It is impossible to conceive of anything in the world good without qualification except the good will". Immanuel Kant

"Two things fill me with wonder, the starry hosts above and the moral law within". Immanuel Kant

"Kant places the stern voice of duty at the heart of the moral life". Robert Arrington

"The highest created good is a world where rational beings are happy and worthy of happiness". Immanuel Kant

"There is more to the moral point of view than being willing to universalise one's rules". William Frankena

Bentham's Act Utilitarianism

Background

The Utilitarians attempted to bring **SCIENCE** to morality by producing an **EMPIRICAL** (testable) method to establishing right and wrong. The approach is **RADICAL** in two senses - there is a radical **EQUALITY** in its method and a radical **SIMPLICITY** which works especially well when assessing **PUBLIC POLICY** (eg whether to reduce road congestion or have legislation pro **EUTHANASIA**). Bentham wanted a new **PRISONS** policy which was centred on character reform, and **MILL** was briefly imprisoned for campaigning for **CONTRACEPTION**. A central difficulty remains: what happens if torturing you makes everyone else happier? Utilitarians argue for **NET** happiness to be **MAXIMISED** (total **PLEASURE** minus total **PAIN**).

Key Terms

- **PLEASURE** the one intrinsic good, according to Bentham

- **GREATEST HAPPINESS PRINCIPLE** to act to maximise the greatest happiness of the greatest number - the fundamental principle of utilitarian ethics

- **HEDONIC CALCULUS** a way of quantifying pleasure by seven criteria

- **TELEOLOGICAL** a theory which relates goodness to ends or purposes

- **CONSEQUENTIALIST** identifying goodness by the results of an action

- **EMPIRICAL** a scientific word implying morality can be tested and measured

Background

BENTHAM (1748-1832) was a social reformer who believed that the law should serve human needs and welfare. Where **JUSTICE** was **RETRIBUTIVE** he wanted to see it **REFORMING** the person and acting as a **DETERRENCE** – there had to be a real social benefit outweighing the pain to the criminal, and with a better **DISTRIBUTION** of resources, but all in the cause of the **GREATEST HAPPINESS PRINCIPLE (GHP)** – the motive was to reduce suffering and increase happiness for everyone. The theory is **TELEOLOGICAL** because it measures likely consequences of **ACTIONS**, and **HEDONIC** because Bentham believed pleasure (Greek: hedon) was the key motive and could be quantified. So there is an **EMPIRICAL**, objective measure of goodness.

Motivation

There is one **MORAL** good – pleasure, and one evil – pain. "Nature has placed mankind under two **SOVEREIGN** masters, pain and pleasure". Right actions are on balance pleasurable, wrong actions are on balance painful. Bentham's is therefore a theory of **PSYCHOLOGICAL HEDONISM** (Hedonism - pleasure-seeking).Hedonic Calculus

The **HEDONIC CALCULUS** is a way of measuring pleasure and pain, so the consequences of an act can be assessed as a score in units of happiness called **HEDONS** (plus for pleasure, minus for pain). The seven criteria are (acronym **PRRICED**): **P**urity, **R**ichness, **R**eliability, **I**ntensity, **C**ertainty, **E**xtent, **D**uration. In this assessment "everyone is to count as one and no-one as more than one" (Bentham), so there is strict **EQUALITY**.

Quantitative Pleasure

Bentham believed "pushpin is as good as poetry" (pushpin – a pub game = playing a slot machine in today's terms). Pleasure is purely **QUANTITATIVE** so we can't award more hedons to listening to Mozart or painting a picture or grasping philosophy. Mill, who was saved from mental breakdown by **WORDSWORTH**'s poetry, really objected to this. According to Bentham, we can compare a small child's delight in a new toy with someone else's delight in a new girlfriend. A **PIG** enjoying a good wallow is of more value than **SOCRATES** having a sightly sad think. Hence "*the pig philosophy*" (Thomas **CARLYLE**).

Pleasure Machines

JCC SMART (1973:18-21) asks us to imagine a pleasure machine where we can be wired up every day and passively enjoy every pleasure imaginable (note-addiction often operates like this as a kind of refuge in a supposed pleasure - like drink). **ALDOUS HUXLEY** wrote of a brave new world where people popped **SOMA** tablets to make them happy (there were 41m antidepressant prescriptions last year in the UK). Bentham can have no problems with this, but **MILL** saw happiness as a wider idea involving **ACTIVITY**, and realistic goals and expectations (closer to what my therapist might advise or what **ARISTOTLE** argues).

Strengths - Bentham

There is a **SIMPLICITY** in Bentham's calculation, and a radical **EQUALITY**. The **TELOS** of increasing human welfare is attractive and **COMMON SENSE**. His ideas drove **SOCIAL REFORM** – and he designed a more humane prison called a **PANOPTICON** – never built in the UK, but in Barcelona. There is a lack of snobbery in his classification of all pleasures as **EQUALLY VALID** – why should Mozart be thought better than Rap music (at least in giving pleasure)?

Labels on the thermometer (Hedon-o-meter): purity, remoteness, reproducability, intensity, certainty, extent, duration

JERRY BENTHAM'S 12 FRUIT SLURPER

Weaknesses

Bentham focuses only on **ACTIONS** so we have to keep on calculating (he doesn't allow us to have **RULES** to make life easier). He equates **PLEASURE** with **HAPPINESS** – but they don't seem to be equivalent (ask the athlete training for the Olympics whether the toil is pleasurable – but it doesn't mean a lack of contentment with training). We can always ask "you're going to the nightclub, but is that a **GOOD** idea?" (Good meaning "promoting your welfare"). Bentham implies pleasure is **MEASURABLE** (it isn't - how can we compare my hedon with yours?). Finally, he has no answer for Smart's **PLEASURE MACHINE** or Huxley's **SOMA** tablet (of course, they were writing two centuries later so even if his stuffed skeleton, residing in a cupboard in London University, could talk, we don't know what it would say!).

Key Quotes - Bentham

"Nature has placed mankind under two sovereign masters, pain and pleasure. It is for them to point out what we ought to do as well as determine what we should do ". Jeremy Bentham, Principles of Morals

"In every human breast, self-regarding interest is predominant over social interest; each person's own individual interest over the interests of all other persons taken together". Jeremy Bentham, Book of Fallacies, p 392

"The community is a fictitious body, " and it is but "the sum of the interests of the several members who compose it ". Jeremy Bentham, Principles of Morals

"Prejudice apart, the game of pushpin is of equal value with the arts and sciences of music and poetry. If the game of pushpin furnishes more pleasure, it is more valuable than either". Jeremy Bentham, Principles of Morals

Mill's Rule Utilitarianism

Background

Following J.O. **URMSON** in 1953, most people describe Mill's form of Utilitarianism **WEAK** (because these aren't hard and fast rules, as with **KANT**), **RULE** (because he argues: follow social rules first, based on past experience of happiness) **UTILITARIANISM** (as it has the one fundamental principle at its core - maximise **UTILITY**). However, it is fundamentally wrong to call his utilitarianism **HEDONIC** (his view of happiness is closer to **ARISTOTLE** than **BENTHAM**) and **RELATIVISTIC** (as there's a non-negotiable **ABSOLUTE** at its core - **UTILITY**). If you read his essay carefully you will find he redefines happiness as he goes along, adding **SOCIAL RULES**, **JUSTICE** and **LIFETIME GOALS** to a list of necessary conditions, and even **PLEASURE** gets a special treatment as Mill distinguishes **HIGHER** and **LOWER** pleasures.

Key Terms

- **ACT UTILITARIANISM** (AU) measuring the utility of an individual act

- **RULE UTILITARIANISM** (RU) focusing on the rules which maximise social happiness

- **RIGHTS** legal obligations which maximise social utility

- **JUSTICE** certain principles, practices and rights which according to Mil guarantee social utility

- **QUALITATIVE PLEASURE** pleasure can be evaluated according to its social value as 'higher' (intellectual) and 'lower' (bodily)

Structure of Thought

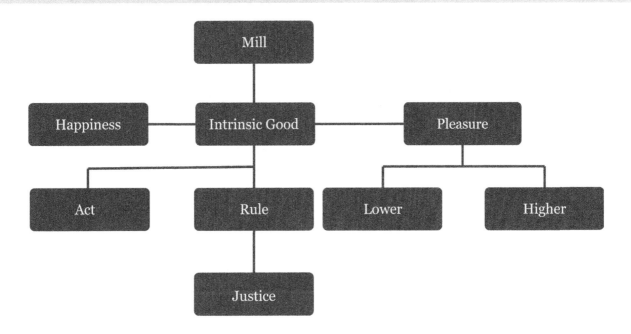

Weak Rule Utilitarianism

The weak **RULE UTILITARIANISM** of John Stuart Mill (1806-73) is a **TELEOLOGICA**L (telos = goal) theory based on a definition of goodness as the **BALANCE** of happiness over misery.

This is a measurable, **EMPIRICAL** idea – measure the happiness effects of likely consequences – giving an **OBJECTIVE** measure of goodness.

Mill was against the **INTUITIONISTS** which he found too **SUBJECTIVE**. Mill argues that happiness is most likely to be maximised by generally following a set of **RULES** which society has found, by experience, maximise utility. But the rules can develop and in cases of moral dilemmas, we should revert to being **ACT UTILITARIANS** (so weak **RU**).

Mill & Bentham

Mill disliked three aspects of **BENTHAM**'s version.

1. The swinish implications of categorising all pleasures as of equal value – drinking beer v. listening to Mozart.

2. The emphasis on pleasure alone, as Mill was influenced by **ARISTOTLE**'s views on virtue (eg the importance of **SYMPATHY** for others). Mill believed Bentham neglected the development of human **CHARACTER**.

3. The problem of **JUSTICE** and **RIGHTS** – how do we prevent one innocent person or group being sacrificed for the general happiness of the majority? So Mill devotes the last chapter of his essay to **JUSTICE**.

Mill on Happiness

Mill's definition of a happy life has three elements – pleasure (varied and rich) and absence of pain, **AUTONOMY** (the free choice of a life goal), and **ACTIVITY** (motivated by virtues like sympathy eg Mill used to hand out leaflets advising about contraception and campaigned for women's rights).

"**HAPPINESS** is not a life of rapture, but moments of such, in an existence with few and transitory pains, many and various pleasures, with a decided predominance of the **ACTIVE** over the passive, and having as a foundation of the whole, not to expect more from life than it is capable of bestowing". JS Mill, Utilitarianism

Higher and Lower Pleasures

Mill was saved from a nervous breakdown in his 20s by the **ROMANTIC MOVEMENT** eg Wordsworth's Lyrical Ballads. To him poetry was infinitely superior to **PUSHPIN** (a pub game). So "better to be Socrates dissatisfied than a fool satisfied".

The **LOWER** bodily pleasures (food, sex, drink, football) were of less value than the **HIGHER** pleasures (reading, listening to Mozart).

So Mill followed **ARISTOTLE** in seeing education as of vital importance (the supreme Greek value is **CONTEMPLATION** to gain wisdom). Only a person who'd experienced both could really judge the difference in

QUALITY (so we say qualitative pleasure is superior to quantitative). He called those who hadn't experienced both "inferior beings". Does this make Mill a snob?

Rules

Mill has been called an "inconsistent utilitarian" (Alasdair MacIntyre) – because as his essay goes on he moves from **ACT** to **RULE** utilitarianism. We use generations of past experience to form rules, so we don't have to do a calculation to know whether murder or theft is "right". We inherit **BELIEFS** "and the beliefs which have thus come down are the **RULES** of morality for the multitude" (JS Mill). These are not fixed but "admit of continual improvement" – so not **ABSOLUTE**.

The **FIRST PRINCIPLE** is utility (or the Greatest Happiness Principle) and then **SECONDARY PRINCIPLES** (rules) come from this and are constantly evaluated against the first principle. Just as navigation is based on astronomy (Mill's own analogy) doesn't mean the sailor goes back to the stars every time – no he uses an **ALMANAC** – so, argues Mill, human beings follow a code book of rules passed down from previous generations as the best way to be happy.

But if the depth sounder disagrees with the chart datum (rules of past chart-plotter's experience) we revert to being act utilitarians (my analogy).

Justice

Bernard **WILLIAMS** argued that Utilitarianism violates our **MORAL INTEGRITY** by encouraging us to do things we would find repulsive – like his example of Jim who is invited to kill one Indian as an honoured guest in order to save nineteen others. This is the problem of **INJUSTICE** – the Southern States may have enjoyed lynching innocent people in the 1920s but this doesn't make it right.

Mill argues that unhappiness is caused by selfishness, by people "acting only for themselves", and that for a person to be happy they need "to cultivate a fellow feeling with the collective interests of mankind" and "in the **GOLDEN RULE** of Jesus we find the whole ethics of utility" (JS Mill).

So we need to defend personal **RIGHTS** and "Justice is a name for certain moral requirements, which, regarded collectively, stand higher in the scale of **SOCIAL UTILITY**, and are therefore of more paramount obligation, than any others", and "justice is a name for certain classes of **MORAL RULES**, which concern the essentials of human well-being". Rights, justice and the virtue of sympathy stop selfish self-interest destroying the happiness of others. So we escape the problem of Jim and the Indians.

Act or Rule?

LOUIS POJMAN argues (2006:111) that we can adopt a **MULTILEVEL** approach (this is what Mill seems to be doing in talking about **PRIMARY** and **SECONDARY** principles). So we can have three levels if we wish: rules of thumb to live by which generally maximise utility, a second set of rules for resolving conflicts between these, and a third process – an

ACT utilitarian one, for assessing a difficult situation according to the Greatest Happiness Principle (eg lying to save a friend). But in this way philosophers like **J.O.URMSON** argue that **RULE** utilitarianism collapses into **ACT** utilitarianism. Mill might counter that we don't have the time, the wisdom, or the resources to keep calculating every action and this multilevel approach is therefore realistic and practical in a way that **KANT**'s deontology is unrealistic and impractical because it cannot handle **MORAL DILEMMAS**.

Strengths - Mill

RATIONALITY and **PRACTICALITY** Utilitarian ethics rests on a rational calculation of numbers of people whose pleasure or happiness is maximised. There is a clarity and simplicity to this.

EQUALITY is central. Bentham wrote "everyone is to count as one, and no-one as more than one". This radical idea implies that everyone has equal weight in the utility calculation.

MILL adds equal **RIGHTS**. Suppose, on an equal vote, you all vote for my dismissal (or even death) in line with maximising general happiness? Mill argues this sort of law would violate rights and such a society would not be one that we'd choose to live in - it would be miserable. "The utilitarian emphasis on impartiality must be a part of any defensible moral theory". (Rachels, 2006:114). Finally, utilitarianism takes account of the **FUTURE** – issues of climate change, potential future wars and famines all suggest we need an ethical theory that takes into account those yet unborn.

Weaknesses - Mill

MOTIVE, "why should I maximise pleasure or happiness?" We can't agree how to define pleasure or happiness. Bentham and Mill don't notice the difficulty of the concept of "pleasure" a fatal objection at the outset", Anscombe (1958:2). Then there is a difficulty in making me think of the interests (happiness) of others. Mill tries to bring "sympathy" in as a kind of virtue or psychological motive.

DISTRIBUTION problems emerge when I try to maximise **TOTAL** not **AVERAGE** happiness – eg low tax for the rich may raise the total but reduce average happiness, because the 10% super rich are much, much happier.

Finally **CONSEQUENCES** are hard to calculate if you don't have the omniscience of God. The **IRAQ WAR** may have seemed justifiable by the Greatest Happiness Principle - but looking with hindsight we might argue - better a Saddam Hussein in power than a million deaths?

Confusions - Mill

1. Was Mill an Act or Rule Utilitarian? He is sometimes described as a **WEAK RULE UTILITARIAN**. Mill believed that generally we should follow the rule as this reflects society's view of what maximises happiness from past social experience. But when a pressing utilitarian need arises we should break the rule and so become an act utilitarian.

2. "Mill took Bentham's view that happiness equates to pleasure". Sometimes Mill seems to argue this, but it's truer to say Mill's view is close to **ARISTOTLE**'s that happiness means "personal and social flourishing". So to Mill the individual cannot be happy without the guarantee of certain rules and rights and clear goals to aim for.

3. "Utilitarianism ignores individual rights". Mill would vigorously deny this: rights are essential for the happy society and the happy society generally, with a sense of security, is essential for happy individuals. However, a Benthamite view of individual **ACT UTILITARIANISM** is subject to this criticism (as is US foreign policy which included Guantanamo Bay and Rendition), because many people's pleasure outweighs one or two people's pain (it's the **BALANCE** of pleasure over pain that matters morally).

4. "Utilitarianism is a form of egoism". Utilitarianism escapes this criticism for two reasons: there is an impartiality as "everyone to count as one" and secondly, because the virtue of **SYMPATHY** as a moral feeling is fundamental to my concern for your welfare.

Possible Exam Questions

1. Evaluate the view that utilitarianism does not provide a helpful way of solving moral dilemmas.

2. "The application of the greatest happiness principle in specific situations is not a sufficient guide to the good action". Discuss

3. "Pleasure is not quantifiable". Discuss

4. To what extent does utilitarian ethics provide a useful guide to issues surrounding business ethics?

Key Quotes - Mill

"It is better to be a human being dissatisfied than a pig satisfied; better Socrates dissatisfied than a fool satisfied". J.S.Mill, Utilitarianism

"Happiness is...moments of rapture...in an existence of few and transitory pains, many and various pleasures, with a predominance of the active over the passive..not to expect more from life than it is capable of bestowing". J.S. Mill, Utilitarianism

"Whatever we adopt as the fundamental principle of Morality refers to the first-order beliefs and practices about good and evil by means of which we guide our behaviour. For morality, we require subordinate principles to apply it by". (Fundamental principle = happiness is good, subordinate principles = rules) J.S. Mill, Utilitarianism

"To have a right, then, is, I conceive, to have something which society should defend me in possession of. If the objector asks why? I can give no other answer than general utility". J.S.Mill, Utilitarianism

"Justice is a name for certain moral requirements, which, regarded collectively, stand higher in the scale of social utility, than any others". J.S.Mill, Utilitarianism

"In the golden rule of Jesus of Nazareth we find the whole ethics of utility". JS Mill, Utilitarianism

Situation Ethics - Christian Relativism

Situation Ethics is a **NORMATIVE** theory (tells you what is right/wrong – what you ought to do), that is **TELEOLOGICAL** and **CONSEQUENTIALIST** (acts are right or wrong if they bring about good/bad consequences, or can be seen as instrumentally good/bad) and **RELATIVIST** (there are no universal rules as actions depend on circumstances; there is just one general universal value – that of agape love). It is also **CHRISTIAN**, based on the principle of sacrificial love (**AGAPE**).

Introduction

Joseph Fletcher (1966) argued there are three approaches to ethics:

1. **LEGALISTIC** – someone who follows absolute rules and laws. Fletcher rejects this as it leads to **UNTHINKING OBEDIENCE** and needs elaborate systems of exceptions and compromises.

2. **ANTINOMIAN** – (nomos is Greek for law, so anti-law) or someone who rejects all rules and laws (Fletcher rejects this as it would lead to social **CHAOS**).

3. **SITUATIONAL** – Fletcher argues that each individual situation is different and absolute rules are too demanding and restrictive. Instead we should decide what is the most **LOVING** course of action (**AGAPE**). The Situationist has respect for laws and tradition, but they are only guidelines to how to achieve this loving outcome, and thus they may be broken if the other course of action would result in more love.

However, Situation Ethics is not **FULLY** relativist: it has an absolute principle (love) that is non-negotiable.

Origins of Agape in the New Testament

William **TEMPLE** wrote "there is only one ultimate and invariable duty; and its formula is this: "thou shalt love thy neighbour as thyself" (1917:206). He went on: "what acts are right depends on circumstances" (1934:405). **FLETCHER** was inspired by Temple but also argues that love is the fundamental controlling norm. There is a case for arguing this from the New Testament.

- Love is the heart of God's **CHARACTER**. "God is love" (1 John 4:8). This echoes the Old Testament description of God as one "abounding in steadfast love and faithfulness" (Exodus, 34:8) in his revelation to Moses.

- Love is the fulfilling of the **LAW**. Love interprets the commandments and allows us sometimes to break them. In John 8 Jesus refuses to allow them to stone an adulterous woman in direct breach of Leviticus 20:10.

- Love is the heart of a controlling **PARABLE** of the Good Samaritan.,(Luke 10). "Controlling" in the sense that Jesus' own sacrificial love mirrors that of the outsider who did all he could to help the victim, as priests and officials passed by, and so the parable 'controls' our interpretation of the entire mission of Christ.

- Love is Jesus' new **COMMAND** (John 13:34) - 'a new commandment I give to you to love one another as I have loved you".

- Sacrificial love (**AGAPE**) is the highest form of love; "Greater love has no man than this, that he lay down his life for his friends". John 15:13

- Love is also the supreme **VIRTUE** in the writings of Paul, with many characteristics (kindness, patience, forgiveness, positivity, hopefulness, perseverance), (1 Corinthians 13).

- Love is given to us by the **SPIRIT** of love, says Paul - the Holy Spirit. (Romans 5:5)

So although the Greeks had several words for love - friendship, family love, erotic love - the greatest moral value is given to **AGAPE**.

Four Working Principles

In Situation Ethics there are **FOUR WORKING PRINCIPLES** (Fletcher's own term).

1. **PRAGMATISM** – (what you propose must be practical – work in practice).

2. **RELATIVISM** – (there are no fixed, absolute rules – all decisions are relative to **AGAPE** love. If love demands that you steal food, then you should steal food. Notice this is special meaning of relativism - Fletcher calls his theory 'principled relativism' because every action is made relative to the one principle of agape love.

3. **POSITIVISM** – (Kant and Natural Law are based on reason as both theories argue reason can uncover the right course of action). Fletcher disagrees with this: you have to start with a **POSITIVE** choice or commitment – you

need to want to do good. There is no rational answer to the question "why should I love?" We accept this norm by faith.

4. **PERSONALISM** – (people come first: you cannot sacrifice people to rules or laws)

Six Fundamental Principles

1. Nothing is good in itself except **LOVE** (it is the only thing that is absolutely good, the only thing with **INTRINSIC** value).

2. Jesus replaced the law with love or **AGAPE** ("The ruling norm of Christian decision is love, nothing else". Joseph Fletcher).

3. Love and **JUSTICE** are the same thing (if love is put into practice it can only result in fair treatment and fair distribution).

4. Love desires the good of **OTHERS** (it does not have favourites, but this doesn't mean we have to **LIKE** them).

5. Only the **END JUSTIFIES THE MEANS** (if an action causes harm, it is wrong. If good comes of it, it is right).

6. Love's decisions are made in each **SITUATION**.

Conscience

Fletcher argues conscience has many potential meanings:

- **THE VOICE OF GOD** - as in the writings of Cardinal John Henry Newman.

- **PRACTICAL REASON** or phronesis - one of two meanings in the writings of Thomas Aquinas.

- **AN INSTINCT** we are born with. Aquinas' other word for conscience is **SYNDERESIS,** meaning an innate conscience.

- **AS A VERB** - Fletcher rejects the idea of conscience as a 'faculty' and argues it is like a verb reflecting our actions in doing loving things: 'there is no conscience; 'conscience' is merely a word for our attempts to make decisions creatively, constructively, fittingly'. (1966:53)

Strengths - Situation Ethics

It takes **INDIVIDUALS** and their needs seriously. It's also **FLEXIBLE** and also allows us to make judgements in situations where two moral principles conflict. **LOVE** is an important value somewhat neglected by other theories, as the motive of sympathy in Mill's utilitarian ethics is not quite as strong as the **AGAPE** of Joseph Fletcher.

Weaknesses - Situation Ethics

LOVE is a very demanding value to place at the centre of your ethics - can anyone love sacrificially all the time? Mustn't we be selfish some of the time? Like all **CONSEQUENTIALIST** theories it's impossible to calculate into the future making this particular love calculation **IMPOSSIBLE**. William Barclay argues that Fletcher fails to realise the value of law - as an expression fo the collective wisdom of generations before us, so the moral law is a guide which we shouldn't throw away so easily. Law also defines the **FABRIC** of society.

Confusions

1. "Situation ethics is a form of relativism". Fletcher denies this as he argues it is 'principled relativism' - meaning that the supreme norm of love is applied to situations and made relative to need and circumstances. There is thus one absolute norm - **AGAPE.** This is not relativism in the sense of the denial of objective truth, it is relativism in the sense of 'goodness is relative to the situation' (a relativism of application not of norms).

2. "Situation ethics is a religious ethic". It is true that **AGAPE** is a controlling norm of the **NEW TESTAMENT**. Also the parable of the Good Samaritan (Luke 10) appears to be a form of situationism 'go and do likewise', says Jesus, which seems to mean 'go and work out love in the situations you find yourself'. When Fletcher gave up Christianity he still argued that the non-Christian will equate goodness with an idea such as Aristotle's **EUDAIMONIA** (flourishing) whereas the Christian would always maintain **AGAPE** as the supreme norm. So there may be a difference there between atheistic situationism and religious forms.

3. "Jesus was a situationist". It is true that Jesus overthrows some elements of the **LEVITICAL CODE** of law such as stoning adulterers, the uncleanness of certain types of food (such as pork), the uncleanness of certain types of people (such as menstruating women). It is also true that the parable of the **GOOD SAMARITAN** promotes a situationist ethic. However, he also said "I came not to abolish the law but to fulfil the law" (Matthew 5:17). This implies that the fundamental principles of the law such as justice, truth and equality are perfectly fulfilled in Jesus, even if he rejects some of the ritualistic practices.

Possible Exam Questions

1. "Situation ethics is too demanding as a system of ethical decision-making". Discuss

2. "Goodness is only defined by asking - how is agape best served". Discuss

3. "Agape is not so much a religious idea as an equivalent to saying 'I want the best for you'". Discuss

4. Evaluate the extent to which situation ethics is individualistic and subjective.

Key Quotes - Situation Ethics

"Love alone is always good and right in every situation". Joseph Fletcher (Situation Ethics, 1966:69)

"Faith, hope and love abide, these three, but the greatest of all is love". 1 Corinthians 13:13

"God is love". 1 John 4:8

"A new commandment I give to you, that you love one another". John 13:34

"There can be and often is a conflict between law and love". Joseph Fletcher (1966:70)

"Too much law means the obliteration of the individual; too much individualism means a weakening of the law...there is a place for law as the encourager of morality". William Barclay, Ethics in a Permissive Society p189

In 1952 Pope Pius called situation ethics "an individualistic and subjective appeal to the concrete circumstances of actions to justify decisions in opposition to the Natural law or God's revealed will'.

"High authority has held that a starving man should rather steal a loaf than die of hunger". William Temple

Euthanasia

Background

There have been numerous appeals to the law courts to get a **RIGHT** to euthanasia established in British law (see for example the Diane **PRETTY** case or Debbie **PURDY**). Interestingly, it is only the **SITUATION** ethicist who unambiguously defends Euthanasia (and then only for certain forms). In the UK we have an approach very similar to what a **WEAK RULE UTILITARIAN** would advocate: we follow the social rule (no euthanasia) but in certain cases we turn a blind eye and become **ACT UTILITARIANS**. For example doctors will increase a morphine dose with a dying patient's permission, having told them it will kill them (**VOLUNTARY ACTIVE EUTHANASIA**) - which corresponds also with the **PRINCIPLE** of **DOUBLE EFFECT** in **NATURAL LAW**. Because the **INTENTION**'s to relieve pain, this is neither illegal nor arguably immoral.

Definitions

- **EUTHANASIA** (Greek = good death) is the practice of ending life to reduce pain and suffering (so "mercy killing").

- **VOLUNTARY** euthanasia = when a patient's death is caused by another person eg doctor with the **EXPLICIT CONSENT** of the patient. The patient request must be **VOLUNTARY** (acting without coercion, pressure) **ENDURING** (lasts some time or is repeated over time) and **COMPETENT** (they have the mental capacity to choose). A variation on euthanasia is **PHYSICIAN-ASSISTED SUICIDE** – this differs from euthanasia as the doctor will help the patient to commit suicide (eg set up the apparatus), but the final act of killing is done by the patient.

- **NON-VOLUNTARY** euthanasia is done without the patient's consent, because they are not competent or able to give the consent (eg in a coma, on a life support machine). The doctor and/or the family may take the decision. A famous test case was that of **TONY BLAND** who was in a persistent vegetative state following the 1989 Hillsborough football disaster.

- **INVOLUNTARY** euthanasia is performed **AGAINST** the wishes of the patient. This is widely opposed and illegal in the UK.

Active or Passive

ACTIVE euthanasia is the direct and **DELIBERATE** killing of a patient.

PASSIVE euthanasia is when life-sustaining treatment is withdrawn or withheld.

This distinction may also be described as the difference between an **ACT** and an **OMISSION** (failing to act) and between **KILLING** and **ALLOWING TO DIE**. Some, such as James Rachels, argue there is no real difference – if anything passive euthanasia (withdrawal of treatment) is worse because it leads to a longer, drawn out death and so more suffering potentially. **DAME CICELY SAUNDERS** (who founded the hospice movement) argues that it is unnecessary for anyone to suffer a painful death with modern drugs. A counter-argument is that many doctors already hasten death (eg by doubling a morphine dose): under the doctrine of **DOUBLE EFFECT** (part of Natural Law theory), if the intention is to alleviate pain and a secondary effect to kill someone, the doctor is not guilty of any crime.

Legal Position

Until 1961 suicide was illegal in the UK. The **1961 SUICIDE ACT** legalised suicide, but made it illegal to assist someone.

The **NETHERLANDS** and **SWITZERLAND** allow voluntary euthanasia (**ACTIVE** and **PASSIVE**) and physician-assisted suicide. The **DIGNITAS** clinic in Switzerland helped 107 British people to die in 2010. **DR ANNE TURNER** (aged 66) was one such person in 2009 – subject of the docu-drama "A Short Stay in Switzerland". No-one has ever been prosecuted in the UK for helping a relative or friend go to Switzerland.

In 2010 Director of Public Prosecutions **KEIR STARMER** confirmed that relatives of people who kill themselves will not face prosecution as long as they do not maliciously encourage them and assist only a "clear settled and informed wish" to commit suicide. The move came after the Law Lords backed multiple sclerosis sufferer Debbie **PURDY**'s call for a policy statement on whether people who help someone commit suicide should be prosecuted.

Keir Starmer concluded: "There are **NO GUARANTEES** against prosecution and it is my job to ensure that the most vulnerable people are protected while at the same time giving enough information to those people like Mrs Purdy who want to be able to make informed decisions about what actions they may choose to take".

The **OREGON RULES** are another attempt to legalise assisted suicide by laying down conditions under which it will be allowed in US law.

Sanctity of Life - Bible

The Bible argues that life is a gift from God. Humans are created in the **IMAGE OF GOD** (Genesis 1:27) and the **INCARNATION** (God taking human form – John 1:14) shows the sacred value of human life. Human life is a **GIFT** or **LOAN** from God (Job 1:21 "The Lord gave and the Lord has taken away"). We should also show **RESPECT** for human life: "thou shalt not murder" (Exodus 20:13). We should also "choose life" (Deuteronomy 30). Finally, Christian love (**AGAPE**) is crucial (1 Corinthians 13 "the greatest value of all is love"). We should protect human life (the parable of the **GOOD SAMARITAN**) particularly as God gave his only son to redeem us (bring us back from sin and death) and give us the gift of "life in all its fullness".

Sanctity of Life - Ethical Theories

- The **NATURAL LAW** view argues that there is a **PRIMARY PRECEPT** to "preserve life" and views life as an **INTRINSIC** good. Euthanasia is therefore wrong and the Catholic Church forbids both active and passive euthanasia as "contrary to the dignity of the human person and the respect due to God, his creator" (Catechism of the Roman Catholic Church). However, the **DOCTRINE OF DOUBLE EFFECT** might accept the shortening of human life (eg if the intention is to relieve pain, secondary effect to kill) so long as it is only a **FORESEEN BUT UNINTENDED RESULT**. The Catholic Church also makes a distinction between **ORDINARY MEANS** (ordinary, usual medical treatments) and **EXTRAORDINARY MEANS** (treatments that are dangerous, a huge burden, or disproportionate). It is morally acceptable to stop extraordinary means, as "it is the refusal of over-zealous treatment".

- **ROMAN CATHOLIC** version of Natural law: "Discontinuing medical procedures that are burdensome, dangerous, extraordinary, or disproportionate to the expected outcome can be legitimate; it is the refusal of "over-zealous" treatment. Here one does not will to cause death; one's inability to impede it is merely accepted. The decisions should be made by the patient if he is competent and able or, if not, by those legally entitled to act for the patient, whose reasonable will and legitimate interests must always be respected." Catholic Catechism 2278

- **HUMANIST ARGUMENTS** Following Mill's **RULE** utilitarianism, we could argue that a. A general rule should be in place for social happiness prohibiting euthanasia (so the elderly don't feel under pressure or depressed people feel the temptation). But, b. In specific cases near the end of life doctor's using their discretion should hasten death. This is the present UK situation, which can be justified by rule utilitarian (non-Christian) arguments, giving a modified humanist sanctity of life view.

Quality of Life - Situation Ethics

JAMES RACHELS argues that the sanctity of life tradition places too much value on human life and there are times (eg with abortion and euthanasia) when this is unhelpful. He makes a distinction between **BIOLOGICAL LIFE** ("being alive" = functioning biological organism) and **BIOGRAPHICAL LIFE** ("having a life" = everything that makes us who we are). He says that what matters is biographical life and if this is already over (for example in a **PERSISTENT VEGETATIVE STATE = PVS**), then taking away biological life is acceptable.

PETER SINGER, a preference utilitarian, argues that the worth of human life varies (the value of human life is not a sacred gift but depends on its **QUALITY**). A low quality of life (judged by the patient) can justify them taking their life or justify someone else doing it for them.

SITUATION ETHICS would also take quality of life as more important than sanctity of life. **PERSONALISM** requires we take a case by case approach, and if someone is suffering in extreme discomfort, then **AGAPE** would dictate that we support their euthanasia. There may however be situations where someone is depressed, for example, where the most loving thing is to persuade them of a life worth living. **PRAGMATISM** demands a case by case and flexible approach. Joseph Fletcher was a himself a pioneer in bioethics and argued: "To bring this matter into the open practice of medicine would harmonise the civil law with medical morals, which must be concerned with the quality of life, not merely its quantity."

Autonomy

JOHN STUART MILL (On Liberty, 1859) argues that individuals should have full **AUTONOMY** (the freedom to make decisions without coercion) so long as it does not harm other people. Individuals cannot be compelled to do things for their own good – "over his own mind-body the individual is sovereign". Those who support voluntary euthanasia believe that personal autonomy and self-determination (choosing what happens to you) are crucial. Any competent adult should be able to decide on the time and manner of their death.

KANT assumes autonomy as one of his three key postulates (together with God and immortality). We are self-legislating, free moral beings. However, he argued in an essay on suicide that suicide was self-contradictory as, if it was universalised, the human race would die out.

DIANE PRETTY argued in a court case in 2002 that Article 1 of the Human Rights Convention (the right to life) included the right to take one's own life. This autonomy argument was rejected by the court. She was paralysed by motor-neurone disease and requested permission for her husband to assist her to die.

Arguments Against Euthanasia

PALLIATIVE CARE – Dame Cicely Saunders argues that there is a better alternative for euthanasia in providing a pain-free death for terminally ill patients. The **HOSPICE** movement may be seen as an alternative, BUT this level of care is not available to everyone, is expensive and cannot fully relieve a patient's suffering (eg for someone who cannot breathe unassisted).

VOLUNTARY AND COMPETENT – some raise questions about voluntary euthanasia. Can the patient ever be free from coercion (eg relatives who want an inheritance or doctors who need to free up resources)? Is the patient likely to be competent (eg when under high doses of medication, or when depressed, or senile). Response would be that there are at least some clear cases when patients **ARE** clearly voluntary (not coerced) and competent. Guidelines such as Starmer's or the **OREGON RULES** require a certain time period of repeated requests to different people, which are then independently confirmed.

SLIPPERY SLOPE – once allowed, the outcome will be a process of a further decline in respect for human life and will end with the practice of non-voluntary euthanasia for the elderly seen as "unaffordable" by the working majority. A response might be that there is a clear difference between voluntary and non-voluntary euthanasia. Is there any evidence of a slippery slope in the US state of Oregon or Switzerland? The rules on assisted suicide are drawn up precisely to stop the slide into widespread disrespect for human life. Note this is an **EMPIRICAL, CONSEQUENTIALIST** argument about probabilities.

DOCTOR-PATIENT RELATIONSHIP – some argue that doctors have a duty to preserve life (the **HIPPOCRATIC OATH**). Euthanasia will undermine the trust between patient and doctor if there is a fear that they will seek to end their life. However, as with abortion, there will remain doctors opposed to euthanasia which a patient could always choose, and it is highly unlikely that GPs will have any say in the process of mercy killing.

Possible Exam Questions

1. Natural Law is superior to situation ethics in its treatment of issues surrounding euthanasia". Discuss

2. "Autonomy as an ideal is unrealistic. No-one is perfectly autonomous". Discuss with reference to the ethical issue of euthanasia.

3. "Sanctity of human life is the core principle of medical ethics". Discuss

4. "There is no moral difference between actively ending a life by euthanasia and omitting to treat the patient". Discuss

Key Quotes

"Euthanasia is contrary to the dignity of the human person and the respect due to God, His creator". Roman Catholic Catechism

"The Lord gave, the Lord takes away; blessed be the name of the Lord". Job 1:21

"God created man in His own image". Genesis 1:27

"God knit you together in your mother's womb". Psalm 139:6

"Discontinuing medical procedures that are burdensome, dangerous, or disproportionate to the expected outcome can be legitimate". Catechism

"Compare a severely defective human infant with a nonhuman animal, we will often find the non-human to have superior capacities". Peter Singer

"We see a life of permanent coma as in no way preferable to death". Jonathan Glover

"The ability to make complex judgements about benefit requires compassion, experience and an appreciation of the patient's viewpoint". British Medical Association

"Once the boundary is crossed it is hard to see how social and commercial pressures do not define the 'volunteers'." Alastair Campbell in Gill, R. ed Euthanasia and the Churches (Cassell, 1998 p 94)

Business Ethics

Introduction

BUSINESS ETHICS is the critical examination of how people and institutions should behave in the world of commerce e.g. appropriate limits on self-interest, or (for firms) profits, when the actions of individuals or firms affect others. We may examine **CODES** which companies publish, or **BEHAVIOUR** of individuals – but also **CORPORATE CULTURE** (which may contradict the code) and responsibilities to the **ENVIRONMENT** and the developing world created by **GLOBALISATION** of markets and free trade between countries. We are asked to apply the Kantian idea of **UNIVERSALISED** duties and categoricals to business ethics, and utilitarian ideas of calculating net happiness or pleasure. according to **CONSEQUENCES**.

Key Terms

- **PROFIT MOTIVE** - the reward for risk-taking in maximising returns on any investment.

- **STAKEHOLDERS** - any parties affected by a business practice.

- **EXTERNALITIES** - costs or benefits external to the company – pollution is a negative externality.

- **GLOBALISATION** - the interconnection of economies , information and culture.

- **MULTINATIONALS** - companies trading in many countries.

Issues

Does the **PROFIT MOTIVE** conflict with ethical practice? Or does good ethics result in good business.

Should the regulation of business be left to **GOVERNMENTS**?

Ben and Jerry's has this **SOCIAL RESPONSIBILITY** statement at its heart: "to operate the company in a way that recognises the role business plays in the wider society and to find innovative ways to improve the life of the wider community". How widely is this view shared?

What happens when **STAKEHOLDER** interests conflict (eg sacking workers to raise shareholder returns?).

In a **GLOBALISED** world should we treat all workers the same irrespective of differences in national laws (think of safety regulations overseas)? Do **MULTINATIONALS** have too much power?

Stake-holders

A **STAKEHOLDER** is any individual or group who has a stake in the success or failure of a company. It includes **INTERNAL STAKEHOLDERS** (managers, employees) and **EXTERNAL** (the local community, customers, shareholders, suppliers, local authorities, Government, other countries). For example, the existence of a Tesco store may mean local shopkeepers do better (if more people visit the town) or worse (if business is taken away).

Stakeholder theory suggest we should consider the interests of all stakeholders in the consequences of a decision.

Codes - Kant's Duty

Most companies have **CODES OF ETHICS** which lay out the rights of different groups and the responsibilities and values of the company. **ETHICAL INVESTORS** only invest in companies that fulfil certain criteria eg **ENVIRONMENTAL** responsibility, and **FAIR TRADE** for overseas workers.

ETHICAL CONSUMERS look for sustainable sources or organic produce. The April 2011 riots in **BRISTOL** against the Tesco local store show how different interests may clash – stakeholders such as local businesses/some customers v. large corporations/ other customers and employees. Does Tesco have an **ETHICAL DUTY** not to destroy local businesses, or a duty to its potential **EMPLOYEES** (jobs) and **CUSTOMERS** (lower prices)? Is there and **ABSOLUTE** principle we can find to judge between them? Most companies have ethics codes. Are they **CATEGORICALLY** followed? (Or just when it suits them?)

Cost/Benefit

COST/BENEFIT analysis is a business equivalent to **UTILITARIAN** ethics, as it seeks to weigh the benefits in money terms of a business decision against the cost. It suffers the same problem: the denial of **INDIVIDUAL RIGHTS** as a moral **ABSOLUTE**.

In the case of **FORD PINTO** (1970s) the cost of a **HUMAN LIFE** was weighed against the number of likely accidents and the cost of a **PRODUCT RECALL**. At $13 a car it was not worth the recall, they decided. But – they didn't calculate **CONSEQUENCES** correctly and valued **HUMAN LIFE** too cheaply – so ended up paying millions in compensation and having to **RECALL** the car anyway.

Unfortunately value has to be placed on a human life in traffic safety, **NHS** budgets etc – it's not economic to place a crash barrier alongside roads adjacent to remote reservoirs – so tragic accidents do occur (e.g in April 2011 four die in a car plunging into a reservoir in Wales).

If environmental costs are too high, will companies pay them or relocate their business?

Externalities

EXTERNALITIES are costs paid (eg pollution) or benefits enjoyed (eg flowers in a roundabout) by someone external to the firm.

Traditionally Governments have taxed and regulated firms to make them comply with their ethical duties: **THE TEN HOURS ACT** (1847 restricts child labour to 10 hrs a day), the **CLEAN AIR ACT** (1956 restricts carbon emissions), the

HEALTH AND SAFETY ACT (1974 – improved safety standards and penalised non-compliance), the **SEX DISCRIMINATION ACT** (1975 – Equal Pay and opportunity for women).

MILTON FRIEDMAN (economist) argues that companies have a duty only to their shareholders (ie profits) – it is for society to set the other ethical rules. But examples such as **ENRON**, the US energy company that went bankrupt in 2003 after massive fraud, indicate that laws are never enough – individuals need to take **RESPONSIBILITY**.

As environmental regulation increases the cost to companies rises. Yet the USA has still not signed up to immediate carbon emission reduction despite the 1996 **KYOTO** protocol and the **COPENHAGEN** (2008)and **DURBAN** (2011) summits. Although China, Russia and America signed the Durban agreement, this only committed countries to define a future treaty by 2015, which will be binding in 2020.Once again immediate action has been postponed. US Senator Jim Inhofe, who has called climate change "the greatest hoax every perpetrated on the American people", applauded the "complete collapse of the global warming movement and the Kyoto protocol".

Rights

ABSOLUTISTS (eg Kantians) argue for universal human rights that apply everywhere for all time – including workers and communities in third world countries.

Because **GLOBALISATION** includes the free flow of **CAPITAL** to least cost countries, this can include those with corrupt governments or lax health and safety laws. Union Carbide (US firm) plant in **BHOPAL** (1986, India) and **TRAFIGURA** oil waste disposal (2008, Ivory Coast, hydrogen sulphide) illustrate how thousands can die (Bhopal – mustard gas) or go sick (Trafigura) when companies pursue least cost choices to boost **PROFIT**.
Worker and community rights often seem to take second place to **SHAREHOLDER** interests.

Individuals

Individual workers may become **WHISTLEBLOWERS** and expose fraud, corruption, lax standards etc. The RBS sacked their finance director who "didn't fit in" = opposed their lending policy before the **GLOBAL FINANCIAL CRISIS**.

UK banks were 24 hours from collapse in 2008 before a Government rescue plan, in taking on their bad debts. The rescue of **ROYAL BANK OF SCOTLAND** cost £43bn. But in the **EUROZONE** crisis countries act like individuals, with David Cameron vetoing a recent treaty change because of Britain's **NATIONAL INTEREST**. Is there such an idea as **COLLECTIVE** (European) interest?

Individual **CONSCIENCE** may serve the **public good,** but at the cost of their own **SELF-INTEREST** (they're fired). Kantian ethics may help us cling to **ABSOLUTES**, but Utilitarian ethics tends to make us pragmatists as at the **NORMATIVE** level we lie or stay silent to serve a **COLLECTIVE** interest (and we may not have enough sympathy with outsiders to care).

However **ENRON**'s collapse in 2003 brought down auditor **ARTHUR ANDERSEN** as it was implicated in the financial fraud which covered up huge debts, and affected shareholders, employees and pensioners. Sometimes **SHORT-TERMISM** in the utilitarian calculation can have terrible long-term consequences, and the courage of **ERIN**

BROKOVITCH in exposing the toxic leaks of **PACIFIC GAS** in an American town shows how a Kantian sense of duty may have much to teach us in Business affairs, even though it can be risky for an individual to take on powerful corporations. There was one Enron whistleblower - Vice-President Sherron Watkins - but she only blew as far as Chairman Ken Lay.

Future Generations

One of the puzzles of ethics is how we account for the interests of future generations and animals, plants, etc. Both **KANTIAN** and **UTILITARIAN** ethics are traditionally weak on environmental issues (Kant stresses rational autonomous beings as having moral worth, not animals, and utilitarianism sees the environment as having only **INSTRUMENTAL** goodness as a means to human happiness. This may suffer from the problem of **SHORT-TERMISM)**.

UTILITARIANISM however can arguably do better because the long term happiness of the human race is clearly one factor to consider – but how do we know how many people to add in to the calculation? How do we assess the environmental effect of the plastic bag "island" the size of Texas which exists in the central vortex of the **PACIFIC** ocean currents? **SUSTAINABLE DEVELOPMENT** is a new idea – and **CHRISTIAN ETHICS** has arguably suffered from an emphasis on **DOMINION** (Genesis 1:26) = exploit, rather than **STEWARDSHIP** = care for the environment.

Can we provide incentives to this generation to protect future rights of the unborn?

Globalisation

Globalisation is the **INTERCONNECTION** of markets, technology and information across the world. There are said to be five global brands: Nike, Coca-Cola, McDonalds, Levis. However globalisation brings the risk that large companies dominate the political agenda working in their own interest, and also force wages down for third world suppliers. For example, multinationals fund **PRESIDENTIAL** campaigns and the oil industry lobbies ceaselessly to stop any rise in **OIL PRICES** and even, it has been alleged, the development of alternative energy sources.

The economist Amartya Sen has argued that the central issue is "the **UNEQUAL SHARING** in the benefits of globalisation" – that the poor receive an unequal gain from any wealth created. Put another way, less developed countries are exploited for cheap labour in the global market place (compare **WAGES PER HOUR** in China and the UK for example).

Finally there is the question of **REGULATION**. Do multinationals export lax safety standards and poor environmental disciplines to the third world? The examples of **BHOPAL** (1984) and **TRAFIGURA*** (2007) are not encouraging. And could any government have stopped a deregulated world banking system bringing the world economy to the brink of collapse in the crisis of 2008? Short-term profit and excessive **RISK-TAKING** in property lending led to the accumulation of huge debts so that Royal Bank of Scotland was only saved from bankruptcy by a £43bn cash injection by the UK Government.

Are multinationals beyond state regulation? Do they have too much power? What incentive do they have to be ethical?

> * In 2007 Trafigura established a foundation to promote environmental concern, rural development programmes and health programmes in the counties where it operated. So far $ 14.5 m dollars has been donated to 36 projects. It

is now seeking to create "a lasting, sustainable model for corporate philanthropy", perhaps trying to counteract the bad publicity generated by the waste dumping scandal.

Possible Exam Questions

1. "Kantian ethic of duty is superior to the utilitarian ethic of happiness in dealing with difficult business decisions". Discuss

2. "Corporate social responsibility is ethical window-dressing to cover their greed". Discuss

3. Evaluate the view that capitalism will always exploit human beings in the pursuit of profit.

4. "Globalisation widens the exploitation of human beings by reducing the need for ethically valid regulation of business behaviour". Discuss

Key Quotes

'Corporate executives do not have responsibilities in their business activities, other than to make as much money as possible for their shareholders" Milton Friedman

"Good employees are good people". Robert Solomon

"The following duties bind the employer: not to look upon their work people as their slaves, but to respect in every man his dignity as a person ennobled by Christian character". Rerum Novarum 1891(p 20)

'It is hard to separate businesses being ethical for its own sake with the fact that being ethical might be good for business". Wilcockson and Wilkinson OCR Religious Studies (Hodder, 2016)

'"Man should not consider his material possessions as his own, but as common to all, so as to share them without hesitation when others are in need." Thomas Aquinas (ST II-II, Q46, A2)

"The rights and duties of the employers, as compared with the rights and duties of the employed, ought to be the subject of careful consideration." Rerum Novarum 1891 (p 58)

Ethics in Year 2 (Spec. sections 4-6)

The Year 1 specification (assuming we follow it sequentially - sections 1-3) introduced **DEONTOLOGICAL** and **TELEOLOGICAL** ethics and asked the question: to what extent is ethics **ABSOLUTE** or **RELATIVE**? We then applied the **NORMATIVE** ethical theories of Situation Ethics and Natural Law to euthanasia, and Kantian Ethics and Utilitarianism to business ethics.

In Year 2 (sections 4-6 of the specification), the theories are now retained and a number of new issues considered in the nature and origin of **CONSCIENCE** (section 5). To deontology and teleology we add a study of the foundation of ethics - **META-ETHICS** (section 4), which includes the study of ethical meaning of the words "good' or "bad".

SEXUAL ETHICS (Section 6) is added as an applied issue (homosexuality, sex before marriage, and adultery). The specification asks us to consider,

"How the study of ethics has, over time, influenced and been influenced by developments in religious beliefs and practices, societal norms and normative theories". OCR H573 Specification

Both our **DEONTOLOGICAL THEORIES** (Kant and Natural Law - though Natural Law isn't pure deontology as it has a teleological aspect in the rational goals we pursue as human beings) and our **TELEOLOGICAL THEORIES** (Utilitarianism and Situation Ethics) are applied to issues surrounding **SEXUAL ETHICS**. Notice the following requirements to understand:

- traditional religious beliefs and practices (from any religious perspectives) regarding these areas of sexual ethics - for example as formed in Catholic **NATURAL LAW** theory and Papal Encyclicals (circulated letters) such as Humanae Vitae (1968)

- how these beliefs and practices have changed over time, including:

  - key teachings influencing these beliefs and practices

  - the ideas of religious figures and institutions

- the impact of **SECULARISM** (see also Christian Thought, paper 3, section 5) on these areas of sexual ethics

Notice that the work of **SIGMUND FREUD** on the unconscious and the **OEDIPUS COMPLEX** may also be relevant here (see section on Conscience). Together with **RICHARD DAWKINS** these are figures in our syllabus who form a basis for considering a secular worldview.

Key Terms

- **META-ETHICS** - concerns the nature and meaning of the words good and right. A key question in meta-ethics is: "Is goodness **OBJECTIVE** (linked to moral facts in the world) or **SUBJECTIVE** (up to me)?"

- **CONSCIENCE** - may come from **GOD**, our **UPBRINGING** or a process of **REASON**. "Where does conscience come from and how does it operate?" **PSYCHOLOGY** merges with philosophy here.

- **INTRINSIC THEORIES OF VALUE** - see something as good-in-itself. Does the pleasure for example have intrinsic value?

- **INSTRUMENTAL THEORIES OF VALUE** - see goodness relative to some end, such as human happiness. But in the debates within ethics, what do **DEONTOLOGISTS** like Kant or **TELEOLOGISTS** like Joseph Fletcher or JS Mill have to say about sexual ethics?

The Ethics Toolkit Revisited

The study of ethical theories so far has equipped us with a toolkit which we can use to assess any ethical issue. In this toolkit we derive insights from different theories.

KANT has given us the **PRINCIPLE OF UNIVERSALISABILITY**, a method of reasoning implying **CONSISTENCY** and a neutral point of view, and **PERSONAL AUTONOMY**, that places human choice and reason as a central ethical concern.

AQUINAS has given us the **PRINCIPLE OF NATURAL RATIONAL PURPOSE:** the idea of an order of being which is appropriate to our unique rational natures. The ultimate **TELOS** is **EUDAIMONIA** – well-being or personal and social flourishing.

UTILITARIANS have given us the **GREATEST HAPPINESS PRINCIPLE** and the **LEAST HARM PRINCIPLE**: the idea that we should always assess consequences in the light of an empirical calculation of the balance of happiness over misery, pleasure over pain or **WELFARE** over harm. In Economics we talk of **COST/BENEFIT** analysis.

RELATIVISTS encourage us to consider the **PRINCIPLE OF CULTURAL DIVERSITY** and to be humble in the face of claims that our own culture is objectively superior. All theories are to some extent children of their times.

Theories overlap to some extent and may not be as opposed as we sometimes think. For example, all of them discuss and claim for themselves the **GOLDEN RULE** "Do to others as you would have them do to you", Matthew 7:18 (is this therefore a good example of a universal ethical **ABSOLUTE**?).

All appeal to **VIRTUE** or character traits (**MILL** appeals to sympathy, **KANT** to dutifulness, **FLETCHER** to love, **AQUINAS** to practical wisdom and the Christian virtues of I Corinthians 13, faith, hope and love).

All theories have a **TELEOLOGICAL** aspect. Kant for example considers consequences in so far as he asks us to universalise the consequences of everyone doing what I do. He also envisages a goal, the **SUMMUM BONUM** which is similar in some ways to Aristotle's **EUDAIMONIA**. Moreover, Aquinas' **NATURAL LAW** is best described as "a deontological theory arising out of a Greek teleological worldview" where the good is defined by the rational end (**TELOS**).

Meta-Ethics

Background

META-ETHICS means "beyond ethics" (metaphysics - beyond physics). Rather than asking how we derive moral principles like "do not kill", meta-ethics asks us to consider what moral statements mean and what the **FOUNDATION** of ethics might be. Here are some of the key issues:

Is there an **OBJECTIVE** principle we can appeal to resolve moral disputes? Or are we inevitably in a world of **RELATIVISM** and **SUBJECTIVISM** where such questions are "up to me"?

When I say "stealing is wrong" am I describing some **FACTS** about the world which we can look at, examine, appeal to, or am I only stating an opinion or expressing a feeling?

Is moral **LANGUAGE** a special type of language where words like "good" and "ought" mean something quite specific and different from other uses of, for example, "good" (**DESCRIPTIVE** meanings, rather than **PRESCRIPTIVE** or action-guiding, moral meanings)? Is the meaning of good in the sentence "that's a good painting" (which applies criteria such as composition, use of colour etc) different from the moral use "good boy!", (praising the child and saying effectively - keep on behaving like that")?

Specification

- **NATURALISM** (the belief that values can be defined in terms of some natural property in the world) and its application to **ABSOLUTISM**

- **INTUITIONISM** (the belief that basic moral truths are indefinable but self-evident) and its application to the term good

- **EMOTIVISM** (the belief that ethical terms evince approval or disapproval) and its application to **RELATIVISM**

Key Terms

- **ANALYTIC** - true by definition "all bachelors are unmarried".

- **SYNTHETIC** - true by observation "John is a bachelor".

- **A PRIORI** - before experience.

- **A POSTERIORI** - after experience.

- **COGNITIVISM** - moral facts can be known objectively as **TRUE** or **FALSE**.

- **NATURALISM** - moral goodness is a feature of the natural world, and so an **A POSTERIORI** fact.

- **NATURALISTIC FALLACY** - you cannot move without supplying a missing **PREMISE** from a descriptive statement such as "kindness causes pleasure" to a moral statement "kindness is good".

Structure of Thought

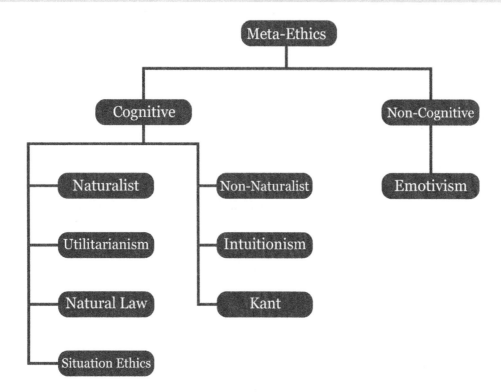

Note: **HUME** was himself a father of the utilitarian **NATURALISTS** as he argued that morality derives from the natural feeling of sympathy. He never said "you cannot move from an 'ought' to an 'is'", but only that if we do so, we must provide a missing **PREMISE** with a value-statement in it, such as "pleasure is good as it leads to a happy life". However Hume's theory of language is developed by **AJ AYER** in the theory of **EMOTIVISM** - a non-naturalist theory of how moral language works and Hume never supplied the missing premise himself (but implies that the origin of morality is found in naturalistic sentiments of approval).

Cognitive or Non-Cognitive

COGNITIVISTS believe goodness can be known as an **OBJECTIVE** feature of the world - where "objective" means "out there where it can be analysed, measured, and assessed". So cognitivism says "ethical statements can be proved true or false".

Something about our reason allows us to do this either by making some measurement (for example of happiness as the utilitarians do) or working out a principle **A PRIORI**, before experience, as Kant argues we do in deriving the **CATEGORICAL IMPERATIVE**.

NON-COGNITIVISTS argue there is no objective, factual basis for morality - it is subjective and up to me to determine. Ethical statements don't have **TRUTH VALUE** - they are empirically unprovable. Put another way - **NON-COGNITIVISTS** can say 'there is no such thing as a moral fact" such as the fact of pleasure or pain identified by Utilitarians.

The **NATURALISTS** argue we can resolve this issue empirically (**A POSTERIORI** - from experience) by looking at some observable feature of an action - a fact such as "it causes pain" (a utilitarian concern) or "it fulfils the natural rational purpose of human beings" (the **EUDAIMONIA** or goal of flourishing of **NATURAL LAW**).

NON-NATURALISTS argue either that the truth is a priori (Kant for example, even though he argues for **COGNITIVISM**) or that there are simply no facts which we can identify as moral facts – so that making a moral statement adds nothing to what we already know from a factual basis. This form of **NON-COGNITIVIST** non-naturalism is called **EMOTIVISM**.

The Naturalistic Fallacy

Developing a point made by David Hume, philosophers like **GE MOORE** have argued that when we move from a description about the real world to a moral statement we make a leap from a naturalistic statement to a **PRESCRIPTIVE** statement (one with ought in it). This prescription is doing something different. What we often fail to do is explain the missing link between a description and a prescription - and this leap from is to ought is what is known as the **NATURALISTIC FALLACY**. A.N. Prior (1949) explains the fallacy:

"Because some quality invariably accompanies the quality of goodness, this quality is identical with goodness. If, for example, it is believed that whatever is pleasant is good, or that whatever is good must be pleasant, or both, it is committing the naturalistic fallacy to infer from this that goodness and pleasantness are the same quality. The naturalistic fallacy is the assumption that because the words 'good' and 'pleasant' necessarily describe the same objects, they must attribute the same quality to them". AN Prior (1949)

MOORE argued that goodness cannot be a **COMPLEX** analysable property of an action. For example a horse can be broken down into animal, mammal, four legs, hairy tail – a **COMPLEX** idea. Because goodness isn't a complex idea, it must be either a **SIMPLE**, indefinable quality or it doesn't refer to anything at all. Since ethics isn't an **ILLUSION**, goodness must consist in a simple **INDEFINABLE QUALITY**, like the colour yellow.

The Open Question

MOORE pointed out that the naturalistic fallacy, of implying that goodness was identical to some specific property such as pleasure, is susceptible to the **OPEN QUESTION** attack. Suppose I say "this ice cream causes me so much pleasure" and then say "ice cream is good!". The open question attack suggests I can always ask the question "it produces pleasure, but nonetheless, is it morally **GOOD**?"

If I can answer "no" to this point then I have proved that goodness is something independent of pleasure.

Moore's Intuitionism

Moore was a non-naturalist **COGNITIVIST** because he believed that goodness could not be defined by its natural properties, but that we know what we mean by good by a special intuition or perception (so **COGNITIVIST**, as goodness can be known as a shared experience).

Moore argues goodness is an **INDEFINABLE PROPERTY** of an action just as the colour yellow is a non-definable property of a lemon - we know what it is and that's the end of it. We can try and reduce yellowness to light waves but that doesn't precisely tell us what yellow is - yellow just is yellow, we know this by intuition. Notice this is a version of non-naturalism as goodness cannot be established as a fact of sense experience, but as a **NON-NATURALISTIC** perception.

Evaluation of Intuitionism

Moral intuitions are said to be like the **ANALYTIC** truths of Mathematics. But moral statements are more than just "true by definition". Peter Singer comments:

"Thus the intuitionists lost the one useful analogy to support the existence of a body of truths known by reason alone".

Intuitionists **CAN'T AGREE** what these moral goods are. So how can they be **SELF-EVIDENT**? Moreover, Moore's theory is also open to his own **OPEN QUESTION** attack on ethical **NATURALISM**: "that may be your intuition (eg genocide is okay), but is it **GOOD**?"

If intuitions are actually **CULTURAL CONSTRUCTS** as Freud suggests, then they cannot be **SELF-EVIDENT**.

Moore is arguing that moral truths are similar to **PLATO**'s ideal forms. John Maynard **KEYNES** once commented that "Moore could not distinguish love, and beauty and truth from the furniture", so enraptured was he by his idealised world of the forms.

Moore also confuses a complex thing (colour) for a simple thing (yellow). Goodness is in fact a **COMPLEX** idea, like **COLOUR** because it includes within it a whole class of principles we might describe as good (like colour includes, red, yellow, green, blue).

Moore has confused a general category (colour, goodness) for a specific quality of that category (yellowness, generosity).

Utilitarian Naturalists

Utilitarians are normative **NATURALISTS** because they argue that goodness is an observable feature of the natural world - part of our **A POSTERIORI** experience of pleasure and pain. So to work out what is good, we need to project into the future and balance the likely pain and pleasure of our choice. That which maximises happiness and minimises pain is good, and actions that do the opposite are bad.

Utilitarians quite openly commit the **NATURALISTIC FALLACY** (which they argue isn't a fallacy at all) arguing that it is obviously good to pursue happiness because that as a matter of fact is the goal that all humans are pursuing. They give a **TELEOLOGICAL** justification for goodness, just as **NATURAL LAW** theorists such as **AQUINAS** follow Aristotle in linking goodness to **HUMAN FLOURISHING**.

The philosopher **JOHN SEARLE** gives us another naturalist way out of the supposed fallacy. If I promise to pay you £500 then I am doing two things - I am agreeing to play the promising game which involves **OBLIGATION** to pay your money back, and I am accepting that part of the rules of the game, fixed by society, in that I can only break this promise if a large, overriding reason appears for doing so (for example, the money is stolen from me and I am bankrupt, so can't pay it back).

So the making of a promise is a **FACT** but because of the logical feature of promising - that I agree to it creates obligations for me - this allows us to move from a descriptive **IS** statement (Brian owes me £5) to a value **OUGHT** statement "you ought to keep your promise".

Ayer's Emotivism ("Expressivism")

A.J. Ayer (1910-1989) formed part of a school of linguistic philosophy called **LOGICAL POSITIVISM** which had at its heart the **VERIFICATION PRINCIPLE**. Truth claims had to be verified true or false by sense-experience. His theory is a theory of **NON-COGNITIVISM** as he argues moral statements add no facts – just opinions which cannot be established true or false empirically. So moral truth cannot be **KNOWN** as objective fact.

"The fundamental ethical concepts are unanalysable inasmuch as there is no criterion by which to judge the validity of the judgements. They are mere pseudo-concepts. The presence of an ethical symbol adds nothing to its factual content. Thus if I say to someone 'You acted wrongly in stealing the money,' I am not stating anything more than if I had simply stated 'you stole the money'". Language, Truth and Logic (1971)

This approach to moral language was a development of **HUME's FORK** - an argument about language developed by David Hume. Hume argued that statements about the real world were of two sorts - they were either analytic or synthetic: either **LOGICAL TRUTHS** or **STATEMENTS OF FACT**.

An analytic statement is true by definition (2 + 2 = 4), a **SYNTHETIC** statement true by experience. So "all bachelors are unmarried" is true by definition, whereas "John is a bachelor" is true by experience (John might be married so that would make the statement **EMPIRICALLY** false). As moral statements are neither **ANALYTIC** (they'd have nothing useful to say about the **REAL** world if they were) or **SYNTHETIC** (not **VERIFIABLE**) they are logically and empirically meaningless.

Ayer put the same point another way.

"The presence of an ethical symbol in a proposition adds nothing to its factual content". (1971:142).

Ayer believed that problems arose when the **NATURALISTS**, such as the **UTILITARIANS** claimed an empirical basis for goodness in the balance of pleasure over pain. What happens when one person's pleasure is another person's pain? Consider that someone steals your wallet. To you, stealing is wrong because it causes you pain. To the thief, stealing is good, because it gives her money to buy food, and she's starving. Stealing appears to be **BOTH** right and wrong at the same time.

This contradictory result indicates there can be no **FACT** of morality – just an **OPINION**.

"It is not self-contradictory to say some pleasant things are not good, or that some bad things are desired". (Ayer, 1971:139)

Ayer means by this that if I say "you were wrong to steal" there is no additional **FACT** introduced by the word "wrong" - only an **EXPRESSION** of a feeling of disapproval. Note he argues the word **GOOD** is not describing a feeling but, in is own words "**EVINCING**" a feeling - like letting out a squeal if you hit your thumb, **"OUCH"**!.

"Stealing money is wrong expresses no proposition which can be either true or false. It's as if I had written "stealing money!!!" where the exclamation marks show a special sort of moral disapproval". A.J. Ayer

Evaluation - Ayer

Ayer's view seems to be a radical **SUBJECTIVISM** suggesting morality is just "up to me". It seems to strengthen the case for **RELATIVISM** that makes moral debate impossible and disagreements insoluble, even though this is not a theory of **NORMS** but of **MEANING**.

Ayer's view is based on a **FALLACY**. Ludwig Wittgenstein demonstrated that language is part of a game we play with shared rules. **MORAL** language is neither analytic nor synthetic but rather, **PRESCRIPTIVE** as Hare suggests (below). Ayer has committed a fallacy like saying "the world is either square or flat". It's neither.

According to Alasdair **MACINTYRE** in After Virtue, emotivism obliterates the distinction between manipulative and non-manipulative behaviour. There is no longer such an idea as a **VALID REASON**. Moral discourse is simply about manipulating you to adopt my point of view.

Absolutism & Relativism

Both these are ambiguous ideas. Relativism has three meanings: **PARTICULAR** to culture, **CONSEQUENTIALIST** and **SUBJECTIVE** (up to me).

Absolutism has three meanings which are the opposite: **UNIVERSAL** (applies everywhere and for all time), **NON-CONSEQUENTIALIST** and **OBJECTIVE**.

Theories may not be consistently absolute in all three meanings as the table demonstrates.

Theory	Universal	Non-consequentialist	Objective
Utilitarianism	YES, it claims we all experience pleasure and pain	NO, as goodness is always relative to maximising happiness	YES, as pleasure and happiness are measurable otherwise they couldn't be maximised
Situation Ethics	YES, as we can all understand and live by agape love	NO, as we maximise the value of love	YES, as there is a measurable test for ethical goodness

Theory	Universal	Non-consequentialist	Objective
Kantian Ethics	YES, as we can all universalise a priori	YES, as categorical absolute rules are created	YES, as the Moral Law exists as an objective truth
Natural Law	YES, as we all share one rational human nature	NO, as secondary precepts are applications of reason and never absolute	YES, the world and human nature is set up in certain way - and operates by objective laws

We may therefore conclude that only **KANTIAN** ethics is absolute in all three possible meanings. The other theories have an **ABSOLUTE** element - they have a non-negotiable principle at their heart. That's why Joseph Fletcher calls his theory ~ **PRINCIPLED RELATIVISM** (the absolute principle is **AGAPE**) made relative always to consequences - the second meaning of relativism given earlier.

Is **EMOTIVISM** a form of **RELATIVISM?** It is a meta-ethical theory, not a normative one, and so in one sense the question is a **CATEGORY MISTAKE** as the term can only be applied to the derivation of norms. However, in stressing the absence of **MORAL FACTS** and arguing that moral statements are neither analytic nor synthetic, and therefore meaningless in empirical terms, emotivism does appear to reinforce **SUBJECTIVISM** (our first meaning of relativism).

C.L. Stevenson's Emotivism

Stevenson argued that three criteria must be fulfilled when we use the word "good":

1. We must be able to agree that the action is good.

2. The action must have a **MAGNETISM** - we must want to do it, and feel an **INTEREST** in its being done.

3. The action cannot be verified empirically by appeal to facts.

So moral language has an **EMOTIVE** meaning and a **PERSUASIVE** meaning – we are encouraging others to share our attitude. This is why we bother to **ARGUE** about ethics, whereas on questions of taste we "agree to differ".

"Good has an emotive meaning...when a person morally approves of something, he experiences a rich feeling of security when it prospers and is indignant or shocked when it doesn't". C.L .Stevenson.

R.M.Hare's Prescriptivism

This is not on the specification, but is useful to evaluate emotivism.

R.M. Hare (1919-2002) argued that moral judgements have an **EMOTIVE** and a **PRESCRIPTIVE** meaning. This implicitly disagrees with the view of **HUME** and **AYER** who argue that meaningful statements are either analytic (true by definition) or synthetic (true by experience.)

Prescriptions are forms of **IMPERATIVE**: "you oughtn't steal" is equivalent to saying "**DON'T STEAL!**".

Hare agrees that you cannot derive a **PRESCRIPTION** such as "run!" from a description "there's a bull over there!" as there is a **SUBJECTIVE** element (I may choose to walk calmly or stand and wave my red rag). I am free to judge, hence the title of his book **FREEDOM** and **REASON**.

Hare follows **KANT** (even though Hare is a preference utilitarian) in arguing that **REASONABLENESS** lies in the **UNIVERSALISABILITY** of moral statements. Anyone who uses terms like "right" and "ought" are **LOGICALLY COMMITTED** to the idea that any action in relevantly similar circumstances is also wrong (see Kant's first formula of the **CATEGORICAL IMPERATIVE**).

So if Nazis say "Jews must be killed" , they must also judge that if, say it turns out that they are of Jewish origin, then they too must be killed. Only a **FANATIC** would say this.

Hare argues for the importance of **MORAL PRINCIPLES** rather than **RULES**. It is like learning to drive a car:

"The good driver is one whose actions are so exactly governed by principles which have become a habit with him, that he normally does not have to think what to do. But all road conditions are various, and therefore it is unwise to let all one's driving become a matter of habit". (Hare, Language of Morals, page 63)

Evaluation - Prescriptivism

Hare is still denying there are **OBJECTIVE** moral truths. We are free to choose our own principles and determine our actions according to our desires and preferences – there is no objective right and wrong independent of our choosing, but then having chosen, we must be able to universalise it. As a **NON-NATURALIST** he avoids reference to any final **TELOS** such as human flourishing.

Philippa **FOOT** criticised Hare in her lecture in 1958 ("Moral Beliefs") for allowing terribly immoral acts (and people) to be called "moral" simply because they are **CONSISTENT**. We cannot avoid approving the statement "If I was a murderer, I would want to be dead too if I support the death penalty". Prescriptivism cannot help justifying **FANATICISM**.

In his later book **MORAL THINKING** Hare brings together **PRESCRIPTIVISM** and his version of **PREFERENCE UTILITARIANISM**. To prescribe a moral action is to universalise that action – in universalising

"I must take into account all the ideals and preferences held by all those who will be affected and I cannot give any weight to my own ideals. The ultimate effect of this application of universalisability is that a moral judgement must ultimately be based on the maximum possible satisfaction of the preferences of all those affected by it". (Peter Singer)

Hare's pupil **PETER SINGER** builds on this idea to give prescriptivism an **OBJECTIVE** basis in his own version of preference utilitarianism. We are asked to universalise from a neutral, universal viewpoint.

So in the end prescriptivism escapes the charge of being another form of radical **SUBJECTIVISM**.

The Legacy of David Hume

David Hume argued that morality was a matter of acting on desires and feelings. Moral reasoning really reduces to the question "what do I want?" – it remains radically **SUBJECTIVE**. If Hume is right, there is no answer to the question "why should I be moral?" or "why should I be benevolent?". If I don't want to be moral, that seems to be the end of the argument.

J.L. MACKIE (Inventing Right and Wrong,1977) argues that the common view of moral language implies that there are some objective moral facts in the universe. But this view is a **MISTAKE**. There are no moral facts. We can only base our moral judgements on **FEELINGS** and **DESIRES**.

The **INTUITIONISTS** (G.E. Moore, H.A. Prichard, W.D. Ross) are arguing that there are **MORAL FACTS** but that we can only know them **NON-NATURALLY** as internal intuitions. This seems to be an attempt to have our cake and eat it.

R.M. HARE does have an answer to the question "why should I be moral?" At least in his later book **MORAL THINKING**, Hare argues that people are more likely to be happy if they follow universal **PRESCRIPTIVISM** and reason from a viewpoint that takes into account the interests and preferences of all people affected by my decision. However, this is an appeal to **SELF-INTEREST** – Hare is still an **SUBJECTIVIST**.

NATURAL LAW suggests a **NATURALIST** reason for being moral : we are moral to achieve personal and social **FLOURISHING**. If we can share the insights of psychology and philosophy we can come to a shared (if still **RELATIVISTIC**, cultural) view of what will build the excellent life. Naturalism has undergone a resurgence in the twentieth century, led by Geoffrey **WARNOCK** (1971, The Object of Morality) and Alasdair **MACINTYRE** (1981, After Virtue).

More recent, subtler, attempts to escape **SUBJECTIVISM** are to be found in John **RAWLS'** A Theory of Justice, which asks us to assume the role of an avatar in a space ship, imagining we are in an **ORIGINAL POSITION** heading to a new world where we don't know our gender, intelligence, race, or circumstances. What rules would we formulate for this world? Rawls, like Hare, brings **KANT** back into the forefront of meta-ethical debate.

Key Confusions to Avoid

1. "Utilitarianism is a meta-ethical theory". No, utilitarianism is a **NORMATIVE** theory that is built upon the meta-ethical view that the foundation of morals is **NATURALISTIC** - out there to be observed in the world **A POSTERIORI** (by experience of pleasure and pain). Meta-ethics has nothing to say about exactly how **NORMS** (values of goodness) are derived.

2. "Normative ethics is more useful than meta-ethics". This old exam question has a central ambiguity - more useful for what and to whom? If you're facing a **MORAL DILEMMA**, meta-ethics has no use at all because it doesn't produce a structure of thought for deciding what to do.

3. "Meta-ethics is boring". This is because it is sometimes badly taught. Actually the structure of morality that builds from meta-ethical **FOUNDATIONS** to **NORMATIVE THEORY** to **PRACTICAL CONCLUSION** is a fascinating one, and we need to think long and hard about how we are to solve moral problems - both **GLOBAL** (war, famine, injustice, poverty, exploitation) and **PERSONAL** (euthanasia, sexual ethics) even though the specification is biased (as in western thought generally) towards the personal.

Possible Future Questions

1. "The meaning of the word 'good' is the defining question in the study of ethics". Discuss

2. Critically consider whether ethical terms such as good, bad, right and wrong have an objective factual basis that makes them true or false.

3. "Ethical statements are merely an expression of an emotion". Discuss

4. Evaluate the view that ethical statements are meaningless.

5. "People know what's right or wrong by a common sense intuition". Discuss

6. Critically contrast the views of intuitionists and emotivists on the origin and meaning of ethical statements.

Key Quotes - Meta-ethics

"As this ought expresses some new relation it is necessary that it should be observed and explained and at the same time that a reason be given". David Hume

"The use of "That is bad!" implies an appeal to an objective and impersonal standard in a way in which "I disapprove of this; do so as well!" does not. If emotivism is true, moral language is seriously misleading". Alasdair MacIntyre

"Good serves only as an emotive sign expressing our attitude to something, and perhaps evoking similar attitudes in other persons". A.J. Ayer

"We have an idea of good ends that morality serves. Even if we are deontologists, we still think that there is a point to morality, to do with better outcomes – truth-telling generally produces better outcomes than lying. These ends can be put into non-moral language in terms of happiness, flourishing, welfare, or equality". Louis Pojman

Conscience

Issues

There are four major issues in a study of conscience.

- What is the **ORIGIN** of conscience: does it come from God, our upbringing or from reason?

- What is the relation between **MORALITY** and **GUILT** feelings? Is guilt a product of certain complexes, such as Freud's **OEDIPUS COMPLEX?**

- How does conscience **WORK**: is it a **MENTAL PROCESS** and so part of our **REASON**, a **FEELING**, or a **VOICE** in our heads (e.g. the voice of God?)?

- Can we go against our conscience and choose to reject it, in other words, is conscience **FALLIBLE** and so likely to make mistakes, or is it inerrant (incapable of error)? What is the relationship between conscience and human **WILL**?

Specification

Requires us to consider **FREUD**'s Psychological approach and **AQUINAS**' Theological Approach, to compare and critically evaluate these two theories. We are at liberty to contrast them with Eric **FROMM**, **BUTLER** or **NEWMAN** or anyone else - the syllabus is open-ended about additional material. We do, however, need to compare and contrast them with philosophers/authors of a different persuasion - so these are included in this guide. Students need to decide which is most relevant to their own approach of critical analysis and evaluation of Aquinas and Freud.

The Psychology of Conscience - Freud (Background)

ENLIGHTENMENT – believed in reason and measurement but also hypothesis tested **A POSTERIORI.** Freud shared this belief that science could probe the deepest unconscious recesses of the human mind and so contribute to the advancement of human welfare.

- **COPERNICUS** taught us that humans were not the centre of the universe.

- **DARWIN** taught us that humans were just another species of animal.

- **FREUD** taught us that humans were not rational actors, but rather are driven by unconscious, primitive, instinctual desires.

Key Terms

- **CATEGORICAL IMPERATIVE** - unconditional demands of the superego whose violation produces guilt.

- **CONSCIENCE** - the part of human consciousness that guides moral decisions and equivalent to the superego.

- **EGO** - the part of the human mind that forms our idea of self and presents a coherent image to the outside world. The ego longs for a moral guide.

- **ID** - the part of the human mind which processes passions and emotions. It is non-moral and is often in conflict with ego and superego.

- **SUPEREGO** - the part of the human mind which regulates behaviour, formed in childhood by relationships with authority figures (father and mother) and by praise and blame.

- **REPRESSION** - the suppression of our real emotions because they do not conform to ego-identity or are categorised as shameful by the superego.

- **EROS** - the creative life-force which is also the mischief-maker as it encourages the ego to take risks and cross boundaries.

- **THANATOS** - the death-instinct in conflict with eros, which appears in destructive patterns of behaviour (self-harm, aggression, and suicide).

- **UNCONSCIOUS** - that part of the iceberg of the human mind which lies unseen but nonetheless influences and even controls behaviour.

- **LIBIDO** - the sexual instinct which forms part of eros and is often repressed or overly controlled by the superego.

- **NEUROSIS** - mental illness which results from a failure to create a coherent and harmonious ego. Examples might be hysteria, obsessive-compulsive disorders (e.g. washing rituals) and phobias (e.g. spiders).

Structure of Thought

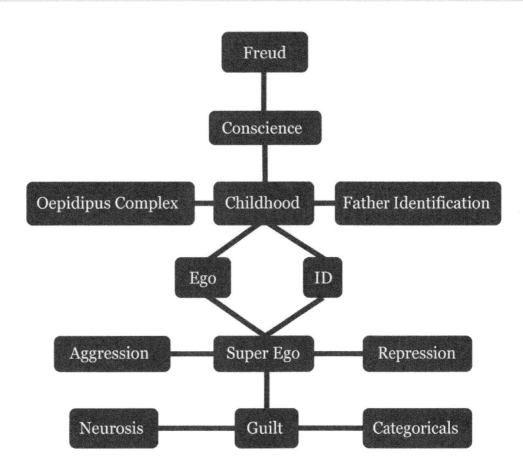

Freudian Revolution

Sigmund Freud (1856-1939) is the **FATHER OF PSYCHOANALYSIS** through his theories of how the conscious and unconscious mind develop and interact. He believed in the **ENLIGHTENMENT** assumption that science could understand all aspects of human behaviour by observing **A POSTERIORI** how patients respond to **PSYCHOANALYSIS** and by positing **THEORIES** (such as **EGO**, **ID** and **SUPEREGO**) which provide a **STRUCTURE** of thinking.

CONSCIENCE for Freud was a product of experiences in childhood which result in the creation of a **SUPEREGO** – an internal guide which seeks to calm our fears, order our world and resolve conflicts between **EGO** and **ID**. The conscience (superego) is the representative of the voice of our parents who in early childhood produced feelings of pleasure (approval/being loved) and pain (shame/punishment). Various attachments either dissolve (the **OEDIPUS COMPLEX**) or strengthen (gender identification with mother or father), and failure to reconcile a feeling of inner conflict or suppressed desire can lead to depression and **NEUROSIS**.

The structure of Freud's thinking is given on the opposite page, and his theory is sometimes referred to as a **STRUCTURAL THEORY** of the human mind and consciousness. He explains behaviour in terms of the

UNCONSCIOUS and the sublimation of desire (for example in ideas of God as **FATHER**), or the repression of desire (such as the **LIBIDO** or sexual desire).

Ego

The child develops a sense of **SELF** in relation to the external world. The **EGO** experiences feelings of pleasure and pain and also conscious and unconscious **DESIRES.** The pain of experience propels us towards change but can arise out of **REPRESSION** of urges which become unconscious.

The sense of self begins in childhood with an **IDENTIFICATION** with either **FATHER** or **MOTHER**. The origins of the relationship with the **MOTHER** are explained by the **OEDIPUS COMPLEX** and with the **FATHER** by a process by which the father (**AUTHORITY FIGURE**) becomes part of the infantile stage of the **SUPEREGO**.

CARL JUNG also proposed an **ELECTRA COMPLEX** in 1913 to explain a girl's psychosexual competition with her mother for possession of her father.

The **EGO** thus assumes a regulatory role - it excludes feelings and memories which don't fit our idea of self. For example, this repression resurfaces in **DREAMS** and also **PHOBIAS** – a fear of spiders, for example, which reflect unconscious sources of anxiety. Freud believed the **EGO** was striving to be moral.

The role of **PSYCHOANALYSIS** is to seek to integrate the "coherent ego and the repressed self which is split off from it" (Freud).

Our behaviour (**ACTION**) is a product of both conscious choices and **UNCONSCIOUS** forces 'which exert a driving force without the **EGO** noticing the compulsion" (Freud). These forces result in behaviour which are driven by a complex **PSYCHIC ENERGY** which can leave the human being baffled and confused by their own behaviour – resulting in a feeling of **ANXIETY** or **GUILT**, and **DEPRESSION** (which Freud called 'melancholia').

Id

The **ID** is the seat of feelings, and passions. It is totally non-moral. The origin of the **ID** lies in our **EVOLUTIONARY** background but also in society itself which has conditioned us over generations.

The **ID** develops two broad categories of desire, according to Freud. **EROS** is the life-instinct, which gives us the desires for food, self-preservation, and sex. **THANATOS** is the death-instinct, which drives desires for domination, aggression, violence and self-destruction. These two instincts are at war within the id, and need to be tempered by ego constraints and by **CONSCIENCE**.

Children learn that authorities in the world restrict the extent to which these desires are satisfied. Consequently, humans create the **EGO** which takes account of the realities of the world and society. The ego Freud referred to as the **REALITY PRINCIPLE**, because our awareness of self and of others is crucial to our interaction with the world around us, and is formed at the age of 3 to 5 years.

Within the **ID** there is a battle going on between **EROS** – the life instinct – and **THANATOS** – the death instinct. **EROS** is the 'mischief-maker' (Freud) – the source of uncontrolled passion and also creativity. It is dominated by the **PLEASURE PRINCIPLE**, and yet not all pleasures are felt as acceptable or 'good'. Hence the irrational guilt that can occur over, for example, masturbation and its presence as a **TABOO** in Christianity. Indeed, **EROS** is often at odds with the demands and **CATEGORICAL IMPERATIVES** (Freud's phrase echoing Kant) of the **SUPEREGO**.

The death-instinct (**THANATOS**) is experienced in the desire to kill the **FATHER** and replace him in the mother's affections in the **OEDIPUS COMPLEX**, but is also present in the destructive desires of the **DEPRESSIVE** or self-harming **NEUROTIC**. The death instinct also emerges in **AGGRESSION**, violence and war. In the individual it can have its final expression in **SUICIDE**. But is the positing of a sexual complex just pseudo-science?

Superego

The **SUPEREGO** represents the **INTERNAL** world of **CONSCIENCE**. *"The superego represents the relationship to our parents"* (Freud) and particularly our **FATHER** as authority figure and source of rules and punishments.

To Freud there is a conflict within the human psyche between **EGO** and **ID** and **EROS** and **THANATOS**. A sense of dread emerges in childhood from a fear of castration, a fear of death and a fear of **SEPARATION** from our parents, particularly a fear of loss of the mother's love. The superego can have a destructive power: causing the **EGO** to feel deserted and unloved, abandoned to an anxious and uncertain world and 'fuelling the death-instinct by making the Ego feel abandoned'. This sense of abandonment and powerlessness resurfaces in **DREAMS** (often of failure or of loss of control).

So the **SUPEREGO** can have both a **POSITIVE** and a **NEGATIVE** role – positive in controlling unbridled and anti-social desires and passions, but also **NEGATIVE** in forming an extreme critical voice "brutally chastising and punishing" with guilt, or shame and ultimately a sense of **SELF-HATRED** which cause self-harm and depression.

We can also experience the **SUPEREGO** as **SAVIOUR** and project our guilt and shame onto a sense of **SIN** and a **FATHER-FIGURE** – whom we call **GOD**, who replaces lost love and provides a **SUBLIMATION** of our sexual desires. Christianity teaches that we deserve death, but that our place is taken by a substitute, Jesus Christ, who removes the **GUILT** and takes on himself the **PUNISHMENT.** (Isaiah 53 "the punishment that makes us whole is upon him"). The **SUPEREGO** in this way grows into a life and power of its own irrespective of the rational thought and reflection of the individual: it is programmed into us by the reactions of other people.

This 'superego', conscience, restricts humans' aggressive powerful desires (**THANATOS** within the **ID**) which would otherwise **DESTROY** us. So guilt "expresses itself in the need for punishment" (Civilisation and its Discontents 1930:315-6). **ERIC FROMM**, quoting Nietzsche, agrees with Freud's analysis of the destructive nature of the **AUTHORITARIAN** conscience.

"Freud has convincingly demonstrated the correctness of Nietzsche's thesis that the blockage of freedom turns man's instincts 'backward against man himself'. Enmity, cruelty, the delight in persecution...- the turning of all these instincts against their own possessors: this is the origin of the bad conscience". Eric Fromm, Man For Himself, 1947:113

Our superego can lead us to **INTERNALISE** shame, and to experience conflicts between the **ID** desires and the shame emanating from the superego responses. The more we suppress our true feelings, the more that which drives us comes from what Freud described as the **SUBCONSCIOUS**, which like an iceberg lies hidden in the recesses of our minds.

Guilt

Freud believed that the more rapidly the **OEDIPUS COMPLEX** succumbed to **REPRESSION** of our desire for our mother, the stronger will be the domination of the **SUPEREGO** over the **EGO** in the form of a severe and dictatorial **CONSCIENCE**.

So "the tension between the demands of conscience and the actual performances of the ego is experienced in a sense of guilt" (Freud). But guilt can itself be **REPRESSED** and so **UNCONSCIOUS**. Unconscious guilt expresses itself in **NEUROSIS** and other forms of **MENTAL ILLNESS**.

SYNOPTIC POINT Freud sees the structure of our Psyche much as Plato describes it in the analogy of the Charioteer (reason) who seeks to harmonise the twin horses of virtue and passion. A man on horseback (the **EGO**) tries to hold in check the superior strength of the horse (**ID**). But unlike the horseman, the **EGO** uses forces borrowed from the **SUPEREGO** – such as shame and guilt. But a result of this is that **EGO**-identity increasingly fails to represent **ID**-desire. The unfulfilled **ID** resurfaces in sick behaviour or **UNCONSCIOUS** forces (**COMPULSIONS**).

Oedipus Complex

Oedipus so loved his mother that he killed his father and assumed his father's role. Infants start with **MOTHER-ATTACHMENT** which is reinforced by the **PLEASURE PRNCIPLE** as the mother satisfies the infants need for sustenance, love and erotic feeling. The hostility to the **FATHER** gradually subsides in healthy children who become more fully identified with the **MOTHER** (girls) or the **FATHER** (boys) as puberty approaches.

However, a failure to identify successfully with one or other parent can lead to transfer of love (Freud saw this as the origin of **HOMOSEXUAL LOVE**). The **EGO** deepens its relationship with the **ID** in rituals which may be associated with shame, such as masturbation, and fantasies that produce guilt. So the **LIBIDO** can be redirected or even suppressed altogether in a sublimation which we call **RELIGION**.

Ultimately, to Freud, Religion is an infantile projection of our desires and longings onto an image which is an **ILLUSION**. In the Christian Thought paper we study more of this theory in Freud's work, The Future of an Illusion.

Evaluating Freud - Weaknesses

REDUCTIONIST George Klein (1973) argues Freud reduces the human mind to an object of enquiry by positing unprovable theories of how conscious and unconscious processes interact. In so doing he reduces human behaviour to a dualism of 'appropriate' and 'inappropriate' behaviour. Like the criticism levelled at geneticist **RICHARD DAWKINS** we can see this as a form of scientific reductionism.

OVERSEXUALISED Freud argues that the relationship of child and parent has sexual desire through the development of the **OEDIPUS COMPEX** as a key factor. The success or failure of a child's sexual feelings for one or other parent as key to child development is highly contentious. For example, a boy's father is his mother's lover, but he's also the disciplinarian. So, assuming boys do harbour feelings of fear toward their fathers, is this because they fear castration by a romantic rival or because they're afraid of ordinary punishment?

SAMPLING Freud's sample is primarily Austrian upper-class woman, who manifested hysteria. The sample is too small and gender-biased to be truly scientific and the emphasis on sex reveals the cultural repression of that age. Scholars argue Freud fabricates the claim that "almost all of my women patients told me that they had been seduced by their father". John Kihlstrom comments: "While Freud had an enormous impact on 20th century culture, he has been a dead weight on 20th century psychology. The broad themes that Westen writes about were present in psychology before Freud, or arose more recently, independent of his influence. At best, Freud is a figure of only historical interest for psychologists".

Evaluating Freud - Strengths

REVOLUTIONARY Freud was the first person to analyse and theorise about the human unconscious. His argument that dreams are a key to unlocking the secrets of the subconscious mind, his belief that hypnotherapy could change behaviour and his invention of **TALKING THERAPIES** have fundamentally changed our treatment of mental illness.

SECULAR Freud believed religion was a neurosis based on delusions and projections – for example God is a father-substitute onto whom we project our desire for an authority figure, our fear of death and our sense of abandonment. This to Freud was infantile. Westen (1998:35) argues "the notion of unconscious processes is not psychoanalytic voodoo, and it is not the fantasy of muddle-headed clinicians. It is not only clinically indispensable, but it is good science".

HUMANE Freud treated the whole human personality rather than condemning aspects of it as shameful, evil or unacceptable. He thereby challenged the old religious **DUALISMS** of good versus evil, monster versus hero, to give a humane alternative and offering hope of cure and transformation to those whose lives were blighted by mental health problems.

Key Quotes - Freud

"In the Ego and the Id Freud abandons the simple dichotomy between instinct and consciousness and recognizes the unconscious elements of the ego and superego, the importance of nonsexual impulses (aggression or the 'death instinct'), and the alliance between superego and id, superego and aggression". Christopher Lasch The Culture of Narcissism page 32

"While Freud had an enormous impact on 20th century culture, he has been a dead weight on 20th century psychology. The broad themes were present in psychology before Freud, or arose in more recently independent of his influence. At best, Freud is a figure of only historical interest for psychologists." John Kihlstrom

"When we were little children we knew these higher natures of our parents, and later we took them into ourselves". Freud

"All that is repressed is unconscious, but not all that is unconscious is repressed". Freud

Evaluation - Psychological Approaches

These psychological accounts of conscience undermine **AQUINAS'** religious theory of conscience (see below) because conscience is **ENVIRONMENTALLY INDUCED** by upbringing, not innate.

Freud's theory is highly **DETERMINISTIC**, because humans are driven, according to Freud, by forces operating out of our subconscious minds.

PSYCHOLOGY doesn't rule out the possibility that God has some involvement with conscience (in originating a moral faculty, for example), but if environment operates so strongly on conscience the religious theories need reworking.

A Theology of Conscience - Aquinas

Key Terms

- **CONSCIENTIA** Aquinas' definition of conscience as 'reason making right decisions".

- **SYNDERESIS** Aquinas' definition of conscience as our innate ability and desire to orientate ourselves towards good ends (aim at the **PRIMARY PRECEPTS**).

- **PHRONESIS** Practical wisdom or right judgement.

- **VINCIBLE IGNORANCE** Blameworthy ignorance of something which we should in principle know about eg a 30 mph zone.

- **INVINCIBLE IGNORANCE** Ignorance which we can't be blamed for - eg a Borneo tribesman's ignorance of Jesus Christ.

Structure of Thought

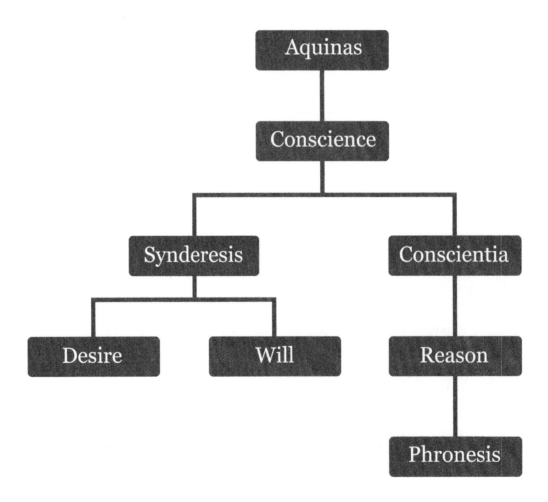

St **PAUL** argued that all human beings, Jew and Gentile (non-Jew), possessed an **INNATE** knowledge of God's law, (we're born with it) written on our hearts. *"I do not do the thing I want, the very thing I hate is what I do"* he wrote in **ROMANS 7** and Gentiles have God's law *"engraved on their hearts"*, (Romans 2:15).

John Henry **NEWMAN** (1801-1890) was an Anglican priest who converted to Rome. How could a good Catholic accept papal **INFALLIBILITY** and still follow his conscience? Newman describes conscience as the innate **VOICE OF GOD** and **ABORIGINAL** (= original or native) **VICAR OF CHRIST**.

"It is a principle planted in us before we have had any training" argued Newman. Newman quoted the fourth Lateran Council when he said *"he who acts against conscience loses his soul"*. John Henry Newman

AQUINAS (1224-1274) agrees with St Paul and with Newman, as he distinguished between an innate source of good and evil, **SYNDERESIS** (literally, one who watches over us) and a judgement derived from our reason, **CONSCIENTIA**. This second idea is, however, closer to **JOSEPH BUTLER**.

Synderesis and Conscience

Thomas Aquinas saw **SYNDERESIS** (first of two words for conscience) as an innate instinct for distinguishing right from wrong that orientates **DESIRE** and forms the **WILL**. Synderesis can be defined as:

"A natural disposition of the human mind by which we instinctively understand the first principles of morality". Aquinas

Aquinas (optimistically) thought people tended towards goodness and away from evil (the **SYNDERESIS** principle). This principle is the starting point or **FIRST PRINCIPLE** of Aquinas' **NATURAL LAW** system of ethics. So these 'first principles' are the **PRIMARY PRECEPTS** which we observe rational human beings pursue as goals. These include preservation of life, ordered society, worship of God, education and reproduction (acronym **POWER**).

CONSCIENTIA is the power of reason for working out what is good and what is evil, the *"application of knowledge to activity"* (Aquinas). This is something closer to moral judgement rather than instinct, close to Aristotle's **PHRONESIS** or practical wisdom or **BUTLER**'s determining process for distinguishing between **SELF-INTEREST** and **BENEVOLENCE**. We cannot flourish without it. In practical situations we have to make choices and to weigh alternatives, and we do so by using our conscience. One way we do this is by looking at consequences and applying the **PRINCIPLE OF DOUBLE EFFECT** (when we have to kill a foetus to save a mother's life we have a good intention but a double effect of one good and one evil consequence).

Conscience can make mistakes and needs to be trained in wisdom. At times people do bad things because they make a mistake in discriminating good from evil. Aquinas believed that if the conscience has made a **FACTUAL** mistake, for example, if I don't realise that my action breaks a particular rule, then my mistaken conscience is not to blame.

But if I am simply **IGNORANT** of the rule (such as not committing adultery), I am to blame. Taking a rather bizarre example, Aquinas argues that if a man sleeps with another man's wife thinking she was his wife, then he is not morally blameworthy because he acted "in good faith".

"Conscience is reason making right decisions and not a voice giving us commands". Aquinas

Conscience deliberates between good and bad. Aquinas notes two dimensions of moral decision making, "Man's reasoning is a kind of movement which begins with the understanding of certain things that are naturally known as

IMMUTABLE principles without investigation. It ends in the intellectual activity by which we make judgements on the basis of those principles". Aquinas

So **SYNDERESIS** is right **INSTINCT** or habit, the natural tendency humans have to do good and avoid evil. **CONSCIENTIA** is right **REASON**, which distinguishes between right and wrong as we make practical moral decisions. We see how conscientia works itself out in the **PRINCIPLE OF DOUBLE EFFECT,** when we solve a genuine moral dilemma, when two 'good things' conflict and we can't have both.

Vincible and Invincible Ignorance

INVINCIBLE IGNORANCE occurs when people (such as non-Christians or tribes in Borneo) are ignorant of the moral law not because they refuse to believe, but rather because they've not yet had an opportunity to hear and experience it. St. Thomas Aquinas discusses the topic in his Summa Theologica 1-1 Q97. Pope Pius IX used the term in his 1854 document Singulari Quadam.

In his 1963 sermon, "Strength to Love," Martin Luther King wrote, *"Nothing in all the world is more dangerous than sincere ignorance and conscientious stupidity."* Intentional **VINCIBLE** ignorance is when I deliberately act on ignorance. For example, if I choose to fire my rifle into a forest without first making sure there's no-one in the undergrowth picking blackberries, I am "vincibly" ignorant and morally culpable for my actions if I wound someone.

Joseph Butler - Innate Conscience Guided by Reason

Note: Butler's and Fromm's theories (see below) are not on the specification, but are useful to evaluate Aquinas.

Butler (1692-1752), former Bishop of Durham, believed human beings had two natural rational guides to behaviour: enlightened self-interest and conscience. Greeks like **EPICURUS** would have recognised the self-interest of the pursuit of **HAPPINESS**, but not the idea of an **INNATE** (inborn) disposition of conscience.

Butler believed we were naturally moral, and that conscience was the **SUPREME AUTHORITY** in moral actions. Morality was part of our human natures.

Human nature has a **HIERARCHY OF VALUES** with conscience at the top which than adjudicates between the self-love and **BENEVOLENCE** (= doing good to others) which define us as human beings. Conscience helps the selfish human become virtuous and so provides a **BALANCE** between these two tendencies.

Butler doesn't deny we have feelings and passions, but it is conscience which **JUDGES** between them as the "moral approving and disapproving faculty" and we act **PROPORTIONATELY** (appropriately to the situation) according to our conscience.

The guidance is **INTUITIVE**, given by God but still the voice of **REASON**. He is arguing that each human being has direct insight into the **UNIVERSAL** or objective rightness or wrongness of an action.

Evaluation - Butler

Butler attacked the **EGOISM** of Thomas Hobbes. **BENEVOLENCE** is as much part of our shared human nature as **SELF-LOVE**. Here there are echoes of Richard **DAWKINS**' argument that we all share a biologically evolved "altruistic gene" (altruism = concern for others).

Butler sees an **OBJECTIVE MORAL ORDER** in the world. Fortune and misfortune are not entirely arbitrary – if we choose **VICE** we naturally suffer misfortune. Following the dictates of conscience usually leads to **HAPPINESS**. But in the end it's **GOD** who guarantees the consequences turn out best. "Although Butler's description of conscience is **UNSURPASSED**, he gives no definition of conscience". D.D.Raphael

"Common behaviour all over the world is formed on a supposition of a moral faculty; whether called conscience, moral reason, moral sense, or divine reason; whether considered as a sentiment of understanding, or as a perception of the heart".
Joseph Butler

Authoritarian Conscience - Eric Fromm

Eric **FROMM** experienced all the evil of Nazism and wrote his books to reflect on how conscience and freedom can be subverted even in the most civilised societies. In order to explain how, for example, Adolf **EICHMANN** can plead at his trial for mass murder in 1961 that he was only "following orders" in applying the final solution, we can invoke Fromm's idea of the authoritarian conscience.

The authoritarian conscience is the **INTERNALISED VOICE** of the external authority, something close to Freud's concept of the superego considered above. It's backed up by fear of punishment, or spurred on by admiration or can even be created because I idolise an authority figure, as Unity **MITFORD** did Adolf Hitler.

As Unity found, this blinds us to the faults of the idolised figure, and causes us to become **SUBJECT** to that person's will, so that "the laws and sanctions of the externalised authority become part of oneself" (1947:108).

So, as with the Nazis, ordinary seemingly civilised human beings do **ATROCIOUS EVIL** because they are subject to a voice which comes essentially from outside them, bypassing their own moral sense. This authoritarian conscience can come from:

PROJECTION onto someone of an image of perfection.

The experience of parental **RULES** or expectations.

An adopted **BELIEF** system, such as a religion, with its own authority structure.

"Good conscience is consciousness of pleasing authority, guilty conscience is consciousness of displeasing it". Eric Fromm
(1947:109)

The individual's **IDENTITY** and sense of security has become wrapped up in the authority figure, and the voice inside is really someone else's voice. This also means **OBEDIENCE** becomes the cardinal virtue, and as the Nazi Adolf Eichmann pleaded at his trial. **AUTONOMY** and **CREATIVITY** are lost.

"Those subject to him are means to his end and, consequently his property, and used by him for his purposes." Fromm (1947:112)

DESTRUCTIVE TENDENCIES emerge, Fromm stresses, where "a person takes on the role of authority by treating himself with the same cruelty and strictness" and "destructive energies are discharged by taking on the role of the authority and dominating oneself as servant". (1947:113)

"Paradoxically, authoritarian guilty conscience is a result of feelings of strength, independence, productiveness and pride, while the authoritarian good conscience springs from feelings of obedience, dependence, powerlessness and sinfulness". Fromm (1947:112)

The Humanistic Conscience

The **HUMANISTIC** conscience, Fromm suggests is "our own voice, present in every human being, and independent of external sanctions and rewards" (1947:118). Fromm sees this voice as our **TRUE SELVES**, found by listening to ourselves and heeding our deepest needs, desires and goals.

"Different from the authoritarian conscience is the "humanistic conscience"; this is the voice present in every human being and independent from external sanctions and rewards. Humanistic conscience is based on the fact that as human beings we have an intuitive knowledge of what is human and inhuman, what is conducive of life and what is destructive of life. This conscience serves our functioning as human beings. It is the voice which calls us back to ourselves, to our humanity". Eric Fromm

The result of so listening is to release **HUMAN POTENTIAL** and creativity, and to become what we potentially are; "the goal is productiveness, and therefore, happiness" (1947:120). This is something gained over a life of learning, reflection and setting and realising goals for ourselves.

Fromm sees **KAFKA**'s "The Trial" as a parable of how the two consciences in practice live together. A man is arrested, he knows not on what charge or pretext. He seems powerless to prevent a terrible fate - his own death - at the hands of this alien authority. But just before he dies he gains a glimpse of another person (Fromm's more developed **HUMANISTIC CONSCIENCE**) looking at him from an upstairs room.

Key Confusions

1. "Conscience is a form of consciousness". No, conscience is only a form of consciousness if it is clearly an exercise of choice and reason, as in Aquinas' **CONSCIENTIA** or Butler's principle of judgement between self-interest and benevolence. But Freud argues **UNCONSCIOUS** forces drive guilt feelings which drive conscience - and these forces may be irrational or **NEUROTIC**.

2. "Without God there can be no human conscience". Only in a certain (narrow) Christian world view that sees even our moral sense corrupted by sin. To Aquinas we all share in **SYNDERESIS** which means conscience is a

UNIVERSAL phenomenon we possess by virtue of our creation in the **IMAGE OF GOD.** It doesn't matter if we believe in God or not.

3. "Science cannot explain conscience". Richard **DAWKINS** would disagree. The **SELFISH GENE** is actually the **SELF-PRESERVING** gene and evolution has given us a genetic predisposition to **ALTRUISM**. So when the conscience of a distinguished Leeds surgeon caused him to jump into the surf off Cornwall to try to save two teenaged swimmers in distress in 2015, he was showing the **ALTRUISTIC** (help others) gene. He tragically died in this heroic moral action.

Possible Future Exam Questions

1. Critically evaluate the theories of conscience of Aquinas and Freud.

2. "Conscience is given by God, not formed by childhood experience". Critically evaluate this view with reference to Freud and Aquinas.

3. "Conscience is a product of culture, environment, genetic predisposition and education" . Discuss

4. "Conscience is another word for irrational feelings of guilt". Discuss

5. "Freud's theory of conscience has no scientific basis. It is merely hypothesis". Discuss

6. 'Guilt feelings are induced by social relationships as a method of control". Discuss

Key Quotes - Conscience

"Freud has convincingly demonstrated the correctness of Nietzsche's thesis that the blockage of freedom turns man's instincts 'backward against man himself'. Enmity, cruelty, the delight in persecution - the turning of all these instincts against their own possessors: this is the origin of the bad conscience". Eric Fromm

"Conscience does not only offer itself to show us the way we should walk in, but it likewise carries its own authority with it, that it is our natural guide, the guide assigned us by the Author of our nature; it therefore belongs to our condition of being, it is our duty to walk in its path". Joseph Butler

"Conscience is reason making right decisions and not a voice giving us commands". Aquinas

"The Gentiles can demonstrate the effects of the law engraved on their hearts, to which their own conscience bears witness". Rom 2.15

"Conscience is the built in monitor of moral action or choice values". John Macquarrie

Sexual Ethics

Issues Surrounding Sexual Ethics

What does it mean to be **HUMAN**? Is there one **UNIVERSAL** shared human nature (as **NATURAL LAW** suggests)?

Are gender equality and same sex attraction equally ethical issues? Or do we evaluate them as good or bad in the light of **CONSEQUENCES** and **HAPPINESS** produced by social policy and individual action, as the **UTILITARIANS** suggest?

What values give meaning to sexual relationships (such as fidelity, chastity and commitment – which seem to be changing)? Are the **VIRTUES** of human character a better way of analysing this issue?

How have developments in understanding the biology and **PSYCHOLOGY** of the human person affected sexual ethics? Sexual ethics thus shares concerns and insights from **PSYCHOLOGY**, **BIOLOGY**, and **SOCIOLOGY**. With the prevalence of pornography, sex trafficking and decline in old models of family life, there can be few more pressing ethical issues facing us. The specification identifies three issues:

- **PRE-MARITAL SEX**

- **EXTRA-MARITAL SEX (ADULTERY)**

- **HOMOSEXUALITY**

Sex & Evolution

Homo Sapiens emerged around 150,000 years ago. As social life developed so a primitive **MORALITY** created rules and boundaries around sexual intercourse. Sex changes its function from **REPRODUCTION** to **SOCIAL REGULATION**.

Religions emerge that created **PURITY CODES**. These involved **TABOOS** (the declaration of certain practices as unclean). For example the purity code of the Hebrew Bible, **LEVITICUS**, lays down a code of uncleanness – which included **BLOOD, INCEST, ADULTERY**, and **SAME SEX RELATIONS**. These are abominations punishable by social exclusion or death.

Such attitudes are reflected in attitudes to **WOMEN**. Women came to be seen as **PROPERTY** of men. Virginity was prized. Up to 1872, married women in Britain had to surrender all property to their husbands; there was no concept of marital rape until 1991 and violence against married women was only outlawed in 1861. In 2011 there were 443 reported incidents of "honour crime" (violence, forced marriage and even murder) in the UK.

A concept of what is **NATURAL** emerged and with it psychological **GUILT** for those who did not conform. It's hard to believe that in 1899 **OSCAR WILDE** was jailed for two years hard labour for a homosexual relationship. **HOMOSEXUAL SEX** was only legalised in 1967. The last people to be executed for sodomy in England were James Pratt (1805–1835) and John Smith (1795–1835), in November 1835.

Kinsey & the Sexual Revolution

The **KINSEY REPORT** of 1945 shocked America. Intimate surveys of real people's preferences revealed:

- 10% of men were homosexual for at least three years of their lives. How then could sexual preference be **UNCHANGING**, fixed and uniform?

- 26% of married women had extramarital experiences of different sorts.

- 90% of men masturbated.

- 50% of men had been unfaithful to their wives.

Christian Views on Sex

Natural Law

Aquinas taught that there were three rational ends of sex, arising from the **PRIMARY PRECEPT** of reproduction:

- To have children.

- To give **PLEASURE**.

- To bind husband and wife together.

His view – that sex was for pleasure, was widely condemned, Aquinas wrote "the exceeding pleasure experienced in sex does not destroy the balance of nature as long as it is in harmony with reason". Right reason involves a delicate balance of the three purposes of sex – and avoidance of irrational or animal extremes. So the following sexual sins were forbidden:

- **RAPE**

- **CASUAL SEX**

- **ADULTERY**

- **HOMOSEXUAL SEX**

- **MASTURBATION**

Aquinas' view echoed the erotic celebration of sexual ecstasy in the **SONG OF SONGS** in the Hebrew Bible where sex is a sacred gift and picture of a mystical union, and one of the highest spiritual as well as physical forms of being.

Behold you are beautiful, my love;

behold you are beautiful;

your eyes are like doves,

Behold you are beautiful my beloved, truly lovely....

Your two breasts are like two fawns,

twins of a gazelle that feed among the lilies...

You have ravished my heart with a glance of your eyes .

(Song of Songs 1:15; 4:2, 5 & 9)

This is one of two parallel strains in the Bible – one positive and one negative, and the positive strain, that sex is to be **CELEBRATED** is echoed by Jesus himself, quoting Genesis 2:24, "from the beginning God created them male and female, and for this reason a man shall leave his mother and father and be united with his wife, and the two shall become one flesh. So what God has joined together, let no-one divide" (Mark 10:6-9). See also Paul in Ephesians 5:31.

The Negative Strain - Theology of the Fall

There is also a negative strain in Christianity which sees sex as dangerous, unclean, and sexual pleasure as sinful.

AUGUSTINE wrote that marriage was the *"first fellowship of humankind in this mortal life"*, and *"good not just for producing children, but also because of the natural friendship between the sexes"*, although primarily *"a remedy for weakness, and source of comfort"*. Ultimately the good of marriage lay in its "goodness, fidelity and unbreakable bond".

Augustine argued against the **PELAGIANS** who saw sexual pleasure as a **NATURAL GOOD**, evil only in excess. Augustine agreed with Paul that since the **FALL** the body had been subject to death, *"our body weighs heavy on our soul"* with its sinful desires. Augustine believed that since the fall desire had been tainted by **LUST**. So sexual pleasure in marriage needed to be moderated by reason.

Sexual desire ("the carnal appetite") outside marriage, and sexual activity that results, *"is not good , but an evil that comes from original sin"*. This evil of carnal lust can invade even marriage – so it is **DANGEROUS** and needs to be treated wisely and carefully.

After the **FALL** (Genesis 3) men and women were *"naked and ashamed"*. The man's member is *"no longer obedient to a quiet and normal will"*. Humankind was in danger of running away with lust for each other.

CONCLUSION: Augustine argues that precisely because the body is created good, it can be used wrongly, and this goodness has been deeply stained by the Fall. Sexual desire has to be circumscribed by **MODESTY**, chastity and wisdom.

Catholic Teaching Today

The Roman Catholic Church teaches that sex has two functions – procreative and **UNITIVE** (binding two people together). Procreation is primary. According to Humanae Vitae (1967) these two elements are **INSEPARABLE**.

"Sexuality becomes fully human when it is integrated into the relationship of one person to the other in lifelong gift of a man to a woman". Catechism 2338

CHASTITY is the virtue of self-mastery (Catechism 2339). It is expressed in friendship towards our neighbour. Sex outside marriage is *"gravely contrary to the dignity of persons and of human sexuality which is naturally ordered to the procreation of children". Catechism 2354*

HOMOSEXUAL ACTS are "intrinsically disordered". *"They are contrary to the natural law. They close the sexual act to the gift of life. Under no circumstances can they be approved". Catechism 2358*

ADULTERY is absolutely forbidden by the sixth commandment and Jesus' words.

CONTRACEPTION - in 1951 Pope Pius XII officially permitted the rhythm method, but otherwise **HUMANAE VITAE** (1967) upholds the view that anything that breaks the natural relationship between sex and conception is wrong.

Evaluation - Catholic View

Professor Peter **GOMES** of Harvard University argues that the Bible bans one **CULTURAL** expression of homosexuality – a promiscuous one and *"never contemplated a form of homosexuality in which loving and faithful persons sought to live out the implications of the gospel with as much fidelity as any heterosexual believer". The Good Book (1997)*

The Catholic interpretation of **NATURAL LAW** implies that the primary function of sex is reproduction. But suppose the primary purpose is **BONDING**, then the argument that sex is purely for reproduction falls down – we can be Natural Law theorists and disagree about the secondary precepts (which Aquinas always argues are relative).

The Catholic **ASSUMPTION** (following Aquinas) is of one human nature. But psychology suggests there are varieties of human nature (heterosexual, homosexual, bisexual) because of genes or environment.

The prohibition on **CONTRACEPTION** seems irrational in a world of overpopulation and **STD**s. If **PRESERVATION OF LIFE** conflicts with **REPRODUCTION**, surely preservation of life is the primary **PRIMARY PRECEPT**?

Situation Ethics - Christian Relativism

Joseph **FLETCHER** sees his own theory as **RELATIVISTIC** (even though it retains one absolute principle, agape love) because any decision is made relative to circumstances.

ABSOLUTE rules must be rejected as authoritarian and unloving.

Biblical prescriptions should be followed as wise **ADVICE** but abandoned in extreme situations if love demands it.

Fletcher argues that many applications of morality are never discussed in the Bible: "Jesus said nothing about birth control, homosexuality, pre-marital intercourse , homosexuality, sex play, petting or courtship". (Fletcher, page 80).

"It seems impossible to see any sound reason for any of the attempts to legislate morality. It is doubtful whether love's cause

is helped by any of the sex laws that try to dictate sexual practices for consenting adults". (Fletcher, Situation Ethics, page 80)

AGAPE love (unconditional love) is the only norm. The situationist is not a 'what asker', ("what sexual practice is allowed?) but a 'who asker'. It's about **PERSONALISM** – people come first.

Evaluation - Situation Ethics (Christian Relativism)

AGAPE is too high a standard for our personal relationships, usually governed by self-interest. Why should I be loving (rather than pleasure-seeking)?

The vulnerable (young, homeless, poor) need the protection of laws preventing **ABUSE** and **EXPLOITATION**.

We cannot predict **CONSEQUENCES** eg unwanted pregnancies or **STD**s happen to people not expecting them who may honestly believe they love the other person.

Homosexual Acts - a Test Case

We have already seen that the Catholic Church condemns homosexual behaviour as intrinsically disordered because of the assumption of one **UNIFORM HUMAN NATURE**. The situationist takes the opposite view; such legalism is unloving and so wrong. Is there a middle way?

In the **ANGLICAN** church there are two gay bishops (in America) and many practising gay priests. **VIRTUE ETHICS** indicates there is a third way of analysing homosexual behaviour. Which **VIRTUES** are present in the relationship? The **EXCESS** of promiscuity is condemned, but faithfulness, care and compassion can apply in any relationship irrespective of orientation. By the same argument the **DEFICIENCY** of abstinence is also a character **VICE**.

The moral issue surrounding homosexuality should therefore be about the promiscuous lifestyle and irresponsible spread of disease (as with heterosexuals). The legalism of natural law or over-emphasis on the code of Leviticus blinds us to the true moral question. What **VALUES** do we need in order to **FLOURISH**?

Kant on Sex

Kant asks us to commit to build the moral world – the **SUMMUM BONUM** or greatest good, by following the rational principle he calls the **CATEGORICAL IMPERATIVE**. This principle has to be applied in all similar circumstances without conditions – it is **ABSOLUTE**. We have to act in such a way that we can imagine a universal law where everyone follows the rule that is generated.

Humans have intrinsic **VALUE** as "ends in themselves". We must be given equal dignity and respect as autonomous rational beings.

We share an irrational nature of passions and instincts with **ANIMALS** but we can rise above these and order our lives by reason. Human sex will be different from animal urges.

LUST disturbs reason. By desiring someone simply as an object of pleasure (rather than seeing them as a whole person, with dignity and reason) we dishonour them and violate their special uniqueness as a free person. We sink to the level of animals.

"Sex exposes mankind to the danger of equality with the beasts...by virtue of the nature of sexual desire a person who sexually desires another person objectifies that person..and makes of the loved person an object of appetite. As soon as that appetite is satisfied one casts aside the person as one casts aside a lemon that has been sucked dry". Kant, Lectures on Ethics

MARRIAGE is the best expression of our sexuality. The pleasure of sex is acceptable (ie not animal) because two people surrender their dignity to each other and permit each other's bodies to be used for this purpose – it is a mutual **CONSENSUAL CONTRACT**. Reproduction is not the end of sex, Kant argues, but lifelong surrender to each other in a context of love and respect.

Evaluation of Kant

Kant appears to separate our **ANIMAL** nature from our **RATIONAL**. This dualism explains why he still sees sex as something belonging to the animal nature. But **FEELINGS** and **REASON** cannot be separated this way, many would argue.

Kantian ethics produces **ABSOLUTES** (Categoricals). So the absolute "no sex before marriage" applies here. But in the modern era such absolutes seem to deny the possibility of a **TEMPORARY** committed relationship – or even sex for fun.

It's possible to be a Kantian and accept **HOMOSEXUAL MARRIAGE** but not **ADULTERY**.

Utilitarianism - Balancing the Positive and the Negative

What do the utilitarians say about our four issues: contraception, pre-marital sex, adultery and homosexuality? Here we contrast two utilitarians: **MILL** (1806-73) and **SINGER** (1946-).

Mill is a **MULTILEVEL** utilitarian who follows a more **ARISTOTELEAN** idea of happiness – **EUDAIMONIA** or personal and social flourishing. He argues that we need **RULES** to protect justice and **RIGHTS**, which are the cumulative wisdom of society. But when happiness demands it, or a **CONFLICT** of values occurs, we revert to being an **ACT** utilitarian – hence multilevel (Act and Rule) utilitarianism.

Mill agreed that **CONTRACEPTION** was moral as it increased personal and social happiness, through family planning and restrictions on population growth. Today the British Humanist association writes "if contraception results in every child being a wanted child and in better, healthier lives for women, it must be a good thing". Mill was imprisoned in 1832 for distributing "diabolical handbills" advocating contraception.

Mill had found a murdered baby in a park. The practice of exposing unwanted children was widespread. Hospitals for **FOUNDLINGS** such as **CORAM** set up in Bristol in 1741, did little except institutionalise **INFANTICIDE** (child killing). Between 1728 and 1757 33% of babies born in foundling hospitals and workhouses died or were killed.

On **HOMOSEXUAL** rights Mill follows Bentham in arguing for "utilitarian equality" by which everyone's happiness counts equally. Bentham was the first philosopher to suggest legalised **SODOMY** in an unpublished paper in 1802. Freedom was a key to personal flourishing, and as long as no harm was done to any but consenting adults, (Mill's **HARM PRINCIPLE** in On Liberty) it is a private matter how people order their sex lives.

In his essay on **LIBERTY** (1859) Mill argues for **SOCIAL RIGHTS** so we can undertake "experiments in living" that give us protection from the prejudices of popular culture and "the tyranny of prevailing opinion and feeling". Mill would have approved of **COHABITATION** and pre-marital sex.

Evaluation - Mill

Mill was a father of the **LIBERALISM** we take for granted where difference is tolerated. His brand of utilitarianism balances social **JUSTICE** and individual freedom and pursuit of happiness.

Utilitarianism works well looking **BACKWARDS**. The Abortion Act (1967), the Homosexual Reform Act (1967) and the Divorce Reform Act (1969) are all examples of utilitarian legislation.

Utilitarian ethics works less well looking forwards. We cannot predict **CONSEQUENCES**. So the **AIDS** epidemic can be seen as a product partly of personal freedom to adopt a promiscuous "unsafe" lifestyle. It is hard to see how a utilitarian can prevent this or even argue it is wrong if freely chosen.

Many of the greatest **SOCIAL** reforms have not been inspired by Christian values, Natural Law or Kantian ethics, but by **UTILITARIAN** considerations of social **WELFARE**. Today relatively few Christian churches accept the complete equality of women.

Key Confusions

- "Sexual ethics is merely up to individual choice". It is a common misunderstanding of ethics that it is purely about personal choice. Yet **MILL** points out, following **ARISTOTLE**, that ethics always has a personal and a social dimension. Laws both reflect social morality and also help to mould it. So when the law was changed on homosexuality, contraception and child protection it both reflected a change in social attitudes (things once thought acceptable are now seen to be abusive and other things once criminalised are now morally accepted) and helped to form those attitudes. And if I choose to be promiscuous that affects every person I am promiscuous with.

- "Sexual behaviour is natural and doesn't do anyone any harm". This is a misunderstanding of what 'natural' means in ethics. For example, the word 'natural" in **NATURAL LAW** means 'in line with our rational natural purpose'. Certain goals are unique to human beings - for example **WORSHIP OF GOD** and even those shared with animals (**REPRODUCTION**) function in a different way to animals - we are **MORAL** beings capable of evaluating consequences, for example, and capable of understanding our social responsibility to build an orderly and co-operative society.

- "There is one heterosexual human nature". This is an **ASSUMPTION** of natural law theory which appears highly questionable. It seems there really is a **HOMOSEXUAL** human nature and also a **TRANSGENDER** human nature. The whole ethics of sexual behaviour has altered radically in the light of empirical research (such as the **KINSEY** report) and also the insights of psychologists such as **FREUD** and **JUNG**. Moreover the criticisms of a type of religious thought that equates sex with **SIN** may well still hang over in the **GUILT** that attends certain expressions of sexual behaviour. Of course, which expression is part of our ongoing ethical debate.

Possible Future Exam Questions

1. "Religion is irrelevant in deciding issues surrounding sexual behaviour". Discuss

2. Critically evaluate the view that the ethics of sexual behaviour should be entirely private and personal.

3. "Because sexual conduct affects others, it should be subject to legislation". Discuss

4. "Normative theories are useful in what they might say about sexual ethics". Discuss

Key Quotes - Sexual Ethics

"The only purpose for which power can be rightfully exercised over any member of a civilised community against his will, is to prevent harm to others". JS Mill

"If a form of sexual activity brings satisfaction to those who take part in it, and harms no-one, what can be immoral about it?" Peter Singer

"The pleasure derived from the union between the sexes is a pleasure: therefore the legislator must do whatever is in his power so that the quantity in society is as high as possible". Jeremy Bentham

"Sex exposes mankind to the danger of equality with the beasts...by virtue of the nature of sexual desire a person who sexually desires another person objectifies that person… As soon as that appetite is satisfied one casts aside the person as one casts aside a lemon that has been sucked dry ". Kant

"It seems impossible to see any sound reason for any of the attempts to legislate morality. It is doubtful whether love's cause is helped by any of the sex laws that try to dictate sexual practices for consenting adults". Joseph Fletcher

Christian Thought H573/3

The OCR 2016 specification H573/3 has posed some challenges for teacher and student, and for this reason this guide represents the foundation of a new approach to integrating Christian Thought with the other papers.

- Christian Thought has key themes which pull the specification together. One theme is how the Bible is interpreted by different generations. For example, feminists and liberationists take a critical **HERMENEUTIC** (interpretation) taking as guiding principles justice and freedom. Was Jesus actually a **POLITICAL LIBERATOR** (see **PERSON of CHRIST** section)? And how do we know God, through **NATURE** or just by **REVELATION**?

- There is no single version of Christianity so an easy way of looking at the question of **WHICH CHRISTIANITY** is to compare the **CONSERVATIVE EVANGELICAL**, **CATHOLIC** and **LIBERAL** views. The Liberal view is rapidly becoming mainstream Church of England and has always been mainstream **EPISCOPALIAN** (US Anglican). But therir views don't just different on ethical issues (such as gay marriage) , but also on the **AFTERLIFE** and role of women (see section on **FEMINISM**). **CONSERVATIVE EVANGELICALISM** can be summed up by reading the **CHICAGO STATEMENT** on Biblical Inerrancy 1976. Textbooks seem not to notice this important document.

- Fundamental to this section is the issue: can Christianity survive in a **SECULAR** age under attack from the **NEW ATHEISTS** (Dawkins for example)? And has Christianity suffered from the **FREUDIAN** revolution in how we understand **SIN** and what it mens to be Human? See the section on **HUMAN NATURE** and link this to the **SEXUAL ETHICS** section of H573/2.

- The textbooks have produced their own interpretation of this specification, in the sense of **ADDITIONAL AUTHORS** and ideas, which you don't necessarily need to adopt or follow. They have overlaid an additional discussion of philosophers and philosophical ideas in order to **EVALUATE** the fairly brief content of the specification. You can add your own: Alistair McGrath on **NATURAL THEOLOGY** is a key modern thinker, for example, textbooks don't mention.

- The three papers need to be integrated to produce what is called **SYNOPTIC** insight. This literally means elements of the three papers that can be 'seen together' or linked up. For example, Kant's **MORAL ARGUMENT** (Philosophy of Religion) links and to his ethics which links to **HICK**'s universal **PLURALISM** (Christian Thought) as Hick is greatly inspired by Kant. The Peped website shows additional ways to integrate the three papers and there will be a **REVISION** section accessible for those who have this guide showing you how to increase your synoptic understanding.

- Our approach is to teach for **STRUCTURES OF THOUGHT**. These are given by the mind-maps in this guide. Notice these are not free-for-all scatter diagrams but are structures that move from **WORLDVIEW** through to **CONCLUSION**. And the same structure will be there in the website and in the other revision materials - with creative and hopefully enjoyable tasks you can use to test your understanding. You need to run with this concept of structures, and if you do so, I believe your chances of an A grade or A* will be greatly enhanced. They remind us to reason from **WORLDVIEW** and assumptions through to a conclusion that follows.

As you revise, think 'process' rather than 'knowledge'. Knowledge is strengthened by process, and so is memory. Those who have this integrated guide should have a head-start, but you need to supplement it with other ideas and sample answers.

Augustine - Human Nature

Background & Influences

Augustine was influenced in his thought on human nature by:

1. **MANICHEES** – each person has a good and bad soul. We escape wrong-doing by using our reason and following positive role models.

2. **NEOPLATONISM** – Plotinus. Good and evil are not distinct realms. Only the Form of the Good exists.

3. **BIBLE** - St Paul's Letter to the Romans – God's grace was necessary.

At AS and A level, you will need to explain and evaluate Augustine's view on human relationships pre-and post-Fall; Original Sin and its effects on the will and human societies, and God's grace.

Key Terms

- **AKRASIA -** paradox of voluntarily choosing to do something we know is against our best interests.

- **CARITAS -** 'generous love', a love of others and of the virtues.

- **CONCORDIA -** human friendship.

- **CONCUPISCENCE -** uncontrollable desire for physical pleasures and material things.

- **CUPIDITAS -** 'selfish love', a love of worldly things and of selfish desires.

- **DOCTRINE -** means 'teaching'. The official teaching of the Roman Catholic Church.

- **ECCLESIA -** heavenly society, in contrast with earthly society.

- **GRACE -** theologically, God's free and unearned love for humankind, embodied in the sacrifice of Jesus on the cross.

- **MANICHEES -** humans have two souls. One desires God, the other desires evil. Evil is not caused by God, but by a lower power. The body is evil and sinful.

- **NEOPLATONISM -** influenced by Plato; the body belongs to the realm of flesh and is necessarily imperfect.

- **ONTOLOGICAL -** the being or nature of existence.

- **OPTIMISTIC VIEW OF HUMAN NATURE -** humans are only immoral because of poor education or psychological fault.

- **ORIGINAL SIN -** Christian belief that despite being made in God's image the human condition means we cannot reach this state.

- **PELAGIANS -** Christians who believed humans could overcome personal sin with free will. No universal guilt.

- **POST-LAPSARIAN -** the world after the fall of Adam and Eve.

- **SUMMUM BONUM -** he highest, most supreme good.

- **THE FALL -** the biblical event in which Adam and Eve disobeyed God's command and ate the fruit from the forbidden tree in the Garden of Eden.

Structure of Thought

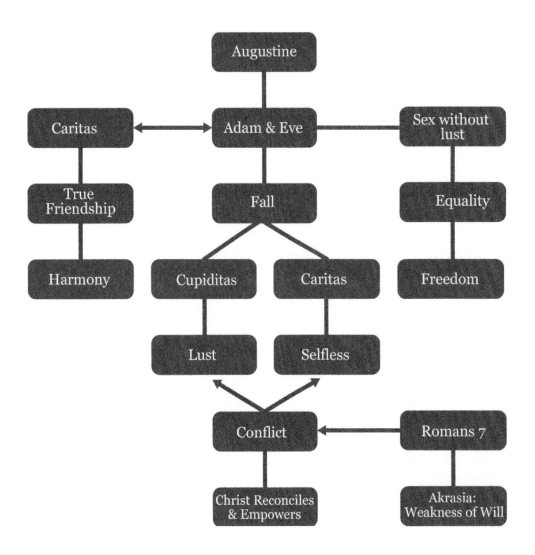

Human Relationships Pre and Post-Fall

The **ORIGINAL SIN** of Adam and Eve ruined the relationship humankind could have had with God.

Augustine teaches that this '**ORIGINAL SIN**' passes on through generations **SEMINALLY** (by sperm), making human nature flawed. However, Jesus' death on the cross was seen as a **SACRIFICE**, paying the price of sin, meaning Christians could be saved through God's **GRACE**.

Christian tradition understands humanity in terms of its relationship with God. This is threefold:

1. Humans are **CREATED** by God.

2. Humans are **FALLEN** in nature.

3. Humans can be **REDEEMED** (bought back by a sacrifice).

Pre-Fall

The shared nature of **IMAGO DEI** means humans can all be seen to be equal. This has sometimes been seen as **EQUALLY RATIONAL**, but at other times women are seen as **COMPLEMENTARY** - but less rational (**AQUINAS**).

In **GENESIS** the second account of creation shows humans as **SPECIAL** in God's creation but simultaneously part of the natural world. God breathes life into man. God animates man - different to **PLATO'S** notion of the soul trapped by the body.

Once created, humans are not programmed to act in a certain way. They have a set of rules to follow e.g. multiply, be stewards, do not eat from the forbidden tree. They have potential to be both obedient and disobedient – made with **FREE CHOICE** and made perfectly.

Humans were made with a **DUTY OF OBEDIENCE** to God's demands and existed harmoniously, observing their duties to other living creatures.

The state of perfection **PRE-FALL** meant that the human will, the body, and reason cooperated with each other entirely. In their **SEXUAL** expression **AUGUSTINE** argues that pre-Fall Adam and Eve had perfect **SELF-CONTROL**.

Humans are naturally sociable and friendship is the highest form of this. **CONCORDIA** is used to describe Adam and Eve's relationship pre-**FALL**. Adam and Eve were not just living together, but were living in a state of the very best of all possible **HARMONIOUS** human relationships.

Post-Fall

The will can be driven by **CUPIDITAS** (self-love typified by **LUST** or **CARITAS** (selfless-love or benevolence).

After the first free decision to disobey, Adam and Eve became aware of their sexual bodies. Through **REASON** the will knows what is good but is often motivated by **CONCUPISCENCE** (sexual lust) rather than by goodness. Concupiscence can distract from God and break up friendship.

Post-Fall, the will became in conflict with itself and could lead to freely choosing what we know to go against our best interests. This is known as **AKRASIA** (weakness of will).

Augustine used his own example of a beautiful, chaste woman –**CONTINENCE**. Not even she could convince Augustine to embrace celibacy – **"Lord, make me chaste, but not yet!"**.

The battle with sin cannot be won without turning to Christ, as shown in Paul's Letter to the **ROMANS,** (chapter 7) and the extracts from **CONFESSIONS**.

SYNOPTIC point: in the Ethics paper, Freud's theory of **CONSCIENCE** suggests a struggle between the **PASSIONS** of the **ID** and the restraint of the **SUPEREGO**.

Original Sin - Effects on the Human Will & Society

Augustine and Pelagius

AUGUSTINE sees sin as an **ONTOLOGICAL CONDITION** of Human Existence. We might appear **VIRTUOUS**, but no one is truly good. Sin was transmitted by **SEXUAL INTERCOURSE**.

PELAGIUS argues that while Adam set a poor example, it was not the one that we had to follow and we could, if we tried, live morally.

Augustine disagreed with Pelagius - human efforts alone were not enough – we need God's **GRACE** and **CHRIST**. Paul said much the same "the things I do not want are the things I do' (**ROMANS 7**). Paul sees human beings as **SLAVES** to sin.

The inherited **ORIGINAL SIN** causes human selfishness and a lack of free will; plus a lack of stability and corruption in all human societies. **CUPIDITAS** (selfish desire) has won over **CARITAS** (the harmonious love of Eden) and the human soul is now in **CONFLICT.**

Human Selfishness & Free Will

The **FALL** left the will divided. Paul's Letter to the **ROMANS** described Paul's struggle between his **SELFISH DESIRES** and his **SPIRITUAL INCLINATIONS**, (see Romans 7).

Paul speaks of Christians as 'forgiven sinners' through their faith and this partially explains how Christians still behave wrongly even after accepting salvation. Paul implies that the release from all sin will come with death of the body.

SEXUAL LUSTS are evidence of sinful **CUPIDITAS. AUGUSTINE** said that even within marriage, a couple should take a vow of **CELIBACY** once they had had enough children. People should live plainly and simply to devote themselves to God.

In '**On the Good of Marriage**' - the physical delight of sex in marriage should be distinguished from **LIBIDO** (misuse of lustful impulse). It is 'pardonable' to enjoy sex without the intention of procreation. Like **ARISTOTLE** and **PAUL**, he stressed 'mutual **OBLIGATION**'.

In 'Free Will' Augustine suggests free will allows us to use reason to aspire to the Good (human flourishing) by living virtuously. This is **PLATONIC**.

However, human reason cannot overcome the punishments of the Fall. Sin is **INVOLUNTARY** and we cannot help but fall into wrong-doing. We prefer to do wrong because our souls are 'chained' by sin. Neither living **ASCETICALLY** (nun/monk) or opting for a **CHASTE** life could enable the will to be free and strong enough to resist **CONCUPISCENCE** in its various forms.

Lack of Stability & Corruption in Human Societies

A forceful political **AUTHORITY** was needed to help society function.

The Bible teaches that humans are appointed to rule over other species, but not each other. **PRE-FALL**, leaders in society were **SHEPHERDS** not kings (Augustine, City of God).

'Earthly peace' is a material and not a spiritual aim. **EARTHLY PEACE** is the best sort of life sinful people can aim for, but even this is **CORRUPTED**. The measures needed for earthy peace (e.g. self-restraint) are only necessary because of the Fall.

Commitment to the common good is a consequence of sinful human nature and not, as **AQUINAS** would say, a **MORAL VIRTUE**. We are '**PILGRIMS** in a foreign land' – we need to live as earthly people out of necessity; but should keep focused on the heavenly destination, the **'CITY OF GOD'**.

This '**HEAVENLY SOCIETY** is called **ECCLESIA** and is 'perfect living'. Heavenly society is known only through death and the **GRACE** of God and is poorly and partially reflected in the **EARTHLY** society**.**

God's Grace

AUGUSTINE argued that the rebellious will and **SIN** could only be overcome by God's grace (his free and generous gifts), made possible through Jesus' sacrifice. Only then can the supreme good (**SUMMUM BONUM**) be achieved.

Augustine's teaching on God's grace laid the foundation for Catholic confession – the Sacrament of **RECONCILIATION**.

The Christian doctrine of **ELECTION** teaches that salvation is possible because God chooses to redeem (literally 'buy back' from the slave market) humans first. God has elected those He knows will answer His love and be restored to paradise. The elected are assisted by the **HOLY SPIRIT.**

Augustine's view contradicts one New Testament suggestion that 'all' are saved – unless this means that God saves across races and cultures (see 2 Peter 3:9).

JOHN 3 ('Jesus said; unless a person is born again of **WATER** and the Spirit they cannot enter the Kingdom of God') led Augustine to believe that heaven could not be reached by anyone deliberately denying baptism. **UNBAPTISED** babies could be condemned to hell. This is not as a result of choice – infants do not 'choose' to deny baptism.

Faith in God's love and an acknowledgement of the failings of human nature are essential on the path to **EUDAIMONIA** - "unless you believe, you will not understand" (Isaiah 7:9).

John 3 showed Augustine that **FAITH** and **BAPTISM** together were needed as human nature is **ONTOLOGICALLY** flawed (flawed in its very essence).

God's **GRACE** is understood as:

- God's **LOVE** and **MERCY**; that He is capable of reaching the heart and will of a person and can give moral guidance to the lives of Christians; something that cannot be deserved by any human on their own merit.

- The quality that enables a person's soul to **RECOGNISE** when it has offended God and when it should praise God.

- Capable of **TRANSFORMING** the human will so that it is capable of obeying God.

- Capable of **OVERCOMING** human pride and can calm the soul with forgiveness and hope.

- **VISIBLE** in Christ's sacrifice and in the gift of the Holy Spirit working in the Church.

MNEMONIC: Lovely Mary Really Transformed Our Vase

Happiness in this earthly life is temporary. Plato's **FORM OF THE GOOD** is similar to **AUGUSTINE**'s understanding of God's goodness in Christianity. The **SUMMUM BONUM** is a state of eternal happiness. It cannot be earned and is the highest goal one can aim for – achievable only through God's grace.

Strengths

1. Close to the reality that people often find themselves **TEMPTED** by material goods, yet wanting to do right.

2. **AUGUSTINE** draws attention to the dangers of uncontrolled sexual behaviour – see how societies restrict it. Recognising human imperfection might lead to more moral progress.

3. The **PELAGIAN** belief that human effort could bring about perfection was optimistic and doomed to fail. Augustine's teaching of our imperfect natures allows us to have genuine hope in God's grace.

4. The **BODY** and human **REASON** can be in tension with the body being willing, but the will not so. This supports the view that sex must have been under the control of the human will pre-Fall. Sex did not come about because of **the Fall**; but rather, was affected by it.

5. Other schools of thought suggest a **SINGLE** human nature. E.g. Buddhism – human nature is characterised by the impermanency of all things and suffering because of attachment and desires. Evolutionary biology suggests the single human nature that is driven by survival instinct.

Weaknesses

1. **ORIGINAL SIN** as 'ontologically present' is difficult to reconcile with belief in a benevolent God. Human nature is not fundamentally corrupt! **ROUSSEAU** argued that humans are, by nature, good and inclined to defend the weak and work for a better society. Rousseau and Locke later asserted the 'blank state' (**'TABULA RASA'**). We are born with – neither a good nor evil state, but readiness to make free choices..

2. **SARTRE**, an **EXISTENTIALIST**, suggests we have the freedom to create our own nature – rather than being born condemned.

3. **PREDESTINATION**/ Election – if our fates are already decided, what responsibility can we have for our moral actions? With no real freedom, what incentive do we have to become better?

4. Richard **DAWKINS** - while the Christian concept of 'original sin' does not wholly contradict evolutionary biology, the idea that human nature could be restored through the death of Jesus is sado-masochistic!

5. **FREUD** (1856-1939) – one of the founders of psychoanalysis – wrote that sex is an important and natural aspect of human development; whereas **Augustine's** link between sex and transmission of sin makes sex only necessary for reproduction. Sex can transmit human disorders but sin is not one of these! Rather than a product of sexual intercourse, sin is a product of our environment (family, religion, education, or lack thereof). Augustine fails to acknowledge the natural enjoyment of sex within marriage.

6. Steven **PINKER** (psychologist) supports **DAWKINS**. God's Grace is not needed as our actions as rational, autonomous beings can succeed and allow us responsibility.

Possible Exam Questions

1. Assess the view that Augustine's teaching on human nature is too pessimistic.

2. Critically assess the view that Christian teaching on human nature can only make sense if the Fall did actually happen.

3. "Augustine's teaching on human nature is more harmful than helpful". Discuss.

4. How convincing is Augustine's teaching about the Fall and Original Sin?

5. Critically assess Augustine's analysis of human sexual nature.

Key Quotes

"For they would not have arrived at the evil act if an evil will had not preceded it". (Augustine, city of God).

"I do not understand what I do. For what I want to do I do not do, but what I hate I do". (St. Paul's Letter to the Romans)

"In vain did I delight in Your law after the inner man, when another law in my members warred against the law of my mind." (Augustine, Confessions).

"No one can enter the kingdom of God unless they are born of water and the Spirit". (John 3)

"Whoever believes in him is not condemned, but whoever does not believe stands condemned already." (John 3)

"What kind of ethical philosophy is it that condemns every child, even before it is born, to inherit the sin of a remote ancestor?" (Richard Dawkins, God Delusion)

Death and the Afterlife

Background & Influences

Jesus' teachings rooted in **JEWISH TRADITION** and **ESCHATOLOGY** (teaching on the end-times) of his time. Influenced by the teaching of the **PHARISEES** who were influenced by **GREEK** ideas of the soul and immortality.

Jesus taught his life was a **SACRIFICE** for sin and his death would bring about a **NEW KINGDOM**.

Some believed the 'new Kingdom' to be **IMMINENT** (about to happen). Different beliefs about the Kingdom of God include whether it is **an actual place, a spiritual state, or a symbol of moral life.**

You will need to show knowledge and evaluation of Christian teaching on Heaven, Hell, and Purgatory, and Christian teaching on Election.

Key Terms

- **ESCHATOLOGY** - discussion of the end-times, including battle between good and evil and God's judgement of the world.

- **PHARISEES** - influential religious leaders at the time of Jesus. Differed to other traditional Jews at the time (e.g. Sadducees) because the Pharisees did believe in angels and bodily resurrection.

- **PAROUSIA** - Greek for 'arrival'. Christ's 'second coming'.

- **KINGDOM OF GOD** - God's rule in this world and the next.

- **HADES** and **GEHENNA**: Hades – for departed spirits awaiting judgement; Gehenna - a symbol for eternal punishment of the wicked.

- **MARANATHA** - Aramaic – 'O Lord, come!' 1 Cor 16:22 (once in NT).

- **PURGATORY** - where those who have died in a state of grace continue to seek forgiveness and receive punishment awaiting Final Judgement.

- **MORTAL SIN** - sin deliberately in defiance of God's law.

- **VENIAL SIN** - errors of judgement, can be forgiven.

- **PREDESTINATION** - Christian teaching that God chooses and guides some people to eternal salvation.

- **DOUBLE PREDESTINATION** - God elects the righteous for Heaven and condemns sinners to Hell - as in **CALVIN**'s teaching.

- **SINGLE PREDESTINATION** - God predestines some to heaven but the wicked elect Hell for themselves. Official **CATHOLIC** teaching.

Structure of Thought

Christian Teaching on Heaven, Hell and Purgatory

1. Heaven, hell, and purgatory as **ACTUAL PLACES**.

2. Heaven, hell, and purgatory as not places, but **SPIRITUAL STATES** that a person experiences as part of their spiritual journey after death.

3. Heaven, hell, and purgatory as **SYMBOLS** of a person's spiritual and moral life on earth and not places or states after death.

Ideas about the Kingdom Taught by Jesus

1. **A present moral and spiritual state**. A call for moral and spiritual reform now. Jesus' healing miracles seem to fulfil prophecies of Isaiah and Jesus presents the Kingdom of God as if it has already begun. This 'nowness' is seen in his parables and examples of how to reach out to the lowly.

2. **A future redeemed state**. Made possible through Jesus' death and resurrection.

3. **A place of punishment and justice**. Where the wicked will suffer and those who suffered will prosper. - **GEHENNA** - a place of **EVERLASTING FIRE** (Matthew 25 - Parable of the Sheep & Goats).

Problems

1. **PAROUSIA** seems delayed. One of the earliest prayers recorded is for the Parousia – **MARANATHA** prayer (1 Corinthians 16:22, 'Come Lord Jesus!'). Jesus emphasises the mystery surrounding this date.

2. **WHERE** is this new Kingdom? On earth or in heaven (or both)?

3. **FINAL JUDGEMENT v INDIVIDUAL** – which is more important? Rich man and Lazarus implies judgement is immediate (Luke 16:13-31). Others suggest it happens at the end-time.

4. **PURGATORY** is not a term used in the New Testament. Arose out of fairness to allow people time to prepare for God's final judgement and as a result of ambiguity surrounding personal and final judgement.

Eschatological Teaching

1. **PAROUSIA** (second coming of Christ)

2. **RESURRECTION** (at the last day a 'trumpet will sound', 1 Cor. 15)

3. **JUDGEMENT** (Matthew 25 - sheep and goats separated)

Hell - Different Ideas

SPIRITUAL STATE: Origen (184-253 AD) – a person's interior anguish separated from God, where "each sinner kindles his own fire ...and our own vices from its fuel" (Cited in Wilcockson & Campbell, 2016, p. 273).

CONSCIENCE: Gregory of Nyssa (335-395 AD) – a guilty conscience when before Christ leads to judgement and torture of Hell.

DANTE (1265-1321): Hell is antithesis to Heaven – "through me the way into the woeful city, through me the way to eternal pain...abandon every hope, ye that enter" (Dante Divine Comedy cited in Wilcockson & Campbell, 2016:274).

SYMBOL OF ALIENATION: Paul Tillich (1886-1965) – hell-type language has a place. Traditional metaphors are reinterpreted as spiritual and psychological descriptions of human alienation: "heaven and hell must be taken seriously as metaphors for the polar ultimates in the experience of the divine" (Tillich, P, Systematic theology III, 1964, p. 446, cited in Wilcockson & Campbell, 2016:275).

HELL AS ETERNAL SEPARATION: Catholic teaching – Hell is real eternal for those who have committed mortal sins.

Purgatory

1. A **CATHOLIC** way of extending the opportunity for repentance beyond this life, even though there is no clear representation of this in the New Testament, just one hint **1 PETER 3:19**. "When made alive, Jesus went to preach to the spirits in prison".

2. Foretaste of Heaven and Hell – **AMBROSE** (340 -397 AD).

3. Probationary school – **ORIGEN**.

4. Redemption of the whole of creation – **GREGORY** of Nyssa – purgatory has a **PURIFYING PURPOSE** for all people to help God complete his purpose of restoring all creation.

Dante's Vision

- For souls who believed in Christ and repented before death; a place for positive **PURGING** since one cannot sin in purgatory.

- The soul ascends terrains of mountain, the goal of which is **BEATIFIC VISION**. Soul is driven by love and later on, reason. An allegory for how life should be lived on earth too with its various temptations before the goal of salvation.

Catholic Teaching on Purgatory

- Ideas of **CLEANSING** of sins by fires implies that forgiveness is possible in this and in the next life.

- A **STAGE** in the soul's journey to salvation.

- Prayers for the dead pre-dates Christianity – **JUDAS MACCAAEUS** (2nd C BC) – prayed that the souls of the dead should be freed from sin. Sale of **INDULGENCES** (masses said for the dead) one reason for **REFORMATION** protest in the sixteenth century.

- St John **CHRYSOSTOM** writes:

"All who die in God's grace and friendship, but still imperfectly purified, are indeed assured of their eternal salvation; but after death they undergo purification, so as to achieve the holiness necessary to enter the joy of heaven". St John Chrysostom

Hick - The Intermediary State

The majority of Protestants reject **PURGATORY** on the grounds of lack of Biblical evidence.

A minority of **LIBERAL PROTESTANTS** are persuaded of the continued journey of the soul after death.

JOHN HICK says that the gap between our imperfection at the end of this life, and the state of perfection is a **SOUL-MAKING** process begun on Earth.

Heaven

This has a number of meanings. The **RESTORATION** of the whole of creation, not just the individual's relationship with God.

DANTE – Heaven is beyond words. Rational soul strives for ultimate good and Divine harmony. God as source of love and governor of universe is experienced.

CATHOLIC TEACHING – Heaven is a "state of supreme, definitive happiness" (Cited in Wilcockson & Campbell, 2016, p. 278). God is wholly revealed in **BEATIFIC VISION**. A community of immortal souls in communion with Christ and obedient.

Election - Who Will Be Saved?

Limited Election

- Only a few Christians will be saved

- '**LIMITED ATONEMENT**' – Christ died only for the sins of the Elect

Unlimited Election

- All people called to salvation, not all are saved

- '**UNLIMITED ATONEMENT**' – Christ died for the sins of the whole world

Universalist Belief (Apokatastasis - Restoration)

- All people will be saved - required by God's goodness and love

- A requirement of human free will – we should all be able to reach salvation

- Upbringing should not exclude people from reconciliation with God

JOHN HICK – The God preached about by Jesus is not one who excludes. Jesus' resurrection is a triumph over death, not eternal damnation.

KARL BARTH - CALVINIST and not strictly universalist but helpful. God is both elected and elector and it is not for humans to speculate on the mystery of salvation.

Predestination

Election and Predestination

AUGUSTINE argued that salvation is only possible because of God's grace. God's grace is unprompted but **FREELY GIVEN.** God calls all to salvation but knows from the beginning that only some are eligible for a place in Heaven (**ELECT**).

Some are not capable of receiving God's grace and are predestined for Hell (**PERDITION**).

Single and Double Predestination

- **SINGLE**: God elects only those for Heaven

- **DOUBLE**: God elects people for both Heaven and Hell.

- **ANTELAPSARIAN DECREE**: God decreed the elect at the moment of creation, pre-Fall (literally **ANTE** - before **LAPSARIAN,** the lapse).

- **POSTLAPSARIAN DECREE:** God decreed the elect post-Fall.

Calvin

Developing ideas in Paul's letter to the Ephesians, Calvin argued God **FOREKNOWS** what will happen but His will is hidden. Calvin believed both saved and damned are **PREDESTINED** from the beginning of time. This is **DOUBLE PREDESTINATION.**

As Human knowledge is **LIMITED**, God's revelation takes this into account. **GOD WILLS** his grace and mercy for all kinds of people.

Even if God has chosen particular individuals, **CHRISTIAN DUTY** is to spread God's words to all kinds of people. Both the **ELECT** and the **NON-ELECT** have a duty to act morally.

Thomas Aquinas and Catholicism

AQUINAS argued the Fall did not wipe out human freedom. THE Catholic Church – argues for **SINGLE** predestination of the saved - damned get to hell by choice.

"God predestines no one to go to Hell; for this, a wilful turning away from God (a mortal sin) is necessary, and persistence in it until the end" (Catechism of the Catholic Church para. 1037).

Parable of Sheep & Goats (Matthew 25)

- **REVERSAL of expectation.** 'Righteous' would have been thought to have meant those who observed Jewish law. Jesus teaches that religious observance is not enough to earn a place in God's Kingdom. One must pursue justice for the marginalised without thinking of heavenly reward.

- **REWARD** is for **ALL** who pursue justice, not just Christians. The God of love rewards all of good will.

- **REVELATION** of Jesus' own ministry of healing and serving the oppressed is reflected in his list of acts that would be rewarded.

- **CHALLENGE** to traditional teaching that you are only obligated to help those in the same social and religious group as yourself. "Just as you did to one of the least of these who are members of my family, you did it to me" (Matthew 25:40).

Possible Exam Questions

1. To what extent can belief in the existence of purgatory be justified?

2. "Heaven is not a place but a state of mind." Discuss.

3. "Without the reward of Heaven Christians would not behave well." Discuss.

4. To what extent is the Parable of the Sheep and the Goats in Matthew 25 only about Heaven and Hell?

5. Assess the view that there is no last judgement; each person is judged by God at the moment of their death.

6. "Purgatory is a vital Christian teaching about the afterlife." Discuss.

Key Quotes

"The time is fulfilled, and the kingdom of God is near" (Mark 1:14)

"Anyone whose name was not found written in the book of life was thrown into the lake of fire" (Revelation 20:15).

"But about that day and hour no one knows, neither the angels of heaven, nor the Son, but only the Father" (Matthew 24:36).

"This is good, and is acceptable in the sight of God our Saviour, who desires all men to be saved and come to the knowledge of truth" (1 Timothy 2:4).

"All who die in God's grace and friendship, but still imperfectly purified, are indeed assured of their eternal salvation; but after death they undergo purification, so as to achieve the holiness necessary to enter the joy of heaven." (Catechism 1030)

"The Church gives the name Purgatory to this final purification of the elect, which is entirely different from the punishment of the damned. The tradition of the Church speaks of a cleansing fire". (Catechism 1031)

Knowledge of God

Background & Influences

NATURAL THEOLOGY is concerned with demonstrating God's existence. Some have assumed God's existence to be logically true. God revealed in the natural world seems removed from Biblical ideas of God as love.

REVEALED THEOLOGY suggests that God allows himself to be known in a special way e.g. in Jesus Christ or the example of the Prophet Muhammad (PBUH).

Problem: God is uniquely different to any other object. Natural theology would have to accept this. Revealed theology seems to neglect reason.

What is 'true knowledge'?

1. **Incorrigible facts** (verifiable)

2. **Wisdom** – understanding life and what gives it value

3. **Knowledge** of God as the source of life

At A level, you will need to show understanding and evaluation of natural knowledge of God's existence as an innate human sense of the Divine, and as seen in the order of Creation; and revealed knowledge of God's existence through faith and God's grace, and in Jesus Christ.

Key Terms

- **NATURAL THEOLOGY** - God can be known through reason and observation of the natural world.

- **REVEALED THEOLOGY** - God can only be known when he lets himself be known e.g. through prophets, scripture, prayer.

- **SENSUS DIVINITATIS** - Latin used by Calvin to mean a 'sense of God'.

- **DUPLEX COGNITIO DOMINI** - 'two-fold knowledge of God' – Calvin's distinction of knowing God as Creator and as Redeemer.

- **ARGUMENT FROM DESIGN** - we must infer a designer (God) of the universe from the universe's complexities.

- **PRINCIPLE OF ACCOMMODATION** - God reveals himself through creation in ways that limited human minds can best understand.

- **SI INTEGER STETISSET ADAM** - Latin used by Calvin meaning 'if Adam had remained upright' – referring to the Fall.

- **IMMANENCE** - 'being part of' – refers to God's participation in all aspects of the world and universe.

Structure of Thought

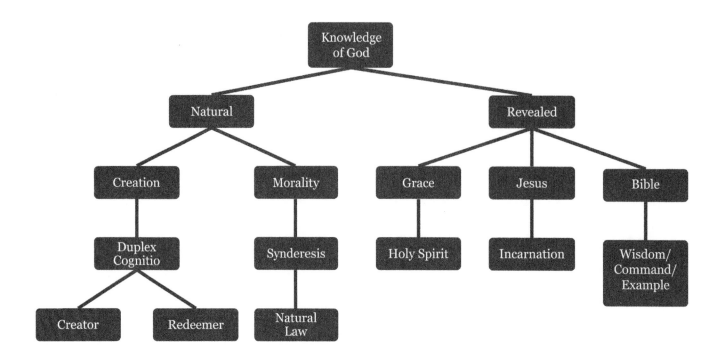

Natural Knowledge of God's Existence as Innate Sense

Sensus Divinitatis

As all humans are made in God's **IMAGE** - they have an inbuilt capacity and desire to know God, including:

- Human **OPENNESS** to beauty and goodness as aspects of God

- Human **INTELLECTUAL** ability to reflect on and recognise God's existence

Both **CALVIN** and the **CATECHISM** of the Catholic Church agree that knowledge of God is **INNATE** (we are born with it).

CALVIN called this innate knowledge of God **SENSUS DIVINITATIS**.

SEMEN RELIGIONIS – seed of religion – human inclination to carry out religious practices e.g. rituals and prayer.

Innate Knowledge

- **UNKNOWN GOD – Acts 17:16-34** – Paul tries to convince Athenians they are worshipping the true God, even if they do not know this.

- **UNIVERSAL CONSENT** – **Cicero, Calvin** – so many people believe in a God/ gods that there **MUST** exist a God/god!

- **HUMANS ARE RELIGIOUS** – religious rituals and meditations are so universal that "**one may well call man a religious being**" (Catechism 28).

Sense of Beauty & Moral Goodness

The foundations of knowledge of God in Protestant and Catholic Christianity.

- **NATURAL LAW** – particularly Catholicism – all humans have an innate awareness of justice and fairness, even if ill-informed. Aquinas calls this innate orientation to the good **SYNDERESIS**.

- **CONSCIENCE** – particularly important to Calvin's ideas about knowledge of God. Conscience is God-given to humans made **IMAGO DEI** with 'Joint knowledge' between us and God. God's presence gives us the sense of moral judgement within us.

Human Intellectual Ability to Reflect on & Recognise God's Existence

Seen in example of **Thomas Aquinas' FIVE WAYS** - God as **UNCAUSED CAUSER** who sustains all things.

Best knowledge we have here is that God exists differently to other beings.

Consider: how can we be **SURE** that this is God?

Natural Knowledge in the Order of Creation

- The idea that what can be known of God can be seen in the apparent design and purpose of nature

- **CALVIN** – **duplex cognitio Domini** – two-fold knowledge of God as **CREATOR** and as **REDEEMER**.

- The **ORDER** and **DESIGN** in the universe are strong sources of revelation.

- **PRINCIPLE OF ACCOMMODATION** – Calvin's explanation that human minds are finite and therefore cannot know God through **REASON** alone. Hence, God manifests himself through creation.

- What we know of God through creation is "a sort of **MIRROR** in which we can contemplate God, who is otherwise invisible" (John Calvin: Institutes I.V.1).

Purpose

- William **PALEY** – watch analogy; God as infinitely powerful maker.

- Challenge- nature seems more cruel than beautiful. Darwin's challenge of evolution too.

- **PROCESS THEOLOGY** developed in response to challenges to Paley's argument and influenced by the principle of **QUANTUM UNCERTAINTY**. Proposes that God works **WITH** the natural processes, not separate to them. Each individual moment is an end in itself – the universe as a whole is not working towards a particular end.

- **GOD IS KNOWABLE** – in contrast with ideas of classical theology. God loves and suffers with creation, helping each aspect to achieve its potential. God's participation in nature is revealed in every moment of creation. Process theology - there is no clear difference between natural and revealed theology.

Revealed Knowledge of God's Existence

As humans are sinful and have finite minds, natural knowledge is not sufficient to gain full knowledge of God; knowledge of God is possible through:

- **FAITH** - "Happy are those that do not see yet believe". (John 20:29)

- **GRACE** - as God's gift of knowledge of himself through the Holy Spirit

The Fall and Human Finiteness

The **FALL** of humanity has been overlooked in thinking about how we can come to know God, if at all.

- *Si integer stetisset Adam* (if Adam had not sinned) – everyone would have known God (**CALVIN'S** view).

- Knowledge of God the **REDEEMER**, mediated through Christ is part of our **REGENERATION** (of being 'born again').

- **CATHOLIC** – the Fall confused human desire for God but did not cut them off from knowledge of God completely – seen through "religious ignorance or indifference" (Catechism para. 29).

Faith

- Faith needs some **REASON** for it not to be meaningless or random.

- **CATHOLIC** – faith is not independent to reason.

- **AQUINAS** – distinguished between **formed** and **unformed** faith.

- **FORMED FAITH** - faith that wills to accept what it can believe through the intellect. Takes time and effort e.g. belief in resurrection based on witness accounts.

- **UNFORMED FAITH** - may find intellectual reasons why to believe e.g. in afterlife BUT cannot accept as truth.

- **CALVIN** – faith is firm and certain knowledge and a willingness to believe.

- **FIRM AND CERTAIN KNOWLEDGE -** Christ is direct object of faith. Firm knowledge only possible revealed through Christ and by the Holy Spirit.

- **WILLINGNESS TO BELIEVE** - an emotional and spiritual experience of assurance – given to anyone willing to accept it.

Grace

- **CATHOLIC** and **CALVINIST** teaching both agree that faith alone is not enough to know God. God's grace completes the relationship.

- **AQUINAS** – faith can only be justified by grace through the Holy Spirit.

- **CALVIN** – the Holy Spirit is a gift repairing the damage caused by Original Sin.

Revealed Knowledge of God's Existence in Jesus Christ

Full and perfect knowledge of God is revealed in the person of Jesus Christ and through:

- The life of the **CHURCH**

- The **BIBLE**

Bible should be read from a **TRINITARIAN** perspective: God as **FATHER** (God spoke **DIRECTLY** by the **PROPHETS**); God as Christ the **MEDIATOR** (clarity and fulfilment to God's promises); **HOLY SPIRIT** (Christians inspired).

CALVIN – Christ is mediator and mirror of God.

CATHOLIC – agrees but adds that the significance should not end with Christ but should continue with our faith, re-thinking God's revelation continuously.

Consider: can God be known by non-Christians?

The Bible and the Life of the Church

- For traditional Catholics and Protestants, *"God is the author of sacred Scripture...[and its words are] the speech of God as it is put down in writing under the breath of the Holy Spirit" (Catechism, 105).*

- Christianity cannot be 'reduced' to the Bible - which is **INSPIRED** not **DICTATED** (contrast with the Qur'an - dictated by angel Gabriel).

- **CALVIN** – the Bible, read from the perspective of Jesus Christ - as revealer of God the Redeemer; prepared for in the Old Testament and culminates in the events of the New Testament.

- Bible is a significant source for knowledge of God, even for those adopting an approach of **NATURAL THEOLOGY** who might say the Bible reveals early experiences people had of God (Hebrew, as recorded in the

OLD TESTAMENT) and to the early Christian communities.

- Knowledge of God revealed is **PERSONAL** and **COLLECTIVE**.

"In you, O Lord, I take refuge; let me never be put to shame...incline your ear to me and save me" (Psalm 71:1-2).

Q. What is the Barth/Brunner Debate?

Brunner

- God's **general revelation** in nature allows humans to become aware of God's commands and the sinful state of humankind.

- **Jesus Christ** reveals **redemption**. Natural theology has limited purpose.

- **Imago Dei** – God's image in humans was materially but not spiritually destroyed in the Fall but not spiritually. This spiritual level allows God to address humans.

- **General revelation** – Innately sinful humans are incapable of seeing God's revelation of his nature through nature – they can know God exists but it remains a **point of contact**, no more.

- **True knowledge** – Faith in Christ is necessary for true knowledge of God.

- **Conscience** – plus guilt bring humans to awareness of God's law.

MNEMONIC: Isabella Gave Temi Cookies

Barth

- There are no points of contact in nature – human nature is absolutely corrupted by the Fall.

- Only God can choose to reveal himself to sinful humans.

Three disagreements with Brunner's interpretation of Calvin:

1. **Formal self (spiritual self)** cannot inform the **material (physical)** self of God's existence. Brunner underestimates the corruption of the material self.

2. **No points of contact**. Nature, conscience and guilt are results of God's grace – they do not provide the points of contact themselves!

3. **Order of creation**. Perception of order in nature should not be basis for morality. God's moral commands are different to any natural laws. We only see order in creation after it is revealed to us through faith and the Bible.

Possible Exam Questions

1. Discuss critically the view that Christians can discover truths about God using human reason.

2. "Faith is all that is necessary to gain knowledge of God." Discuss.

3. "God can be known because the world is so well designed." Discuss.

4. Critically assess the view that the Bible is the only way of knowing God.

5. "Everyone has an innate knowledge of God's existence." Discuss.

6. To what extent is faith in God rational?

Key Quotes

"The desire for God is written in the human heart" (Catechism of the Catholic Church para. 27).

"No-one can look upon himself without immediately tuning his thoughts to the contemplation of God, in whom he 'lives and moves' (Acts 17:28)" (John Calvin: Institutes I.I.1).

"For what can be known about God is plain to them, because God has shown it to them" (Romans 1:19-20).

"In this ruin of mankind no one now experiences God…until Christ the Mediator comes forward to reconcile him to us". (John Calvin: Institutes I.II.1).

"Faith is the great cop-out, the great excuse to evade the need to think and evaluate experience" (Richard Dawkins (Edinburgh International Science Festival, April 1992) cited in Wilcockson & Campbell, 2016, p. 293).

"Yet even if Revelation is already complete, it has not been completely explicit; it remains for Christian faith gradually to grasp its full significance over the course of the centuries." (Catechism para. 66).

Person of Jesus Christ

Background & Influences

Jesus' influence as an authority comes from his teachings, his example, and his relationship with God. Jesus' moral teachings have allowed him to have authority, even for non-Christians.

As teacher of **WISDOM** (and Rabbi), Jesus developed Jewish ethics; as **LIBERATOR**, he challenged political and religious authorities; and as **SON OF GOD**, Jesus came to bring salvation and to carry out God's will on Earth.

At AS and A Level you will need to show understanding and evaluation of the different ways in which Jesus has authority: as a moral teacher of wisdom, as Son of God, and as liberator of the oppressed.

You need to show understanding and **EXEGESIS** of the following Biblical passages:

- Mark 6:47-52   **WALKING ON WATER**

- John 9:1-41   **HEALING OF THE MAN BORN BLIND**

- Matthew 5:17-48 **FULFILMENT OF THE LAW** - revised the **TORAH**

- Luke 15:11-32   **PARABLE OF LOST SON (WAITING FATHER)**

- Mark 5:24-34   **AN UNCLEAN (BLEEDING) WOMAN**

- Luke 10:25-37   **PARABLE OF GOOD SAMARITAN**

Key Terms

- **FORM OF LIFE** - the historical, sociological, moral, and cultural conditions within which language operates. Associated with Wittgenstein.

- **TORAH** - first five books of the Hebrew Bible (Genesis, Exodus, Leviticus, Deuteronomy and Numbers).

- **METANOIA** - repentance, a radical change of heart.

- **PARABLE OF THE LOST SON** - Luke 15:11-32; deals with theme of lost and found.

- **ZEALOTS -** 1st Century Jewish political group. Sought to overcome Roman occupation in the rebellion of 66 AD and committed mass suicide at **MASADA** (AD 74)

- **UNDERSIDE OF HISTORY -** occupies a significant proportion of human existence but often forgotten. Sometimes refers to the oppressed or marginalised.

- **PREFERENTIAL OPTION FOR THE POOR -** Christian duty to side with the marginalised and to act against injustice.

- **SAMARITANS -** from Samaria. Regarded as racially and religiously impure as they had married foreigners and built their own temple.

- **SON OF GOD -** used by followers of Jesus describing Jesus' special relationship with God.

- **COUNCIL OF CHALCEDON -** 451 AD – re-affirm central Christian beliefs, particularly divinity and humanity of Jesus.

- **CHRISTOLOGY -** concerned with nature of Jesus' relationship with God.

Structure of Thought

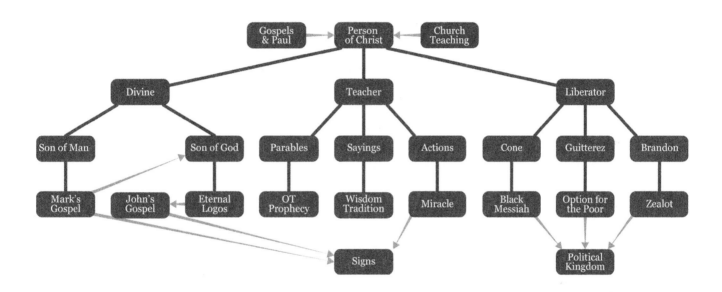

Jesus of History and the Christ of Faith

1. E.P. Sanders

- **FAITH** claims are different to claims made in the realm of reason.

- **HISTORICAL JESUS** shows a man acting within the laws of science and the limits of history. It would be a **CATEGORY MISTAKE** to venture into **HISTORY** as we would confuse history with faith.

- Jesus' teachings on hope for outcasts, non-violence and God's grace did make him significantly different to people at the time but not unique. like the **ESSENES** established desert communities and taught of a coming kingdom.

2. Rudolph Bultmann

- The Jesus of history is less important than the **CHRIST OF FAITH.**

- The most we can know is the preaching/ teaching following Jesus' death (**KERYGMA** - the gospel of the early church).

- We should Evil and suffering can lead to belief without trust. **DEMYTHOLOGISE** the Bible (eg supposed events such as resurrection and ascension have spiritual meaning, not literal).

- The basis of Christian faith is the reflections of the early Church, inspired by their ongoing experiences of Christ; rather than the historical Jesus – of whom we can know **"almost nothing"**.

3. Black Messiah - James Cone

- Starting point is **HISTORICAL** – suffering and oppression of black people

- Link to **PAUL TILLICH** – theology reflects the culture of its day and emerges from it

- Jesus is given many **TITLES** in the NT – 'Son of David', 'Good Shepherd', 'Son of God'. 'Black Messiah' continues this tradition. Jesus would not have been white. Metaphor - Jesus' suffering in unity with the oppressed.

- **CROSS** – not just a symbol, it resonates with the **'lynching tree'**. Both Jesus and blacks died and suffered – on a cross – as a result of injustice.

Jesus Christ's Authority as Son of God

Expressed In his Knowledge of God, Miracles and Resurrection

1. Son of God and Messiah (Mark 6:47-52; John 9:1-41)

In Jewish terms, often used to refer to the King, anointed by God to do His will on Earth. Hoped that an anointed person would deliver Israel politically, morally and spiritually.

- Hebrew for anointed – **MESSIAH**

- Greek for anointed – **CHRISTOS**

- Son of God = **CHRIST**(os)

"Truly this man was God's Son!" (Mark 15:39) – remarked by Roman Centurion at Jesus' death. It is unclear whether the centurion meant Jesus was **the** Son of God or **a** son of God.

Christian leaders accepted Jesus as both fully God and fully human.

2. Christology from Above

- Focus is on Jesus' **DIVINITY** and God's act of bringing humanity back into relationship with him.

- Known as **HIGH CHRISTOLOGY**.

- Relies on faith, cannot be proved.

3. Christology from Below

- Focus is on Jesus' **MESSAGE**, teaching and the example he sets.

- The focus of salvation is on how people **RESPOND** to Jesus and the way this helps to develop their relationship to God and the world.

- Known as **LOW CHRISTOLOGY**.

4. Did Jesus Think He Was Son of God?

- If Jesus thought he was fully human – how can we claim he knew he was God's Son?

- In **EXODUS**, God reveals his identity as "I am who I am"(Exodus 3:14).

- **JOHN**'s Gospel - Jesus uses similar statements - "I am the way, and the truth, and the life. No one comes to the Father except through me" (John 14:6).

- "The Father is **GREATER** than I" (John14:28). Does this imply that Jesus saw himself as limited by his own humanity?

- In **MARK 16:42** Jesus is asked "Are you the **CHRIST**, Son of the Blessed One?". When Jesus replies **I AM** the High Priest tears his clothes with rage and asks "do we need witnesses?" because he recognises the **BLASPHEMY** of invoking **YAHWEH**'s name (I Am who I Am).

5. Miracles do not necessarily indicate Jesus' Divinity

- Miracles - special insights into Jesus' teaching on the nature of God's **KINGDOM**. Example - Rich Man and Lazarus, last are **FIRST** (Luke 16)

- No single word for 'miracle' in New Testament. They might not point to the laws of nature being broken. Instead, 'mighty works', '**SIGNS**' and 'wonders' indicate something deeper about the nature of God and reality.

- **LOW CHRISTOLOGY** – Jesus' miracles understood like parables of **CREATION** (such as stilling the storm) or **REDEMPTION** (such as raising the paralysed man with the words 'your sins are forgiven", Mark 2) raises the issue - is he the **CREATOR-REDEEMER** incarnate?

6. Birth and Incarnation

- **Luke 1:35** – Jesus born of a Virgin, Mary.

- **Chalcedonian Definition** – Mary conceives God in human form – incarnation.

- Mary – **THEOTOKOS** (God-bearer).The Council of Ephesus decreed in 431 that Mary is the Theotokos because her son Jesus is both God and man: one divine person with two natures (divine and human) intimately and **HYPOSTATICALLY** united (humanity and divinity in one hypostasis, or individual existence).

Some Heretical Views

NESTORIUS (d.c.451) – Christ's divine and human natures were completely separate. Humanity and divinity come together as one when Jesus' will becomes one with God's will.

APOLLINARIUS (c.310-390) – Incarnation meant that God's will replaced Jesus' human reason. Jesus was a complete person and experienced suffering, still had a soul but could not sin as he would have no 'inner conflict'.

DOCETIC CHRISTIANS – Incarnation involved God only appearing to assume human flesh. Jesus could not have been fully human as he was fully God, bringing salvation through this knowledge.

Miracles as Signs of Salvation

1. Redemption and Creation Miracles

Agreed by both **HIGH** and **LOW** Christologies.

Echoes vision of **ISAIAH** of a renewed society with new insight.

- E.g. **healing of man born blind** (John 9:1-41) focuses more on the man's awareness of Jesus as saviour, than on the process of the man's sight being saved. **REDEMPTION MIRACLE**.

- **Jesus' walking on water** (Mark 6:47-52) indicates how salvation applies to the whole of the universe; reminiscent of God's spirit hovering over the chaotic water at the point of Creation (Genesis 1:2). **CREATION MIRACLE.**

2. Resurrection as Miracle

A Jewish idea taught by **PHARISEES** that the righteous would be raised to live in God's Kingdom at the end of time.

Jesus' resurrection was different – witnessed by many over a long period; marked the beginning of a **NEW ERA** as early followers experienced a change in their relationship with God.

St PAUL – everything can be brought into completion by God. The resurrection was the '**FIRST FRUITS**' (1 Corinthians

WOLFHART PANNENBURG – Jesus was an ordinary human in his lifetime but the resurrection was a decisive moment in history, a unique sign of God's accomplishment of creation at the end of days, revealing Jesus as God's Son.

3. Doubting Thomas

"Then he said to Thomas, 'Put your finger here and see my hands. Reach out your hand and put it in my side. Do not doubt but believe.' Thomas answered him, 'My Lord and my God!'". (John 20:27-28).

Jesus' body is not just transformed spiritually but also allows the experience of the presence of God. A **RELIGIOUS EXPERIENCE** – Jesus' resurrection allows him to be witnessed to and worshipped as God without being blasphemous. Those who believe '**WITHOUT SEEING**' are commended. (John 20). The resurrection gives authority to proclaim Jesus as God's Son.

Jesus as Moral Teacher

Jesus' moral teaching on repentance and forgiveness, inner purity and moral motivation (Matthew 5:17-48; Luke 15:11-32)

1. The Living Word (John 1)

WITTGENSTEIN - Jesus' authority is derived from him as a teacher of wisdom. He affirmed **AUTHENTIC LIVING.**

Jesus embodied the **MORAL** and **SPIRITUAL** and so was the **LIVING WORD** ('The word became flesh and lived among us', John 1)

2. Jesus' Moral Teaching

Jesus uses **PARABLES**, short sayings, actions, examples and healings to express moral message.

Jesus as the **NEW MOSES** founding a **NEW ISRAEL** (argument of theologian **TOM WRIGHT**). A new community of the Kingdom of God.

"Do not think that I have come to abolish the Law or the Prophets; I have not come to abolish them but to **FULFIL** them." (Matthew 5:17).

3. Forgiveness and Repentance

METANOIA (repentance or radical change of heart) – At the heart of Jesus' teaching on the arrival of the Kingdom of God.

Examples include **ZACCHAEUS** (tax collector) and the **PARABLE OF THE PRODIGAL SON** (Luke 15: 11-32)

Forgiveness brings about mental (end of guilt) and material freedom (forgive our debts) and restores/heals relationships.

Seen in Lord's Prayer.

4. Personal Responsibility

Keeping the Sabbath holy is an important religious law **(Ten Commandments, Exodus 20:1-17).**

It is also an important social law as it is a **foundation for social justice** – everyone is entitled to one day free from work during the week.

Jesus argued people misused Sabbath rules in order to avoid social responsibility. Rabbis had developed 39 different definitions and examples of work (which had to be avoided). Jesus argued that **in focusing on this religious duty, people were avoiding their duty to humanity.**

"The Sabbath was made for humankind, not humankind for the Sabbath" (Jesus, Mark 2:27).

Despite the risk of death penalty for breaking the Sabbath rules, Jesus broke these to heal the sick and allowed his disciples to 'pick corn' to eat.

Morality is not 'blind obedience'. It requires personal responsibility and **PURITY** of mind.

Religious practices should serve human **NEEDS**.

Jesus as Liberator

Jesus' role as liberator of the marginalised, his challenge to political & religious authority (Mark 5:24-34; Luke 10:25-37).

Some Key Authors

1. **S.G.F.BRANDON JESUS AND THE ZEALOTS** (1967) - later writers made Jesus out to be a pacifist, toning down the reality that he was in fact a politically-driven activist – a freedom fighter.

- Preferential Option for the Poor

- The Underside of History

Jesus shows a bias to these groups, despite the Church presenting him as politically neutral, a spiritual teacher.

2. **GUSTAVO GUTIÉRREZ** (1928-) **A THEOLOGY OF LIBERATION**

- Father of **LIBERATION THEOLOGY**

- Seeing Jesus as liberator makes him (the Christ of faith) 'really engaged' in the world and allows us to see the people of the Bible as more than just fictitious characters

- Jesus' historical example as **PREFERENTIAL OPTION FOR THE POOR** sets the expectation for modern Christians

- Jesus more than a **ZEALOT** - did not set himself up as a national leader - encouraged his followers not to think of him in that way. Jesus' mission was also not only to save Israel but **ALL** human societies.

3. **CAMILLO TORRES RESTREPO** (1929-66) **ROMAN CATHOLIC PRIEST**

- Joined communist guerrilla group (National Libertarian Army of Columbia) in their active resistance against the government.

- No longer a priest by the time of fighting but still thought of his actions in a priestly way.

Liberator of the Marginalised

Many parables deal with help of the outcast – often, sinners (**HAMARTALOI**). These include the 'unclean' (diseased, paralysed), tax collectors, sexually impure, religious heretics and the uneducated (fishermen, labourers), as in **LEVITICAL CODE** of OT law.

Jesus - **MORAL MESSAGE** - often delivered through his example towards those considered impure, rather than the religious leaders.

- Luke 10:25-37 (Good Samaritan)

- Mark 5:24-34 (contrast with Leviticus 15:19-28) Bleeding Woman

- "The last shall be first, and the first last" (Matthew 20:16).

Jesus ejected table-fellowship **RITUALS** of the Pharisees (ritual washing, food laws etc.) Indicates his vision of the Kingdom of God as a transformed society. In **MARK 7** he declares all foods "clean".

Possible Exam Questions

1. "There is no evidence to suggest that Jesus thought of himself as divine." Discuss.

2. To what extent can Jesus be regarded as no more than a teacher of wisdom?

3. "Jesus' role was just to liberate the poor and weak against oppression." Discuss.

4. Assess the view that the miracles prove Jesus was the Son of God.

5. "Jesus Christ is not unique." Discuss.

6. To what extent was Jesus just a teacher of morality?

Key Quotes

Christ's blackness is both literal and symbolic. His blackness is literal in the sense that he truly becomes One with the oppressed blacks, taking their suffering as his suffering and revealing that he is found in the history of our struggle, the story of our pain. (J. Cone, God of the Oppressed, p. 136).

Whoever has seen me has seen the Father. (John 14:9)

Jesus accompanies his words with many 'mighty works and wonders and signs' which manifest that the kingdom is present in him and attest that he was the promised Messiah. (Catechism of the Catholic Church para. 547).

Miracles strengthen faith in the One who does his Father's works; they bear witness that he is the Son of God. (Catechism of the Catholic Church para. 548).

Jesus said, "My kingdom is not of this world. If it were, my servants would fight to prevent my arrest by the Jewish leaders. But now my kingdom is from another place." (John 18:36).

The duty of every Catholic is to be a revolutionary. The duty of every revolutionary is to make the revolution. (Restrepo, speech, 1965, cited in Wilcockson, Wilkinson, & Campbell, 2016, p. 311).

If Jesus were alive today, He would be a guerrillero. (Restrepo, cited in Wilcockson, Wilkinson, & Campbell, 2016, p. 311).

Christian Moral Principles

Diversity of Christian Moral Reasoning, Practices & Sources of Ethics

Background and Influences

"All Scripture is inspired by God, and is useful for teaching, for reproof, for correction, for training in righteousness" (2 Timothy 3:16).

The following questions are relevant:

1. If the Bible does reveal God's will and if it is true that only Biblical ethical commands must be followed; then what can be helpful in discerning how to follow scripture?

2. If God is the author of the Bible, does this mean that it, alone, must be used for moral instruction?

3. If the Bible is **INFALLIBLE,** and we cannot understand it, is the problem with the reader rather than with the text?

At A Level, you will need to show understanding and evaluation of the Bible as the only authority for Christian ethical practices; Bible, Church and reason as the sources of Christian ethical practices; and love (**AGAPE**) as the only Christian ethical principle which governs Christian practices.

Key Terms

- **AGAPE** - Greek for 'love'. Also, refers to Jesus' sacrificial and generous love for others

- **BIBLICISM** - belief that the Bible is the revealed word of God and that God directly inspired the writers of the Bible.

- **COVENANT** - God's special promises and agreement made with humans which requires special behaviour from them.

- **HERMENEUTICAL** - study of the principles of interpreting the Bible

- **MAGISTERIUM -** the official teaching of the Church entrusted to the Pope and his bishops (eg in the **CATECHISM** and **ENCYCLICALS**)

- **PAPAL ENCYCLICAL** - letter issued by the Pope to his senior clergy on some significant topic or teaching; has doctrinal authority.

- **SOLA SCRIPTURA -** exclusive following of the Bible.

- **THEONOMOUS CHRISTIAN ETHICS -** God's law or commands govern ethics. Living the good life must be revealed by God, since we are by nature, sinful.Different Approaches to a Christian Moral Reading of the Bible

Structure of Thought

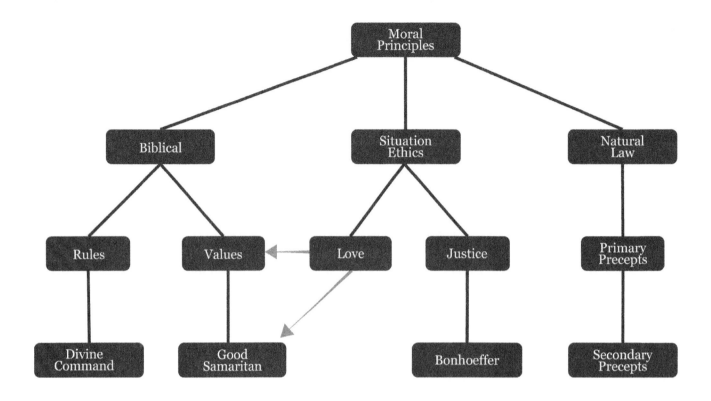

Hermeneutic (Interpretation) Factors

Richard B. HAYS proposes many factors to consider when thinking about how Christians use the Bible to help them to make moral decisions.

1. **Accuracy** different gospels relate slightly different versions

2. **Range** of issues may be limited by cultural context

3. **Frequency** of use of sections

4. **Management** of different texts

5. **Focal images** metaphors can be interpreted different ways

MNEMONIC: Angus Ran For Max's Football

HAYS also proposed questions of interpretation (**HERMENEUTICS**):

1. Is there a focus on **symbolism**?

2. Is there a focus on **rules**?

3. Is there a focus on **principles**?

4. Is there a focus on **paradigms**?

MNEMONIC: Sophie Really Painted Poppies

Propositional & Non-Propositional Revelation

- **PROPOSITIONAL KNOWLEDGE** - knowing or accepting something as true e.g. knowing the date of your birthday. Has a truth value – can be true, false, or somewhere in the middle.

- **PROPOSITIONAL REVELATION** - knowledge revealed by God, not through reason e.g. God's moral standards (such as the Ten Commandments).

- **PROPOSITIONAL APPROACH TO THE BIBLE** - the words in the Bible are messages from God. There are fixed moral messages and meanings e.g. in parables and Sermon on the Mount.

- **NON-PROPOSITIONAL KNOWLEDGE** - other kinds of knowledge e.g. how to do something.

- **NON-PROPOSITIONAL REVELATION** - belief or faith in God through personal encounter or experience.

- **NON-PROPOSITIONAL APPROACH TO THE BIBLE** - God's revelation in Jesus was through Jesus' human life, not through a book. The Bible acts as a doorway into meeting the living God.

The Bible as Sole Authority for Ethics

If the Bible reveals God's will, then only Bible commands must be followed

1. Ethics can be shown in the Bible as **THEONOMOUS**.

2. Ethics can be expressed through **COVENANT** (a legal agreement).

THEONOMOUS ethics are shown through real life situations, rather than as clear commandments.

E.g. King **DAVID**'s adultery with Bathsheba (2 Samuel 11) illustrates what living 'the moral life' is NOT. David is not just judged on his adherence to the commandments but on the type of person he became. Uriah (Bathsheba's husband who was killed in battle) strikes a complete contrast.

Must be understood in the theological context of life lived as a **COVENANT** agreement with mutual obligations, with God.

The **OLD TESTAMENT** establishes ethics as both **SOCIAL** and **PERSONAL**. The **TEN COMMANDMENTS** are evidence of this (Exodus 20:1-17). Other Biblical examples:

- **AMOS** and **ISAIAH** – Old Testament Prophets – focus on social justice and see a proper response to God's covenant to be treatment of the **POOR.**

- New Testament: Jesus' **SERMON** on the **MOUNT**(Matthew 5-7) – the new covenant is not just about following the laws set out in the Old Testament but involves the inner laws of love, peace, faith, and righteousness – "be perfect as your heavenly Father is perfect" (Matthew 5:48).

- Modelled on Jesus' sacrifice, St **PAUL** uses '**LIVING SACRIFICE**' (Romans 12:1) to describe Christian covenantal life. This makes devotion to God and love of neighbour above anything else.

Literalism - Is It Realistic?

"If your right eye causes you to sin, tear it out and throw it away" (Matthew 5:29).

KARL BARTH argued that scripture has high value, but literalism could be dangerous as it gives the bible a divine status that can only rightly be given to God. This is **BIBLIOLATRY** – false worship of the Bible.

Words of the bible are a **WITNESS** to God's Word revealed through the different writers of the Bible over time. It is not the 'Word' itself. Bible writers were 'inspired' but God did not dictate the Bible.

Bible must be read **CRITICALLY** as a source of inspiration. It is not truth itself, despite being a source of moral truth.

HUMAN REASON must be taken into account.

Contradictions

1. Old Testament

There is a contradiction between war and **RETRIBUTIVE JUSTICE**: "an eye for an eye, a tooth for a tooth" (Exodus 21:24) and Jesus' pronouncement to 'love your enemy' (Matthew 5:44) and 'turn teh other cheek'.

The sanctity of human life is contradicted by capital punishment apparent for **BLASPHEMY** (Genesis 9:6).

Capital punishment for those who undermine social and divine order, adultery (Deuteronomy 22:22); dishonouring **PARENTS** (Numbers 1:51), **HOMOSEXUAL** acts (Leviticus 18).

Deuteronomy 20:10-20 – sets out rules of **WAR**, Israelites allowed to kill foreign women and children of the coastal tribes. Again this contradicts the idea of the sanctity of human life, **THOU SHALT NOT KILL.** (Exodus 20:13)

2. New Testament

Sermon on the Mount (Matthew 5-7) – consciously revises old law of **LEVITICUS** (eg 'eye for an eye' becomes 'turn the other cheek') - the **PURITY CODE** is demolished by Jesus eg touching 'unclean women'.

RECONCILIATION replaces retribution (**Matthew 5:38-42**) and love of enemies is taught in addition (**Matthew 5:44**).

Jesus stressing a future ideal – **KINGDOM OF GOD**, similar to how previous prophets in the Old testament had ventured (**Micah 4:1-4**).

Meanwhile, in an imperfect world, violence might be a **NECESSARY EVIL** (Augustine, Luther).

Others argue Biblical **PACIFISM** (Martin **LUTHER KING** Jr) is a Christian duty as it lay at heart of Jesus' teaching on love.

Strengths of Bible - Sole Authority

1. Makes the Bible **INFALLIBLE** (unchallengeable) and **INERRANT** (no mistakes).

2. Can be trusted and relied upon **AS INSPIRED BY GOD** (2 Timothy 3:16).

3. **RICHARD MOUW** – "just because there is one biblical commandment, a law of love, does not rule out the possibility of other biblical commandments on other matters" (Summarised and cited in Ahluwalia & Bowie, 2016, p. 392).

4. Seeing the Bible as infallible can provide a helpful framework for living – decisions about **TAKING LIFE** (Sermon on Mount); attitudes towards **SEXUALITY** (Old Testament, St Paul); attitudes towards **MARRIAGE** (Genesis and Jesus' teachings).

Weaknesses of Bible as Sole Authority

1. We can't separate ourselves from our own reading of the text – impossible not to read **subjectively** and with **interpretation**.

2. If God dictated, then why so many **different styles** e.g. John's Gospel is much more mystical and theological.

3. **Conflicts** arise – Jesus' attitude to Jewish laws eg Leviticus and the bleeding woman of Mark 5 (no longer unclean, as Jesus accepts her).

4. Many Christians do not follow all the 'rules' in the Bible and some do not even appear to refer to moral living e.g. **LEVITICUS 19:27** limits the cutting of facial and head hair; Leviticus 19:19 bans planting two crops in the same field.

Bible Church & Reason

Christian Ethics must involve a combination of Biblical teaching, Church teaching and human reason.

Christian ethics should combine Biblical and Church teaching with human **REASON** to account for new situations.

- **PRIMA SCRIPTURA** – the Bible is the principle source of authority but is understood through and with Church teaching and reason.

- **RICHARD HAYS** and **WILLIAM SPOHN** – you cannot study scripture without reference to the Church communities and traditions. **SPOHN** suggests three interconnecting pillars: 1. the New Testament story of Jesus; 2. the ethics of virtue and character; and 3. the practices of Christian spirituality.

Ethical Heteronomy - Roman Catholicism

HETERONOMY means 'rule by another'. Christian ethics can be accessed through the **NATURAL WORLD, CHURCH AUTHORITY, REASON** and **THE BIBLE**. Together, these make up the **NATURAL LAW**.

Biblical grounding – Romans 2:15 – even **GENTILES** (non-Jews) can behave morally when acting according to their conscience and 'the law of God written on their hearts'.

Thomas Aquinas' Natural Law

Humans are set apart from other animals because of our ability to use human reason to know God's **ETERNAL LAW**.

Human experience of God's eternal law is based on **SELF-EVIDENT** principle – do good, avoid evil - **SYNDERESIS**. Goodness is the **GOAL** of human flourishing.

Magisterium - Roman Catholic

COLLECTIVE WISDOM of Church leaders and teachers, published in **PAPAL ENCYCLICALS** (circulated letters).

In all ordinary circumstances, the **MAGISTERIUM** should be followed – it has authority.

"The Church, the 'pillar and bulwark of the truth', 'has received this solemn command of Christ from the apostles to announce the saving truth'." (Catechism of the Catholic Church, 2032).

Veritatis Splendor (Splendour of Truth)

1996, Pope John Paul II – **VERITATIS SPLENDOR** – **ENCYCLICAL** reasserts centrality of reason, conscience, natural law, and Magisterium in Catholic moral theology.

Moral law = knowable to all through **REASON, NATURAL LAW** and **CONSCIENCE**.

Humans are **SINFUL** and cannot rely on reason alone. Church acts as a guide.

Some moral acts are **INTRINSICALLY** wrong (wrong in **THEMSELVES**). It is never right to contradict the moral order.

Liberation Theology

Developed from1960s onwards - popular in **LATIN AMERICA**.

Bible is seen as the centre of ethics, particularly the **EXODUS** story and other stories of liberation from **SLAVERY**.

ETHICS FROM BELOW– begins with the marginalised, **ENGAGES** with political and economic struggles against the **POWERS**; suspicious of 'top-down' traditional Church teaching.

Some use of **MARXISM**, but criticised, as while it is good at questioning power, it also criticises religion for being exploitative and an **OPIUM OF THE PEOPLE** reinforcing false consciousness (acceptance) of their oppression.

Conscience & Tradition

Protestant **NATURAL LAW** theologians – Richard **HOOKER** (1554-1600); Hugo **GROTIUS** (1583-1645). Bible evolved over time, developing out of the needs of communities and therefore reason and conscience should guide its use in ethics (like Catholicism but no magisterium).

Stanley Hauerwas

Christian ethics can only be done in the Christian worshipping community, called **BASE COMMUNITIES.**

Jesus adapted Old Testament teaching in his **Sermon on the Mount** and we continue to **adapt tradition** today.

Jesus' sermon was aimed at Christian community, not leaders. It includes examples of Christian values that must be developed in communities, in response to God, siding with the **MARGINALISED**.

Christian communities need to question society's values by living and practising Christian **SOCIAL VIRTUES** (loyalty, trust, faithfulness, forgiveness, reconciliation).

Criticisms of the Bible, Faith & Reason

1. Problem of **Sources**: What are legitimate sources for Christian ethics? Are some sources e.g. Marxism, alien to Christian thinking? Do some sources have greater authority than others? If so, what principles determine the hierarchy of these sources?

2. **Deviation** from Bible: some accuse Catholic tradition of breaking away from the Bible e.g. Martin **LUTHER**, German Reformer.

3. Jesus' attitude to **Tradition:** Jesus appears to criticise religious traditions e.g. Pharisees' focus on ritual cleanliness.

4. **Law** of love: should prevail over traditions (Rudolf **BULTMANN**).

5. Justice, love, and wisdom: three ethical norms that should work together for Christians (Paul **TILLICH**), the most important of which is love and not the following of fixed rules that influence '**MORAL PURITANISM**' – the groups that aligns the Christian message with fixed rules about foods, drinks, and sexual relations.

MNEMONIC: Sort David's Traditional Lovely Pie

Agape Love is All

Jesus' only command was to love and human reason must decide how to apply this (Fletcher's Situation Ethics). This is not strictly correct: Jesus describes this as a 'new commandment' but depending how we count them there are around fifty commands Jesus issues to his disciples including 'deny yourself, take up your cross and follow me". (Matthew 16:24)

Autonomous

LOVE should be the only governing Christian principle – summarised in Jesus' own sacrificial life

Hans Küng: supports **AUTONOMY**.

There is nothing in Christian ethics that could not be found in any person with good will.

Pope **FRANCIS** encourages moral guidance rooted in love. The rules of Catholic tradition should be recognised but so should modern challenges of human relationships.

Applied to Euthanasia

Contrary to official Catholic moral teaching but not the principles of Catholic reasoning and conscience to keep someone alive at all costs.

Jesus specifically challenged rule-based ethics and encouraged autonomy. (Mark 7:14-23) - Jesus declares all foods **CLEAN** in opposition to Levitical purity code..

We should not ask if euthanasia is right or wrong but rather, does it respect a person's life?

Rejected by 'faith-ethic' Catholic theologians for undermining Magisterium - official Catholic Church teaching e.g. Joseph **RATZINGER** (Pope Benedict XVI).

Possible Exam Questions

1. How fair is the claim that there is nothing distinctive about Christian ethics?

2. "The Bible is all that is needed as a moral guide for Christian behaviour." Discuss.

3. "The Church should decide what is morally good." Discuss.

4. Assess the view that the Bible is a comprehensive moral guide for Christians.

5. To what extent do Christians actually disagree about what Christian ethics are?

6. "Christian moral principles are not self-evident." Discuss.

Key Quotes

"Prophecy never had its origin in the human will, but prophets, though human, spoke from God as they were carried along by the Holy Spirit". 2 Peter 1:20-21.

"Then the Lord reached out his hand and touched my mouth and said to me, 'I have put my words in your mouth.'" Jeremiah 1:9.

"Just because there is one biblical commandment, a law of love, does not rule out the possibility of other biblical commandments on other matters" (Richad Mouw, surmised and cited in Ahluwalia & Bowie, 2016, p. 392)."

The interpretation of Scripture can never occur in a vacuum". (Richard Hays, The Moral Vision of the New Testament, 1996, p. 209).

"Sacred tradition and Sacred Scripture form one sacred deposit of the word of God, committed to the Church". (Vatican II Council, Dei Verbum, 'Dogmatic Constitution on Divine Revelation,' par. 10. In Vatican Council II: The Conciliar Documents, ed. Flannery, 1975.

"This teaching office [magisterium] is not above the Word of God, but serves it". (Vatican II Council, Dei Verbum, 'Dogmatic Constitution on Divine Revelation,' par. 10. In Vatican Council II: The Conciliar Documents, ed. Flannery, 1975.

"This is my commandment, that you love one another as I have loved you. No one has greater love than this, to lay down one's life for one's friends" (John 15:12-13).

"All Scripture is inspired by God and profitable for teaching, for rebuke and for training in righteousness". (1 Timothy, 3:16)

Christian Moral Action

Background & Influences

- **BONHOEFFER'S ETHICS** - Our sinful nature means that no human decision can with certainty be declared absolutely right or wrong. Sometimes, we can act only **out of despair but in faith and hope.** It is impossible to accurately predict all possible outcomes of an action. Consequentialist approaches to moral action are rejected.

- **MARTIN LUTHER** - State rule brought order to the natural sinful inclination of humans towards disorder. Bonhoeffer was different and emphasised the **AUTHORITY** of God over that of the state. Luther supported the suppression of the **PEASANT**'s revolt in Germany (1534-6).

"They have doubly deserved death in body and soul as murderers... they cloak this horrible sin with the gospel." (Luther,, 1535)

At A Level, you must evaluate the teaching and example of Bonhoeffer on **DUTY** to God and **DUTY** to the State, the Church as community and source of spiritual discipline, and the **COST** of discipleship.

Key Terms

- **CHEAP GRACE** - grace that is offered freely, but is received without any change in the person.

- **COSTLY GRACE** - grace followed by obedience to God's command and discipleship.

- **DISCIPLESHIP** - following the life, teaching, and example of Jesus.

- **NO RUSTY SWORDS** - Bonhoeffer's metaphor to describe the outworn ethical attitudes which the Church has used and have no use for today.

- **PASSION** - Jesus' sufferings at the end of his life.

- **RELIGIONLESS CHRISTIANITY** - Bonhoeffer's description of Christianity without the baggage of the past and contamination by the ideological beliefs of the present.

- **SECULAR PACIFISM** - secular means 'of this world'. Pacifism - violence and war are wrong. Bonhoeffer invented the term 'secular pacifism' to show a false non-religious belief that society can achieve a state of non-violence.

- **SOLIDARITY** - an selfless commitment to stand alongside, and be with those less fortunate.

- **THE WESTERN VOID** - Bonhoeffer's description of the state of the Western secular world without Christianity filled with all kinds of dangerous beliefs and ideas.

- **WORLD COME OF AGE** - used by Bonhoeffer to describe how the Western culture has grown up and in embracing a rational view of the world has discarded a superstitious view of religion.

Structure of Thought

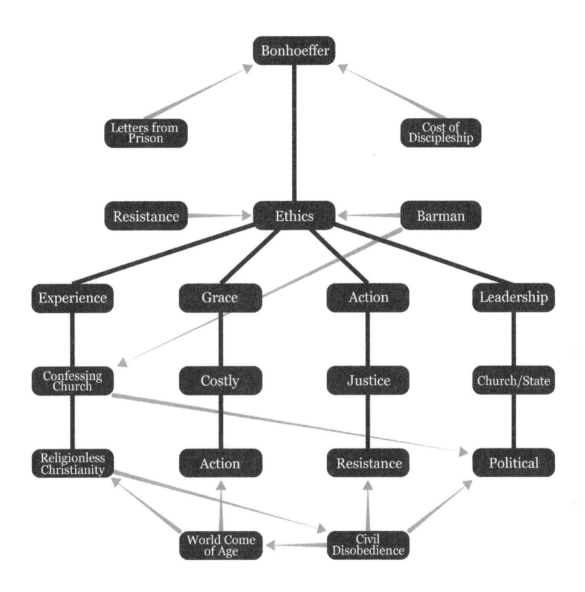

Duty to God & the State

Responsibility to the State

Bonhoeffer taught Christians have a **RESPONSIBILITY** to the state. They must work to ensure the state acts according to **GOD'S WILL**.

Sometimes, the state gains too much power and **JUSTICE** is set below policy. Other times, the state assumes it is 'justice itself' and uses this to justify any action. The state fails to acknowledge its **OBEDIENCE TO THE WILL OF GOD**.

BONHOEFFER – the state can **NEVER** represent the will of God and therefore, the state can **NEVER** adopt ultimate power.

The Church is to keep the state in check – not be a part of it.

Obedience, Leadership & Doing God's Will

Christians have a duty to **DISOBEY** if the state is making reasonable people face difficult situations.

The Church was being fooled into believing **NAZISM** was bringing order to a disordered society.

"Hitler is the way of the Spirit and the will of God for the German people to enter the church of Christ" (Hermann Gruner, quoted in Geffrey B. Kelly et al., Dietrich Bonhoeffer: The Life of a Modern Martyr (Christianity Today Essentials, 2012)

The ostracism of minorities and disrespect for life was a disregard for **GOD-GIVEN ORDER**.

Establishing social order may justify **TYRANNICIDE** as a Christian duty.

A Christian can only act in faith and in hope – influenced by **MARTIN LUTHER** - **'here I stand, I can do no other'.**

LUTHERAN TEACHING – God ordained two kingdoms:

1. The **SPIRITUAL** kingdom of Christ, governed by the Church

2. The **POLITICAL** kingdom of the world, governed by the state

We should ask if obeying the state is the will of God. This will only be clear in the **INSTANT OF ACTION** and as an act of faith.

"You can only know what obedience is by obeying. It is no use asking questions; for it is only through obedience that you come to learn the truth" (Dietrich Bonhoeffer, The Cost of discipleship, 1959, p. 68)

"There is no road to faith or discipleship, no other road – only obedience to the call of Jesus" (Dietrich Bonhoeffer, The Cost of discipleship, 1959, p. 49)

Justification for Civil Disobedience

It is impossible to know whether our actions are truly good or not. No amount of human reason can morally justify killing.

BONHOEFFER argues to kill Hitler and disobey the state is only justified by '**bold action as the free response to faith**'. It cannot be justified in ordinary **ETHICAL TERMS**.

Love is not the only **MORAL PRINCIPLE** by which we can live the moral life. Human ideas **ENSLAVE** humans. Humans are only freed by responding to **GOD'S WILL**.

Consolation for civil disobedience, such as the assassination attempt on Hitler is possible only through God's promises to forgive the '**man who becomes a sinner in the process**' (Letters and Papers from Prison, p. 138).

Duty to God outweighs duty to the State. Need to break away from Luther's idea of advocating of obedience to civil authority.

You would be just as guilty for the destruction of a town if you did nothing, as you would be if you were among those who helped to burn it down. If you are acting out of love, as Christian ethics demands, you need to **actively challenge injustice and resist it** (Link **SYNOPTICALLY** to Fletcher's **SITUATION ETHICS.**

Civil Disobedience - Examples

Bonhoeffer spoke against Nazi ideas in his **UNIVERSITY** position, and then against Nazism at public **LECTURES**. He was banned.

- Criticised **CONFESSING CHURCH** when it wavered under pressure from Hitler to conform.

- Participated in **ILLEGAL SEMINARY** for training pastors.

- Openly spoke about his **PRAYERS** for the defeat of his own country.

Proclaimed Hitler as the **ANTI-CHRIST:**

"Therefore we must go on with our work and eliminate him whether he is successful or not" (Kenny et al., Dietrich Bonhoeffer: The Life of a Modern Martyr [Christianity Today Essentials], 2012).

It is thought he joined the **STAUFFENBERG** plot to **ASSASSINATE** Hitler in 1944 (see the film **VALKYRIE -** the name of the plot**)**.

As a member of the German military intelligence, Bonhoeffer acted as a **DOUBLE AGENT** working with Resistance and Allies.

He was eventually caught when he helped to smuggle **JEWS** into Switzerland, posing as agents of military intelligence.

MNEMONIC: Uptown Lads Create Illuminated Acrobatics During Summer

Church - Community & Discipline

Like **KANT**, Bonhoeffer believed that a Christian can recognise that they act out of **DUTY** when they act along with the rest of humankind.

- The **MORAL AND SPIRITUAL COMMUNITY** of the Church provide the tools needed to live morally in this world. To do this, the Church needs to become **RELIGIONLESS**.

- The **WORLD COME OF AGE** was costly. In discarding Christian values as 'irrational', **LIBERALISM** brought about the **WESTERN VOID** - a **SPIRITUAL VACUUM** that Christianity used to occupy.

Bonhoeffer felt that **NATIONAL SOCIALISM** of the Nazis partly filled this void. Bonhoeffer called for a paradoxical **RELIGIONLESS CHRISTIANITY,** as he argued ethical attitudes used by the Church before have no use today and are 'outworn'- represented by Bonhoeffer's metaphors of **RUSTY SWORDS**. and of **SALT** and **LIGHT** – visible in the **SERMON ON THE MOUNT**. As salt adds flavour to food, Christians must be present among other people and must act as 'light' for the room in their moral actions.

The Confessing Church

When Christianity and National Socialism were blended, forming the German Christian movement, it triggered the founding of the **CONFESSING CHURCH.**

In **1934** Hitler amended the articles of the **GERMAN EVANGELICAL CHURCH** issuing the **ARYAN PARAGRAPH** which made it necessary for all clergy to be of Aryan descent. **BONHOEFFER** and Martin **NIEMOLLER** disagreed with this change and brought together others who also disagreed. This group formed the early **CONFESSING CHURCH**.

In **1934** the Confessing Church met in **BARMEN** and the foundations of **BARTH'S** 'Barmen Declaration' were formed. A Christian's primary **DUTY** is to **CHRIST** and Christians should reject any teaching that is not revealed in Jesus Christ.

The **BARMEN DECLARATION 1934** was a clear denial of Nazi **NATIONAL SOCIALISM** but some say its disobedience against the state was limited and it could have done more politically to aid Jews and other minority groups.

Bonhoeffer tried to take it further to be more **INCLUSIVE** and from this, came his **ECUMENICAL THEOLOGY** – a direct disagreement with the German Christian movement.

In line with '**RELIGIONLESS** Christianity', the confessing Church was not to become 'national' – there must be no racial, political, or national boundaries in a Christian community, as Jesus taught. Bonhoeffer argued "the Church is her true self when she exists for **HUMANITY**".

Finkenwalde

Following his return from the USA in **1935**, Bonhoeffer was responsible for constructing a community at **FINKENWALDE** for training clergy for the Confessing Church.

Nazi control of the German Church and the appointment of a **REICH BISHOP** led to a decline in suitable clergy. The **HIMMLER DECREE** of **1937** made the training of clergy for the Confessing Church illegal and Finkenwalde was shut down by the **THIRD REICH** in September.

The **VIRTUE OF DISCIPLINE** was thought to be the most practical of the Christian virtues and Finkenwalde was intended as a place to develop this through practical Christian living. Key features are listed below:

- *Discipline* - Life was basic and monastic. Both the body and the mind needed to be disciplined and well exercised. The group frequently went on long bike rides together.

- *Meditation* - Foundation of prayer, develops discipline.

- *Community for others* - No one is perfect and so the Church is not there for the righteous but for the forgiven. Needs to be 'outward looking' – Christ dies for all, not just for Christians.

- *Bible* - Heart of daily life for a Christian. An intelligent understanding of the development of Christian teaching was encouraged by debate and discussion.

- *Brotherhood* - Love of and for Christ binds together the community, sustained by the Holy Spirit. Former students Informed of developments and director should change often so that the group does not become 'stuck in its ways'.

MNEMONIC: Dancing Makes Cate's Brothers Bop

The Cost of Discipleship

Bonhoeffer's teaching on Ethics as action

Christianity is grounded in the **EVERYDAY WORLD** – it is not an 'otherworldly institution'. This is affirmed in God's **INCARNATION** – where he took on human flesh, became man and lived among humankind. "*The word became flesh and dwelt among us*" (**JOHN 1**).

Rather than investigating God's nature as human/divine, we should be asking '*who is Christ for us today?*'

Bonhoeffer was influenced by Karl **BARTH**, a Swiss **CALVINIST** theologian. The meaning of Christianity is in action.

BARTH - we do not know God – it is God who chooses to **REVEAL** Himself to humans – always a special and never a general act. **BONHOEFFER** agrees but says we should be careful not to accept the limited role of 'passively receiving' revelation – *we must 'do' as well as 'hear' the law* - e.g. **PHARISEES** (a subdivision of Jewish religious teaches) listened to commands but did not act on God's behalf; and in Luke, Martha acts but fails to listen to Jesus' teaching. Jesus calls the Pharisees "**HYPOCRITES**".

CONSCIENCE is the experience of disunity in the self – it prompts action. Ethics is action. Action is liberating.

Costly Grace

"When Christ calls a man, he bids him come and die...Suffering then, is the badge of true discipleship" (Bonhoeffer, The Cost of Discipleship, 1959, p. 79, p., 80)

Authentic Christianity must be based on:

- **CHRIST**

- **SCRIPTURE**

- **FAITH**

These are the three fundamentals. If we stray from these, then we only have human intervention and nothing else. Religion as an institution is a human invention - like politics.

Church must be **SEPARATE** from State if it is to avoid being politically manipulated.

In taking on the world, the Christian disciple endangers himself.

CHEAP GRACE e.g. rituals, cannot win God's grace. Rather, grace is 'costly'.

"Costly because it costs man his life, and it is grace because it gives man the only true life ... Above all, it is costly because it cost God the life of his Son" (The Cost of Discipleship, p. 5).

God's grace is '**FREELY GIVEN**' not earned. However, it should not be 'cheap' and taken for granted, under the cheap umbrella that Jesus died and saved us from our sins - we take the grace but avoid the cost. Churches are in danger of offering grace without the **COST** of discipleship, which for Jesus meant **SUFFERING** and "giving his life as a **RANSOM** for many" (**MARK 10.45**).

"Cheap grace is effectively a lie, it is not the grace of God but a self-congratulating grace we give ourselves" (Ahluwalia & Bowie, 2016, p. 421)

COSTLY GRACE for Bonhoeffer involved a realisation he might have to die, though he did not seek to suffer and never saw himself as a martyr. He wrote many **Letters from Prison** – affirmed the Christian life, standing against all things evil. He did not dwell on suffering.

In these he calls on Christians to take a stand against **INJUSTICE**- Jesus was '**the man for others**' and so the Church as Christ's body must also be a Church for others. It was failing.

Sacrifice & Suffering

The Cross embodies the suffering of Christ and in human suffering, Christianity engages with the world reflected in this Cross of suffering.

God, too, suffers in Jesus, acting in solidarity with humankind. The ultimate expression of this is the cry of **DERELICTION** from the **CROSS.**

"My God, My God, why have you forsaken me?" (Mark 15:34, Psalm 22:2)

- **KRISIS** (Barth's use of NT Greek) – judgement, decision, verdict.

- **PARADOX** – God reveals His 'crisis' (judgement, redemption) in response to 'crisis' of the world (sinfulness, injustice, murder etc.)

THEOLOGY OF CRISIS - Crisis of human sinfulness can only be triumphed over by God's **JUDGEMENT** and faith in His redemption through Jesus Christ.

The **Passion of Jesus Christ** – his sufferings leading up to and including his death are linked to the call to **DISCIPLESHIP**. 'Those who would come after me must leave self behind, take up their **CROSS** and follow me!" (Mark 8:34) Jesus died without admiration or honour, 'a man of **SORROWS** and acquainted with grief' (Isaiah 53).

Being a disciple means 'picking up the cross' and so suffering and sacrifice are an inherent aspect of the nature of discipleship.

Solidarity

Solidarity with the Jews - Bonhoeffer wrote his essay **'The Church and the Jewish Question'** in response to the boycott of Jewish business in April **1933**. Called for solidarity of those afflicted by Nazism.

BONHOEFFER Publicly rejected the claim that punishment of the Jews was God's work for their rejection and death of Christ. He called it **GODLESS VIOLENCE**– in response to **NIGHT OF BROKEN GLASS (KRISTELNACHT) 1938.**

Living the '**Christian life**' is not to 'become religious' but to be there for other people, sharing in their experiences in a form of **TRANSCENDENCE.**

Strengths

1. Bonhoeffer's focus on **SHARED REFLECTION** and reading of Scripture, alongside shared living and community provide a good basis for understanding the Scripture and not just choosing parts of it.

2. A **COMMUNAL** approach could discourage distorted understanding of God's will. Church exist as **SALT** and **LIGHT** for everyone.

3. Bonhoeffer's account of true Christianity and what was wrong with the German Christians being misled by the Nazi-Controlled German Church would seem **ACCURATE** and attracts sympathy today.

4. Calls into question the nature of civic authorities and what they are doing – Bonhoeffer proposed an **ETHIC OF ACTION.** This action needed to be **COSTLY** - so Christians emerge from the shadows and become visible agents of change.

Weaknesses

1. Interpreting God's will might be **MISTAKEN.** Action that includes violence (as in some forms of **LIBERATION THEOLOGY**) opposed by **MARTIN LUTHER KING**'s theology of **NON-VIOLENT** resistance.

2. It is not always clear how God will want us to act in any given situation - requires God-like **WISDOM.**

3. If someone has a distorted view of God's will, Bonhoeffer's teaching could be **DANGEROUS** and even support genocide as in the book of **JOSHUA** where entire peoples were wiped out in cities of Jericho and Ai.

4. St Paul's Romans 13:1-2 suggests that **OBEDIENCE** to the state is important as state leaders have been established by God. Bonhoeffer differs from this.

5. Even Jesus did not openly challenge the rule of **PONTIUS PILATE** and he did not encourage people not to pay their taxes, even though he did challenge religious authorities and social norms. Contrast with the **ZEALOTS** who fostered a disastrous rebellion against Rome in **66AD** which led directly to the destruction of the Jewish **TEMPLE** in **70AD.**

Possible Exam Questions

1. "Using the will of God as a guide for moral behaviour is impractical, as in most circumstances it is impossible to know what God wants us to do." Discuss.

2. To what extent, if at all, does the theology of Bonhoeffer have relevance for Christians today?

3. "Bonhoeffer's most important teaching is on leadership." Discuss.

4. "Christian ethics means being obedient to God's will." Discuss.

5. To what extent was Bonhoeffer's religious community at Finkenwalde successful?

6. "Costly grace is the key to Bonhoeffer's theology and action". Discuss

Key Quotes

"Whoever wishes to take up the problem of a Christian ethic must ... ask 'what is the will of God?'" Dietrich Bonhoeffer, Ethics, p. 161.

"The nature of this will of God can only be clear in the moment of action"." Dietrich Bonhoeffer, No Rusty Swords, p. 43.

"We make again and again the surprising and terrifying discovery that the will of God does not reveal itself before our eyes as clearly as we had hoped." Dietrich Bonhoeffer: No Rusty Swords (1965), p. 46

"And Jesus answering said unto them, Render to Caesar the things that are Caesar's, and to God the things that are God's. And they marvelled at him." Mark 12:17

"Let everyone be subject to the governing authorities, for there is no authority except that which God has established. The authorities that exist have been established by God." Romans 13:1

"Costly because it costs man his life, and it is grace because it gives man the only true life ... Above all, it is costly because it cost God the life of his Son' (The Cost of Discipleship, p. 5).

"There is no road to faith or discipleship, no other road – only obedience to the call of Jesus" (Dietrich Bonhoeffer, The Cost of discipleship, 1959, p. 49)

"The followers are a visible community; their discipleship visible in action which lifts them out of the world" Dietrich Bonhoeffer, The Cost of Discipleship, 1959, p. 106

"Who will speak up for those who are voiceless?" Psalm 31:8

"When Christ calls a man, he bids him come and die...Suffering then, is the badge of true discipleship" (Bonhoeffer, The Cost of Discipleship, 1959, p. 79, p., 80)

Religious Pluralism and Theology

Background

Christianity has always existed alongside other religions. In its growth out of **JUDAISM**, Christians had to decide the extent to which they would continue with beliefs and practices of others, and what was it that was going to make them distinctively Christian. The question of whether other religions contain valuable truths remains, as well as the extent to which Christians can be seen to have a unique **EXCLUSIVE** relationship with God. Issues within religious pluralism and society also arise, for example, should Christians work to convert others or is it possible for non-Christians to achieve salvation too.

Specification

At A level, you will need to explain and evaluate the teaching of contemporary Christian theology of religion on exclusivism, inclusivism, and pluralism. You need to show knowledge and understanding of:

1. The view that only Christianity fully offers the means of salvation

2. The view that although Christianity is the normative means of salvation, 'anonymous' Christians may also receive salvation

3. The view that there are many ways to salvation, of which Christianity is one path (OCR A Level in Religious Studies Specification, 2016, p. 36)

Key Terms

- **EXCLUSIVISM:** the view that only one religion offers the full means of salvation

- **INTER-FAITH DIALOGUE:** discussing religious beliefs between members of different religious traditions, with an intention of reaching better understanding

- **INCLUSIVISM:** the view that although one's own religion sets the standard (is 'normative') for means of salvation, those who accept its fundamental principles may also attain salvation

- **PLURALISM:** the view that there are several means of salvation through different religious traditions

- **PARTICULARISM:** another name for exclusivism, meaning that salvation can only be found in one particular way

- **VATICAN II:** the Second Vatican Ecumenical Council, held from 1962 to 1965 to deliberate the place of the Catholic Church in the modern world

- **NOUMENA:** a Kantian term to describe reality as it really is, unaffected by the human mind

- **PHENOMENA:** a Kantian term to describe reality as it seems to us, filtered by the human mind

Structure of Thought

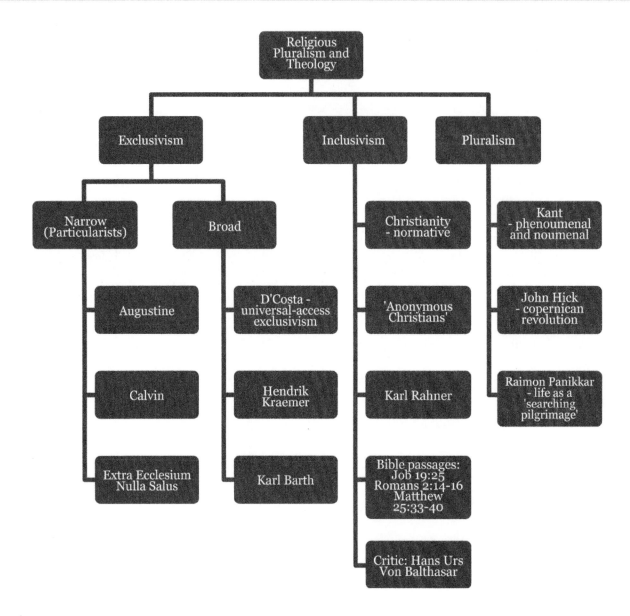

Christian Teaching on Exclusivism

EXCLUSIVISM is the belief that only Christianity offers the means of salvation. It comes from the belief that Jesus is 'the' way, not 'a' way to salvation. Another word for exclusivism is **PARTICULARIST**.

Christ's **SACRIFICE** was **UNIQUE**. Salvation can only reach those who hear the gospel and respond to this with faith. A sign of this acceptance is **BAPTISM**.

NARROW EXCLUSIVISM is the belief that salvation is possible only for those of a particular Christian denomination (Baptist, Catholic, Lutheran, Anglican). **AUGUSTINE** and **CALVIN** are examples of **PARTICULARISTS**. They believed God only elects – through grace - a small number of Christians for salvation. **Catholics** believe there is no salvation outside of the Church – **EXTRA ECCLESIAM NULLA SALUS**. The Catholic view has been considered less narrow since **LUMEN GENTIUM** – "many elements of sanctification and of truth are found outside of its visible structure" (1964).

BROAD EXCLUSIVISM is the belief that salvation is possible for all who accept Christ, regardless of denomination. Other religions may contain some truth, but not enough for salvation. Gavin **D'COSTA** asserted **UNIVERSAL-ACCESS EXCLUSIVISM –** that salvation is possible after death. **1 TIMOTHY 2:3-4** supports this – "this is good, and pleases God our Saviour, who wants all people to be saved and to come to a knowledge of the truth".

HENDRIK KRAEMER – The Christian Message in a Non-Christian World. Kraemer was part of the **ECUMENICAL MOVEMENT** aiming to bring different Christian denominations together. Worked among missionaries in non-Christian countries, spreading the message that salvation could only be achieved by converting to Christianity. We should evaluate religions **HOLISTICALLY** to see if 'as a whole', the religion accepts Christ's salvation or not.

KARL BARTH – Church Dogmatics. Emphasised the importance of Christ for salvation. Humans cannot achieve salvation on their own. Presents **'THEOLOGY OF THE WORD'** – God can only be known where He chooses to reveal this knowledge through His Word – through Christ's life, death, and resurrection; through the Bible and through Church teaching. Revelation is always God's choice. **CHRIST** is the **FULLY UNIQUE** way God has chosen to reveal himself and so is the only fully reliable way of gaining knowledge of God.

Christian Teaching on Inclusivism

INCLUSIVISM is a middle path between exclusivism and pluralism. Christianity is a **NORMATIVE** means of salvation but '**ANONYMOUS**' Christians may also receive salvation (Karl **RAHNER**).

Salvation can be reached by people who turn to Christ in the **AFTERLIFE**. Salvation is possible for those who follow God sincerely, albeit in a wrong religious context. Truth in other religions could be from Christ – even if they do not recognise this.

KARL RAHNER – Christianity sets the **STANDARD** by which other religions should be measured. An **OMNIBENEVOLENT** God should be able to offer salvation to those who have not been able to freely accept Christ. Christianity holds the truth, but people can follow Christ unknowingly. People who do not know Christ can still have a relationship with God – e.g. **JOB 19:25**. Such people are called **ANONYMOUS CHRISTIANS**.

HENDRIK KRAEMER - disagreed with Rahner. **NON-CHRISTIAN RELIGIONS** were **CULTURAL CONSTRUCTS**, not responses to God's revelation through Christ.

The **BIBLE** can be seen as a source of authority:

1. **JOB 19:25** – Job appears to refer to Jesus – "I know that my redeemer lives".

2. **ROMANS 2:14-16** – non-believers can have an innate sense for Christ, even if they do not recognise it – "They show that the requirements of the law are written on their hearts".

3. **MATTHEW 25:33-40** – the Parable of the Sheep and the Goats implies anyone living by altruistic love is working for Christ – whether they realise it or not. "What you do for the least person, you do for me" says Jesus.

HANS URS VON BALTHASAR – CRITIC of the '**ANONYMOUS CHRISTIAN**'. Multi-culturalism should not be an excuse to 'water down' the importance of Christ's crucifixion and resurrection.

Christian Teaching on Pluralism

PLURALISM is the view that there are many ways to salvation. Christianity is one of these. Human culture causes differences in beliefs and practices, but religions share the same ultimate goal.

KANT – there is a difference between the **NOUMENAL WORLD** (world as it really is) and the **PHENOMENAL WORLD** (world as it appears to us). Nature of God belongs to the noumenal world.

JOHN HICK – called for a **'COPERNICAN REVOLUTION'** in theology: to put God central – not Christianity. This call **AWAY FROM** a **CHRISTOCENTRIC** approach to theology is driven by our observations of the world, just as the **COSMOLOGICAL COPERNICAN REVOLUTION** was.

Religion is a **PHENOMENAL** attempt to understand God (by experience). All religions fall short of the truth. Christianity's 'truth claims' e.g. Virgin Birth, should be understood as myths expressing human relationship with 'the **REAL**'. God is **BENEVOLENT** and so salvation must be extended to all.

Hick's call for **DEMYTHOLOGIZATION** of the Bible has origins in **RUDOLF BULTMANN**. This is the idea that the Gospels do contain essential truths but these are revealed through **MYTHS**.

Hick argues it is impossible to create rational arguments for God e.g. **NATURAL THEOLOGY**. People are given reason to believe by **RELIGIOUS EXPERIENCES**. Knowledge of God is similar to our other knowledge of the world – through our experiences. Since individual experiences provide the grounding for belief, we must respect all religions, since none of them can provide universally-accepted argument for their beliefs. Experiences of God can be interpreted through the lens of different religions and faith is how we interpret these events. An **ANALOGY** is how different people respond differently to the same **MUSICAL STIMULUS**, influenced by their cultural background. Cultural influences might explain the differences in how people interpret the divine. Human projection shapes the experience but does not cause it.

Challenges to Pluralism

Supporting Hick

- **FEUERBACH -** religious belief is projection. No genuine external cause of the religious experience

- **CUPITT -** challenges existence of God

- **PHILOSOPHICAL ARGUMENTS** – if 'the Real' is unknowable, we can't say anything meaningful about it and it cannot reveal itself deliberately to humans – this would make the revelation come from the human mind.

- Hick's theology allows for a **GLOBAL** theology and does not exclude polytheistic or non-theistic religions

Opposing Hick

- **INCARNATION** is regarded as central to Christianity, affirmed in the creed. Hick challenges traditional doctrines.

- **CHRISTIANS** might argue Hick undermines the essence of Christianity and reduces the Bible to fiction with morals.

- **LEE STROBEL** – 'the Case for Christ' – the gospels are eyewitness documents. But we know very little of Jesus' early life and the gospels were written after Jesus' death.

CONCLUSION OF HICK's PLURALISTIC HYPOTHESIS Empirical evidence, practical considerations and philosophical logic lend themselves to a Copernican revolution in theology.

How Was Hick Influenced by Kant?

The distinction between **NOUMENA** and **PHENOMENA** helps us to comprehend how different religions are talking about the same reality (noumena) but do so in different ways since our mind shapes our perception of our experiences (phenomena).

SYNOPTIC connection **PLATO** (Forms) -> **KANT** (noumena) -> **HICK**

RAIMON PANIKKAR – we need to be 'open' about the truth, rather than making claims about it. Life is a **'SEARCHING PILGRIMAGE'** and we might need to let go of traditions in order to find our identity. **CHRISTOPHANY** is God's way of making Himself known to people. **RELIGIOUS PLURALISM** is a **SPIRITUAL POSITION** not an intellectual position.

Confusions to Avoid

1. Hick is NOT calling for one religion with everyone having the same beliefs – **GLOBAL THEOLOGY** is NOT the same as a **GLOBAL RELIGION**. He is emphasising that people necessarily have different ways of experiencing the divine.

2. Hick is NOT saying all religions are correct – rather, that they **CONTAIN TRUTH**. They also contain human projection and error and since we cannot know all truth, we must respect all religions.

3. For the belief system to be valid, it ought to lead people away from selfishness and towards ethical living. Therefore, not every belief system reflects the Divine.

Possible Exam Questions

1. "A theologically pluralist approach significantly undermines the central doctrines of Christianity." Discuss.

2. To what extent can non-Christians who live morally good lives and genuinely seek God be considered to be 'anonymous Christians'?

3. Critically assess the view that only Christianity offers the means of salvation

4. "Christianity is one of many ways to salvation." Discuss.

Key Quotes

"Those also can attain to salvation who through no fault of their own do not know the Gospel of Christ or His Church, yet sincerely seek God and moved by grace strive by their deeds to do His will as it is known to them through the dictates of conscience". (Catechism, paragraph 19)

"I know that my redeemer lives, and that in the end he will stand on the earth" Job 19:25

"All that matters (metaphysically) is that Jesus did rise from the dead, and that this act made salvation possible for all, irrespective of one's particular religion." (Religion, Key Concepts in Philosophy, 2007, p. 154)

"This is good, and pleases God our Saviour, who wants all people to be saved and to come to a knowledge of the truth". (1 Timothy 2:3-4)

"They show that the requirements of the law are written on their hearts". (Romans 2:14-16)

"Whoever believes in him is not condemned, but whoever does not believe stands condemned already because they have not believed in the name of God's one and only Son." (John 3:18)

"For it is by grace you have been saved, through faith—and this is not from yourselves, it is the gift of God— 9 not by works, so that no one can boast." (Ephesians 2:8-9)

"You see that a person is considered righteous by what they do and not by faith alone." (James 2:24)

Religious Pluralism and Society

Background

In the 21st Century, a question that concerns many Christians is how they relate to people who follow no religion, or non-Christian beliefs. This goes together with the **MULTI-CULTURALISM** of Britain, leading it to become a multi-faith society. Issues arise for a Christian who might ask themselves whether to tolerate, or try to convert other people. Issues of religious expression in the workplace and attitudes towards sexuality have also made the public eye in the media. Christians might be unsure of how to voice their opinion without being discriminatory. Some Christians have become involved in **INTER-FAITH DIALOGUE**.

Specification

At A level, you will need to explain and evaluate:

1. The development of contemporary **MULTI-FAITH** societies – the reasons for this development, for example, migration

2. Christian responses to, including:

    a. Responses of Christian communities to inter-faith dialogue

    b. The scriptural reasoning movement (its methods and aims; and how the mutual study and interpretation of different religions' sacred literature can help understanding of different and conflicting religious truth claims)

3. How Christian communities have responded to the challenge of encounters with other faiths, for example:

    a. Catholic Church: **REDEMPTORIS MISSIO (ENCYCLICAL**, pp. 55-57)

    b. Church of England: Sharing the Gospel of Salvation (OCR A Level in Religious Studies Specification, 2016, p. 37)

Key Terms

- **ENCYCLICAL** an open letter sent by the Catholic hierarchy to the churches, endorsed by the Pope

- **MISSIONARY WORK** activity that aims to convert people to a particular faith or set of beliefs, or works for social justice in areas of poverty or deprivation

- **MULTI-FAITH SOCIETIES** societies in which there are significant populations of people with different religious beliefs

- **SOCIAL COHESION** when a group is united by bonds that help them to live together peacefully

- **SYNOD** the legislative body of the Church of England

The Development of Multi-Faith Societies

Example - Migration

Christianity was introduced by the **ROMANS**. Before this, religious practices concentrated around worship of ancestors, fertility and agriculture. Christianity was established as the **PRIMARY FAITH** in Britain in **7th CENTURY**. Western development in **TRAVEL** and **COMMUNICATION** has increased **CULTURAL** and **RELIGIOUS DIVERSITY**. In the 1950s and 60s, the Textile industry was short of labour - encouraging immigration from **PAKISTAN** and the **CARIBBEAN**. **IDI AMIN** expelled the **ASIAN** population from **UGANDA** in 1972. This led to arrival in Britain of **HINDUS, MUSLIMS** and **SIKHS.**

People have travelled more for holiday and work and this has led to greater contact with different beliefs and traditions. 'Pockets' of religious groups were caused by religious people choosing to live near where others who practised the same religion. **SIKHS** arriving in 1950s for work tended to settle in **LONDON, BIRMINGHAM** and **WEST YORKSHIRE**; while the **JEWISH** population is higher in **NORTH LONDON** and **LEEDS**. When travelling, local etiquette needs respecting and for this, further education about beliefs is also needed.

MAX MULLER'S 19th century translations of Hindu texts into English (**THE SACRED BOOKS OF THE EAST**) increased interest in meditation and ideas such as **REINCARNATION**.

The changes have resulted in **MIXED-FAITH MARRIAGES,** the teaching of world faiths in schools, people working among **RELIGIOUS DIVERSITY**, the stocking of multi-faith **FESTIVAL FOODS** in supermarkets, **PRAYER ROOMS** in airports and hospitals, and an acceptance of **ATHEISM** and **AGNOSTICISM**, allowing religious beliefs to also be challenged.

Some argue that this new opportunity for the sharing of beliefs has helped to dispel prejudice and to **PROMOTE PEACE**. Others say it has helped **DEEPER REFLECTION** on one's own beliefs; while others still, claim tolerance is promoted at the expense of the **UNIQUE MESSAGE** of **SALVATION** through **CHRIST** promoted by the Christian mission.

Responses to Inter-faith Dialogue

Inter-faith dialogue is also known as inter-belief dialogue and inter-religious dialogue. It aims for mutual peace, respect, and cooperation. It aims to understand:

- Common ground and points of difference

- One's own faith while learning about, and from, beliefs of others

It is NOT about **CONVERSION** but serves renewed interest in the wake of migration and human responses to tragedies such 9/11.

David Ford: The Future of Christian Theology

Inter-faith dialogue has new direction due to two major historical strands:

1. **HOLOCAUST**: the role played by Christianity in spurring on anti-Semitism in contrast with those that opposed Nazism. **DABRU EMET ('SPEAK THE TRUTH')** – was an invitation from Jewish leaders to Christians, calling for **CO-OPERATION**.

2. Rising **TENSIONS** between Islam and the West: **A COMMON WORD BETWEEN US AND YOU** – a call from Muslim leaders to Christianity outlining the responsibility of both to work for the common good of all.

Catholic Church - Redemptoris Missio (Mission of the Redeemer)

JOHN PAUL II – encouraged perseverance with the Christian mission in a multi-faith world. **PAPAL ENCYCLICALS** – letters from the Pope to Church leaders, are considered to be an authority and a 'final word.' **REDEMPTORIS MISSIO** (1990) re-visited the issues of **VATICAN II** and affirmed the essential place of Christian mission in a multi-faith world.

All religions provide spiritual opportunity, despite gaps and errors. The **LAITY** understand Christianity as lived through everyday life and so have a key role in dialogue.

All **CATHOLICS** have a duty to engage in **RESPECTFUL DIALOGUE**. This dialogue gives an opportunity to bear witness and is an 'expression' of Christian mission – not an opposition to it. The unique path to salvation through Christ is still offered by Christianity and should be emphasised.

Church of England - Sharing the Gospel of Salvation

1. **'THE DIALOGUE OF DAILY LIFE'** – informal discussions of differing beliefs

2. **'THE DIALOGUE OF THE COMMON GOOD'** – different faiths cooperate to help the community

3. **'THE DIALOGUE OF MUTUAL UNDERSTANDING'** – formal debates e.g. Scriptural Reasoning

4. **'THE DIALOGUE OF SPIRITUAL LIFE'** – meet for prayer and worship

This **FOURFOLD PLAN** to **SHARING THE GOSPEL OF SALVATION** is in response to **PAUL EDDY'S** 2006 question asking the Church to clarify the position of the Church of England on converting others. The plan affirmed that Jesus uniquely offers salvation and the Church of England has a mission to testify to this.

Christians should make efforts to speak about their beliefs openly and honestly but should not treat this as a 'marketing' exercise. Conversions are God's work – not the result of a 'good sell'.

Christians should make efforts to engage with members of different faiths – **MORE THAN JUST TOLERANCE.** Christians should follow the **GOLDEN RULE** – to 'treat others as you would like to be treated' (**LEVITICUS 19:18**) and should listen to others and leave judgement to God.

The Scriptural Reasoning Movement

How the mutual study and interpretation of different religions' sacred literature can help understanding of different and conflicting religious truth claims.

The movement began as a **JEWISH ACADEMIC FORUM** in the USA. In the mid-1990s, Christians asked to join to learn and found the conversations to be engaging. **MUSLIMS** were asked to join because of shared roots (**COMMON GROUND**) and together, the three religions can be known as **RELIGIONS OF THE BOOK** because each religion claims to have a holy text that is authoritative and revelatory. The movement now welcomes people of **ALL FAITHS**.

Cambridge Inter-faith Forum

This involves a discussion of themes considering scriptures of the Abrahamic faiths (those that come from a common origin in the **HEBREW** Scriptures) – Judaism, Christianity, Islam. Discussions are held in English in order to be inclusive. Discussions will concern earning, clothing, modesty, fasting, differing truth claims (e.g. Prophethood and Trinity) among other topics. The forum will consider how beliefs that appear similar are understood in their own contexts. Honesty and openness are encouraged.

Strengths

Brings together people of different faiths, aiding **TOLERANCE** in a multi-faith society.

IDEAS - Collaboration socially and academically is encouraged.

Face-to-face discussion is encouraged, as well as joint research. This further promotes inter-religious harmony and **SOCIAL COHESION** through raised awareness and understanding of one's own views and those of others.

Weaknesses

INDIVIDUALISTIC - Participants represent themselves – it is possible we lose sight of the normative teaching of each religion.

It is difficult to decide if an interpretation is **REASONABLE**.

It is **QUESTIONABLE** – the extent to which theological **EXCLUSIVISTS** can engage fully in inter-faith dialogue.

Although open to all faiths, the extent to which non-Abrahamic faiths with varied origins and traditions can partake fully and benefit, is questionable.

Some will criticise the **RELATIVIZING** of religious groups by treating all beliefs as equally valid.

Confusions to Avoid

1. There is some debate as to whether conversion of those of no faith is significantly different to conversion of those of a previous faith. On the one hand, those converting from a previous faith might face bigger challenges because

of their **FAMILY** and social group.

2. This tension might not be the same for someone of no religious background – thought, their social group might change. On the other hand, some **INCLUSIVISTS** might argue that the non-religious have a greater need to know God than the 'anonymous Christian' does. The non-religious might never have encountered the opportunity to become religious; while others might have actively opposed religion.

Possible Exam Questions

1. To what extent should Christians seek to convert others to Christianity at every opportunity?

2. "Inter-faith dialogue is of little practical use." Discuss.

3. To what extent does scriptural reasoning relativise religious beliefs?

4. "Converting people of no faith should be equally important to a Christian as converting people of non-Christian faith." Discuss.

Key Quotations

From Redemptoris Missio (paragraphs) and the Bible:

"Every person has the right to hear the 'Good News' of the God who reveals and gives himself in Christ" Para. 46

"In the light of the economy of salvation, the Church sees no conflict between proclaiming Christ and engaging in inter-faith dialogue" Para. 55

"The Church gladly acknowledges whatever is true and holy in the religious traditions of Buddhism, Hinduism and Islam as a reflection of that truth which enlightens all people" Para. 55

"Dialogue should be conducted and implemented with the conviction that the Church is the ordinary means of salvation and that she alone possesses the fullness of the means of salvation" Para. 55

"Dialogue leads to inner purification and conversion" Para. 56

"Inter-religious dialogue is a part of the church's evangelising mission" Para. 55

"Therefore go and make disciples of all nations, baptising them in the names of the Father and of the Son and of the Holy Spirit." (Matthew 28:19)

The Challenge of Secularism

Background

The role of religion in Western Europe has changed and is changing. Christianity in Britain has been in decline – seen in Church attendance and solemnisation of fewer marriages. This reduction has led to questions from **PSYCHOLOGY** and **SOCIOLOGY** about the role of religious institutions in public life and culture. It has been suggested that religion should be seen as part of the '**PRIVATE**' rather than 'public' sphere while the relationship between Christianity and British culture is diminishing.

Specification

At A level, you will need to explain the rise of **SECULARISM** and **SECULARISATION**, and know and evaluate:

1. The views that God is an illusion and the result of wish fulfilment

2. The views of Freud and Dawkins that society would be happier without Christianity as it is infantile, repressive and causes conflict

3. The views that Christianity should play no part in public life

4. The views of **SECULAR HUMANISTS** that Christian belief is personal and should play no part in public life, including education and schools, and government and state (OCR A Level in Religious Studies Specification, 2016, p. 40). Be aware that there are two different approaches to secularism, and one of these argues that **SECULARISM** is absolutely necessary for religious toleration and diversity, (the other, argued by **DAWKINS**, argues that religion should be completely excluded form public life).

Key Terms

- **SECULAR** not connected or associated with religious or spiritual matters

- **SECULARISM** various meanings – a belief that religion should have no role in public or government life; a belief that no one religion should have a superior position in the state; a belief in a public space and a private space, and that religion should be kept apart from public power

- **SECULARISATION** a theory rising out of Enlightenment thinking, developed in the 1950s and 1960s, that proposed that with the advancement of democracy and technology, religious belief would progressively decline. Such a linear decline is now doubted by sociologists

- **WISH FULFILMENT** according to Freud, the satisfaction of a desire through a dream or other exercise of the imagination

Structure of Thought

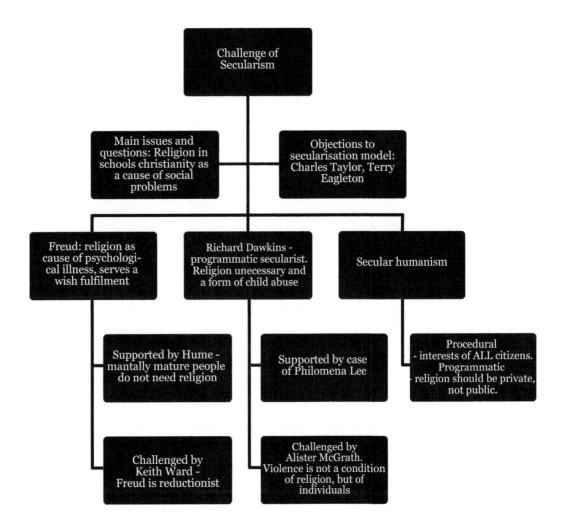

The Rise of Secularism and Secularisation

1. Reasons for the rise of secularism and secularisation and the views that God is an illusion and the result of wish fulfilment

2. The views of Freud and Dawkins that society would be happier without Christianity as it is infantile, repressive and causes conflict

Difficulty in Defining Secularism

1. **Measuring and defining terms**: less Church attendance does not mean less spirituality

2. **Influence and authority**: new movements are being accepted by society, even with a decline in mainstream religions

3. **Religious commitment and evidence of the past**: Church attendance in previous years was not the best test of religious commitment. Today, people attend because they want to, not because they must. So, what really is an appropriate way of measuring secularisation?

AUGUSTE COMPTE - civilised society develops progressively from:

1. *Theological* perspective

2. *Metaphysical* (abstract) view of the world

3. *Positive* (scientific/rational) view of the world

Sigmund Freud

Religion is a key cause of **PSYCHOLOGICAL** illness. Tradition and conformity **REPRESS** natural instincts, and this leads to **NEUROSES**.

Freud considered that religion belongs to the **INFANTILE** – belief is formed in the early stage of human social development. This stage is before the person has developed the ability to reason and at this stage, needs external care and security provided by a **FATHER** and **MOTHER** figure (by **PROJECTION**, God and the Virgin Mary).

Supported by Hume

Mentally mature people do not need religion – it is practised by the uneducated.

Freud went further to say that religion was a **SICKNESS** and could be proven as such by his use of psychoanalysis.

When instinctual life wins and religion ends, humans will be content.

Wish Fulfilment

As children, there is a **VULNERABILITY** and helplessness that is fulfilled 'by a belief that injustices will be corrected, that life has a purpose, and that there is a moral code' (Freud, The Future of an Illusion). God – or belief in God – represents a **PERSONIFICATION** of our needs. Religion can answer questions that humans have that cannot be answered by studying 'what is real?'

Religion causes conflict as it creates unreliable and harmful answers to human uncertainty and matters outside of our control.

Challenges to Freud

KEITH WARD labels Freud a **REDUCTIONIST** because he appears to reduce everything to material terms. This is an **INADEQUATE** explanation for the spiritual experience of existence.

Truth claims about religion cannot be disproved.

Freud emphasises the **DESTRUCTIVE** nature of religion but for others, religion is an aide rather than a harm. It can assist understanding and acceptance of life. Religion can help to form communities rather than to divide them.

Freud **GENERALISES** religions – while some are hierarchical and controlling, not all are and therefore, not all religions can be seen to perpetuate guilt.

Wish fulfilment might not always lead to illusion – it can lead to creativity such as that seen in **DREAMS** and daydreams.

Richard Dawkins - Programmatic Secularism

In **THE GOD DELUSION**, Dawkins makes the case for:

1. Imagining a world without religion

2. Accepting that the God hypothesis is weak

3. Realising that religion is a form of child abuse

4. Accepting atheism with pride

Dawkins argued that life can be meaningful without reference to religion. The processes of nature can be most clearly explained by Charles Darwin and his **THEORY** of **EVOLUTION**.

Belief in God is **DELUDED** and unnecessary. Religion is delusional since it represents a persistent false belief going against the main body of evidence. The supernatural world cannot be subject to empirical study and therefore, Dawkins rejects **STEPHEN JAY GOULD'S** attempts to argue that religion and science are '**NON-OVERLAPPING MAGISTERIA'**. For Dawkins, all things must be able to be studied empirically. (Link with **VERIFICATIONISM** in Religious Language).

RELIGION IS A FORM OF CHILD ABUSE – A child lacking understanding should not be labelled as religious. Dawkins criticised the state for allowing a child below the age of consent and reason to be labelled as religious. They have been unable to think about the beliefs they are labelled as possessing. This could be seen in school admissions, for example.

Dawkins used the example of **CATHOLICISM** as a form of long-term psychological abuse. He gave the example of Catholic women who had experienced sexual abuse, who found the fear of hell to be greater than the abuse itself. Another example was the '**HELL HOUSE**' thought of by a pastor in Colorado. Here, children were terrified by actors role-playing the sins of abortion and homosexuality, followed by the torture of Hell. Dawkins suggests that the power of belief in religion becomes greater than the physical abuse suffered.

Example- Philomena Lee

Had her child, born out of wedlock, taken from her by the Catholic Church. She stayed with her boy for three years at the **SEAN ROSS ABBEY** in Roscrea – a place for unwed mothers. Philomena's boy was then sold, to be adopted by a Catholic family.

Responses to Dawkins - Alister McGrath

The Dawkins Delusion

Many Christians think faith is not irrational. Furthermore, religion and science are not necessarily in conflict. Science can explain the intelligible universe and so **DAWKINS** is right to criticise the '**GOD OF THE GAPS**'. However, the intelligible universe could still point to an intelligent designer.

The relationship between science and religion can be **COMPLEMENTARY**, reflecting different aspects of human experience.

Dawkins' **LIMITED POSITIVIST VIEW** that metaphysical questions are outside of scientific enquiry and therefore meaningless is criticised by many scientists. Science, theology and philosophy can provide useful insights.

MCGRATH also criticised Dawkins' claim that violence was a necessary condition of religion. Jesus taught against violence – "turn the other cheek". Violence is a condition of certain individuals, not religion as a whole. McGrath also notes that atheism has also been a part of violence and repression, e.g. in communist regimes.

Secular Humanism - Christian Belief is Personal

Two Types of Secularism

1. **PROCEDURAL**: the interests of ALL citizens – religious and non-religious, should be considered by the state. Religion should be treated equally to other institutions but not with preference.

2. **PROGRAMMATIC**: in a **PLURAL** society, the state should be solely secular. This means religious views and practices should be kept apart from public institutions – schools, universities, public holiday and government.

The main aims of modern humanism were set out in the **AMSTERDAM DECLARATION** of 1952:

1. Humanism is **ETHICAL**: all humans are of worth, have dignity and autonomy

2. Humanism is **RATIONAL**: science should be used imaginatively and as a basis for solving human difficulties.

3. Humanism supports democracy and human **RIGHTS**: the best way in which humans can develop their potential.

4. Humanism insists that personal **LIBERTY** must be combined with **SOCIAL RESPONSIBILITY**: no dogmatic beliefs, the autonomous person has a responsibility to society and the natural world

5. Humanism is a response to the widespread demand for an alternative to dogmatic religion: continuous observation will build our reliable understanding of the world and revision of **SCIENTIFIC** understanding.

6. Humanism values artistic **CREATIVITY** and imagination: enhancing human existence. Novelist **E.M. FORSTER** defined the humanist as someone with "curiosity, a free mind, belief in good taste, and belief in the human race."

7. Humanism is a **LIFESTANCE** aiming at the maximum possible fulfilment: creative and ethical living can help us to achieve the challenges of the present

Education and Schools

Government and State

1776 – Formation of the USA – Church and State made separate.

Keeping Church and State separate might be seen as one way of avoiding conflicting political aims between Christian denominations and even with other religions with the increase in migrants.

Alternative ideas about theocracy are seen in:

1. **DOMINIONISTS**: America should be ruled according to Biblical laws – based on Genesis 1:28 where humans are said to have dominion – this includes over the state. A view held mostly by Protestant, evangelical and conservative groups.

2. **RECONSTRUCTIONISTS**: Similar Dominionist notion. Seen in the Old Testament when the life of Israel was

ordered according to laws given to Moses. Followed by Calvinists.

In England, the Queen is the Head of the Church of England. 26 Bishops sit as '**LORDS SPIRITUAL**' in the **HOUSE OF LORDS**. Regardless of faith, church of England Parish Churches can be used for marriages, funerals and baptisms. This is a way of the state providing a spiritual life for everyone.

NOTE: England is NOT a **THEOCRACY.**

Some **PROGRAMMATIC SECULARISTS** believe the government should go further in separating Church and State.

ROWAN WILLIAMS – the Church has a role to play in resisting the apparent threat of secularism felt by some religious fundamentalists who are anti-democratic (as they oppose democratic consensus on laws such as legalisation of abortion and homosexuality reform)

CHRISTOPHER DAWSON – secular education systems bring challenges. They deprive people of the ability and right to make sense of their own culture – a culture which, to a large extent, is immersed in religion.

Objections to the Secularisation Model

CHARLES TAYLOR – the '**SUBTRACTION STORIES**' of **DAWKINS** and **FREUD** show how the world can be explained with stories that show neither God, nor any 'greater being' is needed for us to live fulfilled lives.

This is '**SELF-SUFFICING HUMANISM'**. This humanism fails because it emphasises the individual and in so doing, loses the **COMMUNAL** aspect of society (notice though, a counter-argument, that humanists argue for **SOCIAL RESPONSIBILITY**). Rather than a discovery that God does not exist, our exclusion of God from our explanation of the world reflects a **WESTERN PHASE**. In order to live a full life, we need to embrace a sense of the divine and distance ourselves from secularism.

TERRY EAGLETON – a **MARXIST** and **CHRISTIAN** approach. Marxist in the sense that he thought it wrong to exclude religious imagination and its contribution to human existence. Eagleton thought the harm of religion should be weighed up against its positive contributions.

The **SPIRITUAL** aspect of human experience can be captured by religion, but not by secularism. People have been prepared to make ultimate sacrifices for truths about existence but not for **AESTHETIC** reasons e.g. sport/ music. Secularist privatisation has seemed to make religion and morality irrelevant. 9/11 showed the dangers of a **POSITIVIST** view of the world without religion where dangerous extremists interpret the Western secularists as trying to turn the world anti-religious.

Key Confusions to Avoid

1. The discussion concerning whether spiritual values are just 'human values' can sometimes lead to confusion. To say spiritual values are just 'human', implies that there is '**NO SIGNIFICANT OTHER**' to which they are directed or from which they come.

2. Arguments to support this include the belief that values often labelled as 'Christian' are actually fundamental values of being human and part of flourishing in society. Such values include those of **COMPASSION,**

FORGIVENESS, JUSTICE, AND PEACE. Furthermore, those who argue that these spiritual values are no different to 'being human', might add that the aforementioned values do not require a belief in God or an afterlife in order to be endorsed.

3. On the other hand, there are arguments that spiritual values are much more than simply 'human'. For example, some spiritual values such as self-sacrifice and 'love your enemies' do not always benefit the human. Spiritual values are untainted by human, material desires, and express a commitment to something 'other'. Furthermore, it has been suggested that the **UNIVERSAL DECLARATION OF HUMAN RIGHTS** is based on the belief that humans have 'ultimate worth', and so values are **ABSOLUTE**.

4. Lastly, there is an argument that human and spiritual values cannot be made separate and this was shown in the **INCARNATION**.

Possible Exam Questions

1. "Christianity has a negative impact on society." Discuss.

2. To what extent are Christian values more than just basic human values?

3. "Christianity should play no part in public life." Discuss.

4. Critically assess the claims that God is an illusion and the result of wish fulfilment.

Key Quotes

"Faith is the root of freedom and programmatic secularism cannot deliver anything comparable". Rowan Williams, Faith in the Public Square, 2012, page 32

"9/11 highlights two extremes of anxiety: faithless Western secular atheism and its fear of religion (and hence its reaction as the 'war on terror') and faithful religious fundamentalism and its fear of positivism, capitalism and secularisation". Michael Wilcockson, Religious studies for A Level Year 2, 2017, page 277

"No, our science is no illusion. But an illusion it would be to suppose that what science cannot give us we can get elsewhere". Sigmund Freud, The Future of an Illusion, 2001, page 56

"Dawkins' naïve view that atheists would never carry out crimes in the names of atheism simply founders on the cruel rocks of reality". Alister McGrath and Joanna Collicutt McGrath, The Dawkins Delusion?, 2007, page 78

"There is something infantile in the presumption that somebody else (parents in the case of children, God in the case of adults) has a responsibility to give your life meaning and point." Richard Dawkins, The God Delusion, 2006, p. 404

"The religions of mankind must be classed as among the mass delusions". Sigmund Freud, Civilisation and its Discontents, 1930, page 81

"Children, I'll argue, have a human right not to have their minds crippled by exposure to other people's bad ideas". Nicholas Humphrey, 'What Shall We Tell the Children?' Amnesty Lecture, 21 February 1997.

Liberation Theology and Marx

Background

Marx introduced the idea that when humans are unable to live fulfilling lives due to being 'dehumanised', this results in a form of **ALIENATION**. Humans are **DEHUMANISED** when they are **EXPLOITED,** and this is a result of being treated as objects and used as a means to an end.

Marx's teachings on alienation and exploitation have been used by **LIBERATION THEOLOGY** to analyse the **'STRUCTURAL'** causes of **SOCIAL SIN** that have led to poverty, violence, and injustice. Such 'structural' causes include capitalism and institutions (schools, churches, and the state).

The analysis of structural sin has led to a call for the **'PREFERENTIAL OPTION FOR THE POOR'** – a thought calling for Christians to act in solidarity with the poor, rooted in the Gospel. The implication of this teaching is to place **ORTHOPRAXIS** (right action) before **ORTHODOXY** (official Church teaching).

Specification

At A Level, we explain and evaluate liberation theology and Marx, including:

1. Marx's teaching on **ALIENATION** and exploitation

2. **LIBERATION THEOLOGY**'s use of Marx to analyse social sin

3. Liberation theology on the '**PREFERENTIAL OPTION** for the poor'

Key Terms

- **ALIENATION:** The process of becoming detached or isolated

- **BASIC CHRISTIAN COMMUNITIES:** Christian groups that gather to try to directly resolve problems in their lives

- **CAPITALISM:** An economic system in which the means of production are privately owned and operated for profit, in contrast with communism where the state controls trade and industry

- **ORTHODOXY:** Right belief

- **ORTHOPRAXIS**: Right action

- **PREFERENTIAL OPTION FOR THE POOR:** Acting in solidarity with the poor and oppressed

- **STRUCTURAL SIN:** Social dimension of sin, beyond individual sin. It is an attitude of society that contributes to oppression

Marx's Teaching on Alienation and Exploitation

Marx taught that alienation occurs when humans are dehumanised and unable to live fulfilling lives. **EXPLOITATION** occurs when humans are treated as objects and used as a means to an end. Note the similarity to Kant's second formulation of the **CATEGORICAL IMPERATIVE** here (treat people not just as a means to an end but always also as an **END** in themselves).

For example, consider a recent purchase from someone you might not know. You might have bought a sandwich from a local supermarket. Did you stop to think about the person serving you at the till? Or, in today's times of 'self-service' – have you thought of the people involved in the building and maintenance of the machines, the famers producing the ingredients needed for the bread and filling of your purchase?

Marx's teaching on **ALIENATION** and exploitation help us to think about the people involved in the **PRODUCTION** of things we value. Marx would say it does matter and should matter that we appreciate the persons involved in the stages of production and do not just see them as a means of production. If we do the latter, we alienate them from society.

Furthermore, technology has revolutionised the world but with the more apparent power we have in this development, the less in control we actually feel. Marx said there is a **HUMAN CAUSE** behind this feeling of powerlessness.

When humans reached the ability to produce **SURPLUS TO REQUIREMENTS**, the favour was granted to those who controlled the means of production and herein begIns class division. This division is evident through the ownership of land, where labour is bought and sold – people are treated as means and not 'ends'. Marx laid the foundations for **SOCIALISM** and **COMMUNISM** through his criticism of **CAPITALISM** – the private ownership of land. This private ownership changed the relationship between people and the means of production, leading to the exploitation and alienation of the workers.

What does this look like?

1. **FEUDAL LORDS** own the land and the means of producing food.

2. **SERFS** work on the land but don't own it. They rely on feudal lords for access and must give surplus to feudal lords.

3. **SUBSERVIENT** Serfs alienated from the land on which they work.

This system can be likened to working in a factory. Here, people only understand the part they work on and do not have sight of the whole process. In this way, they are **DEHUMANISED**. The work is necessary as without it, we could not pay for our survival. In this way, exploitation becomes a means to an end. Workers form part of a supply chain and do not know the 'purchasers'.

Neither do those purchasing know the workers - people are **ALIENATED** from their work. Our 'happiness' at cheap prices comes at the expense of other people's happiness - at the expense of the exploitation of others.

Liberation Theology's Use of Marx and Social Sin

Liberation theology began as an **INTELLECTUAL** and **PRACTICAL THEOLOGICAL** movement among those who worked with the poor.

PAULO FREIRE described the process of **'CONSCIENTISATION'** – a process by which someone becomes aware of the power structures in society. **FREIRE** argued that education should teach people to read the power structures and should work to **TRANSFORM** society and not to just transmit information.

Traditionally, theology had focussed on passing on information. **LIBERATION THEOLOGY** focused on **ACTION** before **EXPLANATION** – **ORTHOPRAXY** before **ORTHODOXY**. Liberation theology became, therefore, a **THEOLOGY OF ACTION**.

Liberation theology proposed that the **KINGDOM OF GOD** is not a place we go to when we die; but is something to work for in this life.

GUSTAVO GUTIÉRREZ, one of the founders of liberation theology, proposed that liberation occurs two-fold:

1. **SOCIAL AND ECONOMIC** – poverty and oppression are the consequence of human choices and therefore humans can resolve as well. Hence an idea of **SOCIAL SIN**.

2. **FROM SIN** – to be reconciled with the Divine.

Both 'social and economic' and 'from sin' aspects of liberation must happen together. Gutiérrez claimed that **POLITICAL LIBERATION** is the work of salvation. He emphasised earthly liberation, whereas **JUAN SEGUNDO** emphasised spiritual liberation.

The Bible extracts in the 'key quotations' section allow you to consider how each teaching might have influenced the development of liberation theology. For example, **MATTHEW 25:40** - "whatever you did for one of the least of these brothers and sisters of mine, you did for me" – encourages the **PREFERENTIAL OPTION FOR THE POOR** in the call to side with **'ONE OF THE LEAST'**, i.e. an outcast.

Liberation theology has its origins in 1960s Latin America, a place of corrupt governments and poverty. Christian groups formed to discuss experiences and practical solutions. Liberation theology therefore became a **THEOLOGY OF HOPE**, with God's love extending both to creation and to liberation.

LATIN AMERICA had found itself at a crossroads, a significant battleground in the cold war conflict between the USA and USSR. Marx had predicted a violent uprising of the oppressed – this seemed to be happening. Liberation theology focused on increasing **HUMAN WELL-BEING** rather than **HUMAN MATERIAL WEALTH**. This links to Marx's understanding that industrialisation can sacrifice the well-being of humans, despite the increase in wealth.

Liberation theology's use of Marx here, seems to be that the process of industrialisation is supported by a structure of sin that then forms part of the organisation of society, and in turn, part of the systems of government and education.

GUTIÉRREZ warned against using every aspect of Marxism but mentions his theories of alienation and exploitation. Gutiérrez also utilises Marx's suggestion that human beings can change the world they inhabit. Gutiérrez considered that people of Latin America wanted to be liberated from capitalism and so he called for the Church to stand with such movements for liberation – **BEING CHRISTIAN NECESSITATES BEING POLITICAL**. Gutiérrez went as far as to say that to not get involved in politics would be equal to helping to keep things the same, even if this situation was wrong/undesirable.

The **STRUCTURAL SIN** that must be changed can be seen in the injustices experienced by the oppressed. The current social system is one of structural inequality. By failing to address the class struggle, we legitimise the existing system, and in so doing, we act as a part of it. Perhaps Marx's most important contribution to liberation theology is his emphasis on recognising the class struggle against the structures of sin.

Liberation Theology's Teaching on "Preferential Option for the Poor"

The **GOSPEL** demands that Christians must give priority to the poor and act in **SOLIDARITY** with them. Liberation theology demands we put **ORTHOPRAXIS** before **ORTHODOXY**.

The teaching on **PREFERENTIAL OPTION FOR THE POOR** refers to a **BIBLICAL TREND** to show favour to the oppressed and outcasts. This follows the example set by Jesus – "whatever you did for one of the least of these brothers and sisters of mine, you did for me" **(MATTHEW 25:40)**. The phrase was first coined by **FATHER ARRUPE**, **SUPERIOR GENERAL OF THE JESUITS** in **1968**, and was later picked up by the Catholic bishops of **LATIN AMERICA**. **JUAN SEGUNDO** taught that a preferential option for the poor shows an **AUTHENTIC CHRISTIAN RESPONSE**, avoiding the dangers of neutrality.

JUAN SEGUNDO wrote that the Church "intends to struggle, by her own means, for the defence and advancement of the rights of mankind, especially of the poor". Since we are made in **GOD'S LIKENESS**, **HUMAN DIGNITY** should be central to what we do. By failing to intervene and by allowing an ongoing social divide, we would prove incompatible with the peace and justice advocated in the Bible.

SEGUNDO differed to **GUTIÉRREZ** because he argued that liberation from sin (**SPIRITUAL LIBERATION**) should come before **SOCIAL LIBERATION**.,as social liberation might not be possible. Even Jesus taught *"the poor you will always have with you, but you will not always have me" (Matthew 26:11)*. Segundo still taught we should prioritise the preferential option for the poor - now gained acceptance beyond liberation theology.

JOHN PAUL II used the term in his encyclical **CENTESIMUS ANNUS** (1991). In this, he argued that support of the poor is an opportunity for the moral and cultural growth of humankind. However, this also includes a care for **SPIRITUAL POVERTY** – not just a focus on material wealth:

"This option is not limited to material poverty, since it is well known that there are many other forms of poverty, especially in modern society – not only economic but cultural and spiritual poverty as well". (Centesimus Annus para 43)

This spiritual poverty can be caused by focusing too much on the material goods. **POPE PAUL II** referenced drug and pornography addiction as an indication of a broken social structure. A destructive reading of human needs leaves a spiritual void that is filled by exploitation of the weak. **POPE FRANCIS** encourages the Catholic Church to be a **'POOR CHURCH FOR THE POOR'**.

The **CATHOLIC CHURCH** was concerned about the theological use of Marx as some of Marx's ideas were considered intolerable and thus a danger to use in theology **(CARDINAL RATZINGER)**. Furthermore, Ratzinger (later Pope Benedict XVI) also claimed that using Marx interfered with the **EUCHARISTIC CELEBRATION** of power struggle. Evangelism was in danger of being superseded by violent revolution. Christian liberation should focus on **LIBERATION FROM SIN**, with God being the ultimate liberator. Marxism, Ratzinger claimed, was inherently un-Christian.

BONAVENTURE (1221-74), in **TEMPTATIONS FOR THE THEOLOGY OF LIBERATION (1974)**, criticised liberation theology for prioritising action over the Gospel. He claimed that liberation theology equated theology with politics, and as a result, side-lined Christian evangelism. Bonaventure highlighted that liberation theology focused on structural and not personal sin – despite Jesus' emphasis on **PERSONAL RECONCILIATION** with God.

However, for the starving and oppressed, one can question whether liberation from sin is more important than social liberation. Jesus did teach the importance of inner spiritual change, but he also called for real action – seen in the **PARABLE OF THE SHEEP AND THE GOATS (MATTHEW 25)**. The election of a Latin American Pope might signal the beginning of real impact of liberation theology. Pope Francis named **OSCAR ROMERO** a martyr and asked Gutiérrez to be a keynote speaker at a Vatican event in 2015.

However, in a 2017 visit to **MYANMAR** Pope Francis failed to explicitly denounce the persecution of the **ROHINGYA** Muslims by supposedly pacifist Buddhists.

Confusions to Avoid

1. Liberation theology would claim it is not Marxist, but rather, makes use of Marx's analysis of society. Within liberation theology, Marxism is not treated on its own – it is always considered in relation to the situation of the poor. Marxism is of '**INSTRUMENTAL**' use to liberation theology – an instrument in understanding and responding to the needs of the oppressed. For more on this, read **BOFF** in 'recommended reading'.

2. Christianity would claim that its 'preferential option for the poor' came from the Bible and that Marx's criticism of religion was based on corruptions in which the Church had contributed to oppression.

3. Liberation theology's call for **ORTHOPRAXIS** (living) before orthodoxy (dogma) might imply that the church had not advocated Christian action. This is not true. Christianity had always advocated putting beliefs into practice (see **JAMES** "faith without works is dead'). Liberation theology brought to attention the need of religion to affect the whole life – including an active role in the traditionally more secular areas of politics and **ECONOMICS**. This is what made liberation theology distinctive.

Possible Exam Questions

1. To what extent should Christianity engage with atheist secular ideologies?

2. "Liberation theology has not engaged with Marxism fully enough." Discuss.

3. Critically assess the claim that Christianity has tackled social issues more effectively than Marxism.

4. Critically assess the relationship of liberation theology and Marx with particular reference to liberation theology use of Marx to analyse social sin.

Key Quotes

"The growth of the Kingdom is a process which occurs historically in liberation". (Gutiérrez, A Theology of Liberation, 1973, p. 177)

"Then the Lord said to Moses, "Go to Pharaoh and say to him, 'This is what the Lord, the God of the Hebrews, says: "Let my people go, so that they may worship me." (Exodus 9:1).

"Blessed are the poor in spirit, for theirs is the kingdom of heaven. (Matthew 5:3).

Social division exists whereby the worker "is depressed...both intellectually and physically, to the level of a machine" (Karl Marx, Early Writings, [1833-4] 1975, p.285

"Liberation theology used Marxism purely as an instrument. It does not venerate it as it venerates the gospel". Leonardo Boff and Clodovis Boff, Introducing Liberation Theology, 1987

"Let us recall the fact that atheism and the denial of the human person, his liberty and rights, are at the core of the Marxist theory". Congregation of the Doctrine of the Faith 1984, para 7.6

Gender and Society

Background

The Christian Church has lagged behind changes in social attitudes (and UK laws) in recent years, particularly on sexual issues such as **CONTRACEPTION**, **ABORTION** and **PRE-MARITAL SEX**, and gender issues such as attitudes to **HOMOSEXUALITY** (including gay marriage). For example, the Church of England still formally disallows homosexual gay partnerships in the **CLERGY** whilst professing to welcome gay church members. Gender issues also include attitudes to **TRANSEXUALS** and the political implications of **FEMINISM**.

Key Terms

- **ESSENTIALIST THEORIES:** Gender is fixed by objective human nature, either by God or by our inherent biology (eg genes)

- **EXISTENTIALIST THEORIES:** Gender is determined by social discourse (Foucault), by upbringing (Freud), or by social conditioning (including religious conditioning)

- **FEMINISM:** A movement and a philosophy emerging form the Enlightenment emphasis on equal rights, but embracing theories of power and social conditioning.

- **SEX:** Refers to the biological and physiological characteristics that define men and women

- **GENDER:** The state of being classified as male or female or transgender (typically used with reference to social and cultural differences rather than biological ones).

- **FALSE CONSCIOUSNESS:** Beliefs and behaviour induced by social attitudes and values which contradict the true interest (economic, political or social) of a person

- **PATRIARCHY:** A system of society or government in which men hold the power and women are largely excluded from it.

- **ETERNAL FEMININE:** Simone de Beauvoir's term to describe the role of woman as some ideal imposed by men (submissive housewife, sex object etc).

Specification

A Level requires us to study the effects of changing views of **GENDER** and gender roles on Christian thought and practice, including:

- Christian teaching on the roles of men and women in the family and society

- Christian responses to contemporary **SECULAR** views about the roles of men and women in the family and society including reference to:

    - **Ephesians 5:22–33**

- **Mulieris Dignitatem 18–19**

The ways in which Christians have **ADAPTED** and **CHALLENGED** changing attitudes to family and gender, including issues of:

- motherhood/parenthood

- different types of family (single parent, extended, nuclear etc)

Note: there is not one, but **MANY** Christianities. The specification mentions just one Bible passage of many that need to be taken, and one Roman Catholic Document, Mulieris Dignitatem, in the context of a history of **PAPAL ENCYCLICALS**. Roman Catholics and Evangelical Christians argue against women leadership for different reasons. **QUAKERS** have always espoused strict gender equality and are pacifist.

Gender – Essentialist or Existentialist

ESSENTIALIST gender is essential to biology eg Biblical account of creation "God created them male and female'. Often includes conclusions about roles and/or intelligence eg men are stronger and wiser (**AQUINAS**).

EXISTENTIALIST gender is a product of **CIVILISATION** (de Beauvoir), male expectation, a cultural interpretation of gender roles, or an interpretation of the Bible. E.g. body image is a cultural construction (modern anorexic images very different from Rubens portraits).

Exploitation and Power (Michael Foucault)

The idea that human beings have a **SEXUALITY** is a recent western social phenomenon.

At the start of the 18th century, there was an emergence of "a political, economic, and technical incitement to talk about sex,"with experts speaking about the morality and rationality of sex, fuelled by Catholic teaching on sex, sin and confession" (Foucault).

ENLIGHTENMENT emphasises the empirical nature of sex and gender eg biological differences between men and women, the nature and source of sexual pleasure and supposed **OBJECTIVE** measures of intelligence and emotion

The "world of perversion" that includes the sexuality of children, the mentally ill, and homosexuality all subject to more vigorous prosecution. The labelling of **PERVERSION** conveyed a sense of "pleasure and power" for academics studying sexuality and the 'perverts' themselves.

HYPOCRISY as Middle Class society exhibited "blatant and fragmented perversion," readily engaging in perversion but regulating where it could take place. In 18th century Britain 1 in 5 women were prostitutes – Nelson's mistress Emma **HAMILTON** started out as a 'courtesan'.

The mythical idea that previous generations were **REPRESSED** feeds the modern myth that we now live in a 'garden of earthly delights'. (Foucault)

Culture changes by "interconnected mechanisms" and there has been a proliferation of possible sexualities and forms of **DESIRE**, "a deployment quite independent of the law".

Jimmy **SAVILE** sex abuse scandal (2016) and Harvey **WEINSTEIN**'s alleged abuse of power (2017) illustrate Foucault's argument in 1964 A History of Sexuality, as Foucault argues that power relations define how we see sex and sexuality – the powerful **SUBJUGATE** the weak and convince them of the benefits of compliance (the silence of Weinstein's victims is bought by money, jobs or intimidation).

Roger **SCRUTON** (Sexual Desire, 1986) rejects Foucault's claim that sexual morality is culturally **RELATIVE** and criticises Foucault for assuming that there could be societies in which a "problematisation" of the sexual did not occur.

"No history of thought could show the 'problematisation' of sexual experience to be peculiar to certain specific social formations: it is characteristic of personal experience generally, and therefore of every genuine social order". Roger Scruton, Sexual Desire

The fact that Leviticus chapter 18 defines a **PURITY CODE** which causes to stone to death adulterous women and homosexuals as evil doesn't mean that we don't have our own purity code (for example, found in the extreme disgust of paedophilia – a view different from the Greeks).

Gender as a Fluid Concept – Judith Butler (Gender Trouble)

Christianity has encouraged society to impose a **BINARY** (two-sided) relation of women and men. This is then **IDEALISED** as a **HETEROSEXUA**L form, and in the ideal of a two parent family.

Feminists reject the idea that **BIOLOGY** is **DESTINY** (link this to the **TELEOLOGICAL** view of human identity in Natural Law) , but then develop an account of patriarchal culture which assumed that masculine and feminine genders would inevitably be built up from 'male' and 'female' bodies, making the same destiny just as inescapable.

Butler (1956-) argues (with Simone de Beauvoir) that gender is a **SOCIAL CONSTRUCT**. The idea is not fixed, but fluid. Gender is created by repetition of a type of **BODY LANGUAGE** and social attitudes to rebellion (such as disgust at cross-dressing). With Foucault she sees sex (male, female) as causing gender **STEREOTYPES** (masculine, feminine) which is seen to cause desire (towards the other gender).

'There is no gender identity behind the expressions of gender; ... identity is performatively constituted by the very "expressions" that are said to be its results.' (Judith Butler, Gender Trouble, p. 25)

PERFORMATIVITY of gender is a stylised repetition of acts, an imitation or miming of the dominant **CONVENTIONS** of gender. "The act that one does, the act that one performs is, in a sense, an act that's been going on before one arrived on the scene" (Gender Trouble).

"Gender is an impersonation and becoming gendered involves impersonating an ideal that nobody actually inhabits" (Judith Butler, interview with Liz Kotz in Artforum).

"Performativity has to do with **REPETITION**, very often the repetition of oppressive and painful gender norms" (Judith Butler, Gender Trouble).

Butler calls for **SUBVERSIVE ACTION** in the present: 'gender trouble' -- the mobilisation, subversive confusion, and proliferation of genders -- and therefore identity. She would approve of the transgender movement and its forms of direct action and protest in the UK.

Gender and Women's Liberation

PARADOX in a world of liberation and increased rights we still have the silence surrounding Savile and Weinstein, incidence of domestic and other violence against women, and the continued inequalities in pay and promotion in the workplace. Key dates include:

- **1885** Married women could keep hold of their wealth which previously passed to the husband, so restricting divorce.

- **1864** Contagious Diseases Act reacts to prevalence of venereal disease amongst the armed forces (30%) by permitting "policeman to arrest prostitutes in ports and army towns and bring them in to have compulsory checks for venereal disease. If the women were suffering from sexually transmitted diseases they were placed in a locked hospital until cured". **JOSEPHINE BUTLER** launches protest movement at the labelling and degrading of women.

- **1914-18** Women occupy many men's jobs in armaments factories, but in 1918 Unions insist they are made redundant to make way for returning men.

- **1918** Women over 30 obtain the vote after eight year suffragette struggle.

- **1928** Women over 21 obtain the vote.

- **1960s** the Pill allows women to regulate fertility, (Queen Victoria had eight children) experienced by both upper and lower classes.

- **1967** Abortion Reform Act allows termination up to 28 weeks if certain criteria fulfilled. Mental health criterion easily the most popular.

- **1969** Divorce Reform Act allows divorce for 'irretrievable breakdown' rather than just proof of adultery.

- **2004** Gender Recognition Act allows you to apply for a Gender recognition Certificate and so legally change gender after psychiatric assessment for gender dysphoria.

- **2014** Gay couples can be legally married (but not in church).

- **2017** Church of England issues transgender guidance for its 4,700 schools - "pupils need to be able to play with the many cloaks of identity' and should be able 'to explore the many possibilities of who they might be" including gay, lesbian and transgender. "Transphobic bullying causes damage and leads to mental health disorders", Archbishop of Canterbury.

- **2017** a A Bill to make gender identity a protected characteristic under the Equality Act 2010 in place of gender reassignment and to make associated provision for transgender and other persons halted due to the election.

The Changing idea of Family

Comparing 2005 and 2015, we see a snapshot of a profound change in the concept of family continuing (from nuclear to reconstituted, and from **EXTENDED** to nuclear, and from two parent to one parent and from married to cohabiting).

You don't need to learn detailed statistics for A level.

However it may be worth knowing that the fastest growth has been in **COHABITING** couples followed by **LONE PARENT** families in the decade 2005-15. Married and civil partner families have not grown significantly in the ten year period. However, they are still the largest group overall at 8/19 million (42%). Only around a third of households have two people in them.

So we can say with confidence – families are much less likely to be presided over by a married couple than they were forty years ago – family life is far more **FRAGMENTED** and disparate (lone parent, reconstituted, gay or cohabiting, rather than married). Moreover there are many people of any gender living alone. There may be psychological and social **CONSEQUENCES** of these changes.

From **2014** gay people can legally marry (2% of total) – but overwhelmingly in non-religious services (gay couples can't get married in Church by church law).

Christian views on Gender Roles

Augustine on Gender Roles

In Confessions Augustine list of the qualities of his mother Monica - patience, mildness, obedience, selfless service of others, temperance, piety, and even an aversion to gossip, are **STEREOTYPICAL** feminine virtues and vices.

He also describes his long-term relationship with a **CONCUBINE**. Women have one of two roles – mother or lover. Unlike Aquinas, Augustine sees men and women of equal rational capacity , but women by nature submissive because they are **WEAKER**.

Elaine **PAGEL**'s (1989) analyses of the cultural implications of the doctrine of **ORIGINAL SIN** , especially the role of the story of the Fall in Genesis 3. Pagels lays the blame for Christian sexual repression and misogyny (woman hatred) on Augustine, arguing that Augustine's pessimistic views of sexuality, politics, and human nature would come to dominate in Western culture, and that

"Adam, Eve, and the serpent—our ancestral story— would continue, often in some version of its Augustinian form, to affect our lives to the present day." (Elaine Pagels, Adam, Eve and the Serpent, page 34)

Aquinas on Gender Roles

Aquinas follows **ST PAUL** (*1 Corinthians 11:10 "woman was created for the sake of man"*) in seeing women as **INTELLECTUALLY** inferior. Aquinas sees Ephesians 5:22 "the husband is head of the wife" by virtue of greater intellectual wisdom."Men are wiser and more discerning, and not so quickly taken in", he says.

In attempting to interpret **ARISTOTLE** Aquinas accepts his biological assertion that men are the **ACTIVE AGENT** in reproduction, and women the passive (submissive). It is part of **NATURAL LAW** that women are placed in submission to men – and have to obey men.

Luther (1483-1536) on Gender Roles

The creation of Adam and Eve is God's way of preventing human loneliness (**GENESIS 2**).

Adam and Eve were equals before God, and equally culpable in the **FALL**.

But (like Aquinas) Luther saw men as **SUPERIOR** and more guided by reason and destined to lead in life, and women destined to **SUBMIT.** Women had responsibilities for children and the home. The Lutheran view included equality in principle, but superiority and subordination in practice echoes the contradiction in **ST PAUL** (*Galatians 3:28 'there is neither male nor female'* **versus** *Ephesians 5:22 "wives submit to your husbands"*).

Luther formulated the doctrine of three estates, which divided society into church, family and state each governed by a **PATRIARCHAL** household as their ideal, i.e. a structure in which the father exercised authority but was also a caring protector. But the **REFORMATION** picture overall is more ambiguous.

MELANCTHON (1497-1560) had theological discussions with highly intelligent women. Luther emphasised that a father performs a Christian act when washing his children's dirty nappies, for example. He also expressed his patriarchal respect for his own wife by calling her Mr Kathy.

Modern Church on Gender Roles – Catholic, Liberal Protestant (USA)

The **EPISCOPALIAN** Church of America is the most **LIBERAL** of the Anglican communion of churches. They argue that gender matters because of language, imagery and power relations.

ESCHATOLOGICAL hope is for a future where gender ceases to matter – meantime we make small steps towards **JUSTICE** and **EQUALITY** for women.

"The expression of gender and sexuality are conditioned by culture and by experiences of oppression, especially as racial and ethnic diversity are considered" (Episcopalian Church, USA)

The structures of leadership, the language and the practices need to work together to transform the present.

In the Church of England, women priests were first ordained in **1993** and the first woman Bishop, Libby Lane, consecrated in **2015**. Currently there are 12/78 women Bishops (October 2017).

Christian Views on Social Changes

Linda **WOODHEAD** argues that a gap has opened up between Church Teaching and social attitudes on issues such as contraception and gay marriage. The church, faced with the challenge of **RELATIVISM,** has made increasingly tentative steps towards reform – and in the case of the **CATHOLIC** church, has held steadfastly in public to an orthodox (patriarchal) line.

So the increase in UK citizens identifying as **NO RELIGION** (in 2016 51%) does not equate to a lack of **SPIRITUALITY** but a rejection of orthodox forms of Christianity and the embracing of new forms of spirituality (such as New Age, meditation, mindfulness etc).

The Church of England continues to reject gay marriage in church, whilst taking a contradictory view on homosexual sex – gay priests must be celibate (but often in practice are not) whereas church members generally should be encouraged to be faithful to their partner.

In the Catholic church, research suggest only around 11% of Catholic women in the USA follow the prohibition on contraception and abortion, and 31% are on the pill – so fuelling allegations of **DOUBLE STANDARDS**. Meantime, in Africa **AIDS** infection remains endemic and safe sex officially discouraged by the Church.

CATHOLICS FOR CHOICE argues that "Abstinence before marriage and faithfulness in a marriage is beyond the realm of possibility here. The issue is to protect life. That must be our fundamental goal. African people must use condoms."

Christian Teaching – the Bible

Ephesians 5:22-33

EPHESIANS 5 needs to be interpreted in the context of a revolutionary document presented to a patriarchal culture. *"The apostolic letters are addressed to people living in an environment marked by that same traditional way of thinking and acting". "All the reasons in favour of the "subjection" of woman to man in marriage must be understood in the sense of a "mutual subjection" of both "out of reverence for Christ". Mulieris Dignitatem p 24*

Christian Teaching- Roman Catholic Mulieris Dignitatem (MD)

1971 Pope appoints commission to ensure "effective promotion of the dignity and the responsibility of women" culminates in 1988 in **MULIERIS DIGNITATEM** (of the vocation and dignity of women).

Reaffirms **IDEAL** of Mary as obedient and submissive handmaid of the Lord (Luke1:38), and pure virgin. Like Jesus himself, she is called to **SERVE**. She is the new **EVE** and the prototype of a **NEW CREATION**.

Also confirms the Creation order that "both man and woman are human beings to an equal degree, both are created in God's image". Genesis 1:28

Acknowledges the contradiction between two creation accounts (Genesis 1:28 versus Genesis 2:18-25). MD asserts, against traditional teaching, that

"The biblical text provides sufficient bases for recognising the essential equality of man and woman from the point of view of their humanity".
(Mulieris Dignitatem p14)

Word equality here does not mean 'equal rights' to exercise leadership in the church. Interpretation here is **RELATIONAL** and **TRINITARIAN**.

"Man - whether man or woman - is the only being among the creatures of the visible world that God the Creator "has willed for its own sake"; that creature is thus a person. Being a person means striving towards self-realisation (the Council text speaks of self-discovery), which can only be achieved "through a sincere gift of self". (Mulieris Dignitatem p16)

The model for this interpretation of the person is God himself as **TRINITY** (God in Three Persons) as a communion of Persons. To say that man is created in the **IMAGE** and likeness of God means that man is called to exist "for others, to become a gift", (Mulieris Dignitatem).

Affirms the feminine and masculine qualities of God eg "Can a woman forget her sucking child, that she should have no compassion on the son of her womb? Even these may forget, yet I will not forget you". (Isaiah 49:14-15).

The **FALL** 'obscures' and 'diminishes' the image of God but does not eliminate it. But consequences include pain (for women) and death for all. Man also 'shall have **DOMINION** (power) over women" (Genesis 3:16) as a part of the consequences of sin.

However, all 'unjust situations' should be remedied because the fundamental equality of Genesis 2 overrides the effects of the Fall in Genesis 3.

Gender differences need to be preserved as part of the **NATURAL CREATED ORDER**. even the rightful opposition of women to what is expressed in the biblical words "He shall rule over you" (Genesis 3:16) must not under any condition lead to the "masculinisation" of women. In the name of liberation from male "domination", women must not appropriate to themselves male characteristics contrary to their own feminine "originality".

Despite evidence of a new relationship to women reflected in Jesus actions and teachings, and the presence of women as the first witnesses of resurrection , MD reaffirms that

"Virginity and motherhood are two particular dimensions of the fulfilment of the female personality". (Mulieris Dignitatem p 17).

MARY DALY would see the depiction of women as virgin, mother or whore as part of the conditioning of **PATRIARCHY** whereas **DAPHNE HAMPSON** would see the complex interpretations of Mulieris Dignitatem as part of the **IRREDUCIBLY** patriarchal nature of historical Christianity, the Bible and all its interpretations which justify inequality (such as the Catholic teaching against women priests and bishops).

Possible Exam Questions

1. "Christians should resist current secular views of gender" Discuss

2. Evaluate the view that secular views of gender equality have undermined Christian gender roles

3. "Motherhood liberates rather than restricts". Discuss

4. Critically evaluate the view that idea of family is entirely culturally determined.

5. "Christianity follows where culture leads". Discuss

Key Quotes

"One is not born, but rather one becomes a woman…it is civilisation that produces this creature." Simone de Beauvoir.

"Gender is an impersonation . . . becoming gendered involves impersonating an ideal that nobody actually inhabits." Judith Butler, Gender Trouble

"My argument for the "moral significance" of gender is an extensive attack on the Kantian assumption behind modern feminism—the assumption that what I am essentially is a person, and that persons are essentially genderless." Roger Scruton, Sexual Desire

"There is no gender identity behind the expressions of gender; ... identity is performatively constituted by the very "expressions" that are said to be its results." Judith Butler, Gender Trouble

"Within Christianity, more than in any other religion, women have had a special dignity, of which the New Testament shows us many important aspects." Pope Paul VI

Gender and Theology

Background

Paradoxically, Christianity presents itself as a prophetic movement of liberation and belief in a **NEW HEAVEN** and a **NEW EARTH** redeemed by the faithful. Mary **DALY** and Daphne **HAMPSON** are post-Christians feminists who reject the very basis of Christianity and the Christian God-concept. Rosemary **RUETHER** remains a Catholic calling the church to repent and change.

A word of warning though: Christianity isn't one entity and it is dangerous to **GENERALISE**. The **MONTANISTS** of the second to sixth century had women leaders and prophets, and the **QUAKERS** of the past 400 years have always followed a priestless equality where anyone can speak a word from God. Perhaps Christianity (following Emperor **CONSTANTINE**'s conversion in 316) have become too enmeshed in the power structures of many societies to be a prophetic movement and has become a rather laggardly reflection of its times.

Specification

A level requires that we study Ruether's discussion of the maleness of Christ and its implications for salvation including:

- Jesus' challenge to the male **WARRIOR MESSIAH** expectation

- God as the female **WISDOM** principle

- Jesus as the **INCARNATION** of wisdom

Daly's claim that *'if God is male then the male is God' (1996:76)* and its implications for Christianity, including:

- Christianity's 'Unholy Trinity' of rape, genocide and war
  - spirituality experienced through nature

Key terms

- **APOCRYPHA:** That part of the Bible rejected by Protestant Christianity, but containing Wisdom literature which exalts the feminine.

- **ESCHATOLOGY:** The end times, traditionally a time in the future when God judges the world. In feminism, eschatology is realised now with judgement on patriarchy and formation of a new society.

- **FEMINISM:** A movement campaigning for the rights, empowerment and equality of women.

- **GENOCIDE:** The attempt to eliminate a race or a religious group by extreme violence and murder

- **GOD/ESS:** Ruether's genderless term for God

- **HERMENEUTICS:** The study of methods of interpretation and the textual generation of meaning

- **INCARNATION:** Embodiment of some value of goodness or aspect of God

- **MESSIAH:** The 'anointed one' sent by God in fulfilment of Old Testament prophecy to liberate and redeem Israel

- **MONTANISM:** prophetic movement in the second century where women prophesied and claimed visions directly from Christ.

- **PATRIARCHY:** (Two Latin words, pater/arche) rule of the male. A form of society where men dominate, denigrate and oppress women.

- **SEXISM:** Prejudice, stereotyping, or discrimination, typically against women, on the basis of sex.

- **SHEKINAH:** The glory of God which traditionally shone forth from the altar, expelled by patriarchy and rediscovered in the Exodus community of women.

- **SPIRITUALITY:** Response to the metaphysical reality beyond the physical, where the individual forms patterns of self-determination that build the common good.

Structure of Thought

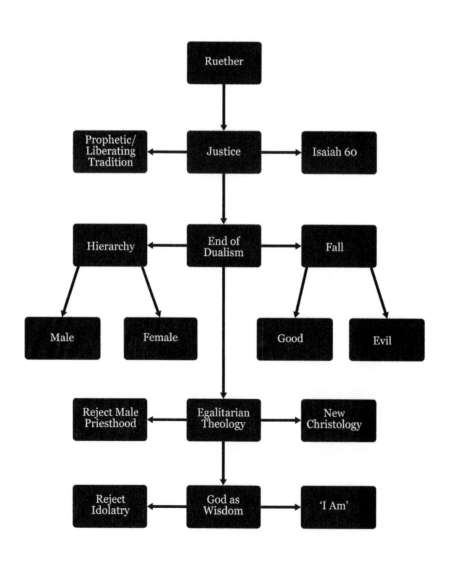

Hermeneutics of Suspicion

Paul **RICOEUR** (1913-2005) asks us to adopt a **HERMENEUTIC OF SUSPICION** when reading a text such as the Bible. We need to be suspicious of the **MOTIVES**, the **VALUES**, the culture of those who wrote it, and not just project our own values onto the text. James O'Donnell comments

"Liberation means, therefore, to opt for the exercise of an ideological suspicion in order to unmask the unconscious ideological structures which dominate and which favour a powerful, privileged minority." (O'Donnell 1982:32)

There is a **WORLD BEHIND** the text (the culture of Jesus' day) and there is a world **IN FRONT** of the text, our own culture. These **TWO HORIZONS** (Gadamer's term) need to merge in a valid interpretation that is **CRITICAL**.

Elizabeth Schüssler **FIORENZA** argues that theology is the product of each writer's experience and that this is determined by the historical and **SOCIAL CONTEXT** of every theologian. Theology is culturally conditioned and shapes, reflects, and serves a particular group's or individual's interests, (Fiorenza 1975:616).

Ruether argues that the Bible is riddled with **PATRIARCHY** and emerged from a world of hierarchy with males in charge. The **FEMININE** is constructed from these patriarchal values.

The social relationships are **ARCHAIC** and inappropriate for our time: they are reflected in a male clergy and a continued tolerance of **INJUSTICE** and **INEQUALITY**.

Behind the interpretation of the Bible lies the acceptance of **ARISTOTLE**'s biology that sees men and women as two separate classes of human and whereby

"The female is not only secondary to the male but lacks full human status in physical strength, moral self-control, and mental capacity. The lesser "nature" thus confirms the female's subjugation to the male as her "natural" place in the universe". (Ruether 1985:65)

Ruether's Hermeneutic

Controlling principle – whatever denigrates women is rejected, whatever builds up and values women is accepted. Then it is **EXPERIENCE** (rather than history) which is the starting-point of theology. The Bible needs to be interpreted anew, and the story of **REDEMPTION** retold in the light of women's experience. This may be linked to the **EXISTENTIAL** theology of Paul **TILLICH**.

There is a **PROPHETIC PRINCIPLE** in the Bible which can be rediscovered and brought to the fore: emphasising **JUSTICE** and the call to be a new people of **LIBERATION. ISAIAH 60** gives a radical vision of a just world order.

"God's Shekinah, Holy Wisdom, the Mother-face of God has fled from the high thrones of patriarchy and has gone into exodus with us". Ruether, 1985:87

The counter-culture of early Christianity which emphasised this were suppressed, for example, the female **PROPHETS** Priscilla and Maximilla in **MONTANISM.** Priscilla claimed a night vision in which Christ slept by her side "in the form of woman, clad in a bright garment". She adopted a priestly ministry with direct voices and visions from God. Montanists were persecuted and ultimately suppressed with violence in the sixth century.

SEXISM is a sin against God/ess and against the fundamental golden thread of **JUSTICE** within the Bible.

"The dominant Christian tradition, if corrected by feminism, offers viable categories for interpreting human existence and building redemptive communities" Ruether, 1985:123

Ruether's God-Concept

GOD/ESS is the ground of all being. God is **GENDERLESS** and to turn God into the **MALE** is a form of **IDOLATRY** that serves men's interests.

In the **OLD TESTAMENT**, **YAHWEH** is the name of God – it means 'no name' or I **AM WHO I AM**.

Patriarchy encourages **HIERARCHY** with the idea of **TRANSCENDENCE**. Ruether emphasises **IMMANENCE** – God as **BEING** within all things.

Ruether sees God as **WISDOM** – the Greek word **LOGOS** and the idea in **WISDOM** literature (the Book of Wisdom is part of the **APOCRYPHA** – not in the Protestant Bible). **GOD/ESS** has sources in **PAGANISM**, and Babylonian **CREATION** myths – but the **MOTHER NATURE** idea was suppressed by the early Church.

LANGUAGE reflects patriarchal values – **FATHER**, Lord, King. "**OUR FATHER…THY KINGDOM COME**".

Can a Male Saviour Save?

Jesus' **GENDER** is irrelevant. Maleness of Christ has no **THEOLOGICAL** significance. The **MESSIAH** is an iconoclastic (idol-smashing) **PROPHET** in the tradition of **ISAIAH** or **AMOS**.

The real Jesus needs to be rediscovered and the Church should **REPENT** and cast off patriarchal values and images. Jesus is the I**NCARNATE WISDOM** of God (**LOGOS**, John 1).

Such a rediscovery embraces a new relation to the earth (link with Mary Daly's **GYN/ECOLOGY**). Feminism is, says Daly, **BIOPHILIC** (loves life). This creative thinking creates communities of liberation who engage in play of ideas. Ruether agrees.

The New Age and the Eschatological Community

Does not lie in the future, **ESCHATOLOGICALLY** as in patriarchal ideas – beyond the grave. Link with theological **IMMANENCE** (God is here now, the new community is realised here, now)

It is brought into being now in the **REDEEMED COMMUNITY – REALISED ESCHATOLOGY**.

Ruether believes church can be redeemed by forming new **BASE COMMUNITIES** with **JUSTICE** at their heart. **CLERICALISM** (male priesthood) is a product of patriarchy and should be rejected.

Early Church experiments such as **MONTANISM** (2nd century) had women leaders: in Acts there is a prophetess, and Paul's argument "I do not allow women to have authority in the Church" (1 Corinthians) only makes sense in context of the rise of women **PROPHETS** in Corinth and discord that surrounded it.

Criticisms of Ruether

In a 1986 debate, Daphne Hampson makes three criticisms of Ruether's position (acronym **HIS**).

- **Historical** Roots of Christianity are Sexist. Ruether ignores the historically-entrenched nature of Christianity, which 'necessarily has one foot in the past'. Incarnation means that God became a human being at a particular time, within a patriarchal worldview. That Jesus only chose male apostles may be no accident. Hampson concludes that 'it cannot be the case that God is related in a particular way to a certain history'. Like Daly, Hampson is a post-Christian. Anthony Thiselton agrees:

"Some texts, by their very nature, draw part of their meaning from the actions, history and life with which they are inextricably interwoven"; Thiselton, New Horizons pg 66.

- **Incarnational** Doctrine is sexist. God 'sent his son'. Metaphors for God are male (with a few exceptions that are never developed). God calls Jesus 'My Beloved Son, whom I have chosen,' and asks Jesus' followers to 'listen to him' (Luke 9:35). Christian creeds ask us to affirm belief in "Jesus Christ, his only Son, our Lord'. Lord and Son are both patriarchal images.

- **Symbolic** world is sexist. The revelation of Christ in history is full of patriarchal symbols and messages. The Prodigal Son is having property divided between two men (Luke 15:11-35). The Good Samaritan is a male. When Jesus visits Martha and Mary, Mary is busy cooking and Martha commended for sitting passively at Jesus' feet, (Luke 1:38-42). Women who were Resurrection witnesses were not believed because the testimony of women is unreliable. Moreover, Paul is a Rabbi and retains some of the Levitical symbolic world of Rabbinic Judaism. Hampson points out 'we do not have stories of a man sitting at the feet of a female teacher'. When stories circulate in Corinth of women prophets, Paul seeks to suppress the upsurge by writing two letters to the Corinthians, both against women's liberation, insisting 'women keep silent in church' (1 Corinthians 14:34-5).

Hampson therefore accuses Ruether of misrepresenting the profoundly historical nature of Christian patriarchy, which still affects Christian theology and practice. Hampson is a **POST-CHRISTIAN**, Ruether a Christian **LIBERATION** theologian.

Mary Daly - Radical Feminism

Mary Daly (1928-2010) was a radical lesbian feminist theologian who taught at **BOSTON COLLEGE**. She almost always refused to let men into her classes, in 1999, a male student sued the school for discrimination. Daly was suspended and ultimately refused to comply. She also stated she found men disruptive. Lawrence Cunningham calls her 'the gold standard of **ABSOLUTE FEMINISM**."

The Myths that Bolster Patriarchy

Daly argues that male **MYTH-MAKERS** constructed an image of the feminine to mould women for their own purposes. The male is the **ROBBER** who robs women of "their myths, their energy, their divinity, their very selves". **PATRIARCHY** has 'stolen our **COSMOS** and turned it into Cosmopolitan magazine" and is the prevailing religion of the entire planet, whose essential message is **NECROPHILIA** (love of **DEATH** eg crucifixion and **MORTIFICATION** - putting our sins to death by self-flagellation).

She calls women to have the courage 'to see and to be' and represent the greatest challenge to the religions of the world. The ultimate **SIN** is patriarchal religion; yet women are **COMPLICIT** by living out the role of the submissive **OTHER**, represented in Christianity as **WEAK, OBEDIENT, DEPRAVED**. As in **AQUINAS'** thought, men are **SUPERIOR, WISE, STRONG, RATIONAL**.

The Patriarchal God

The language of the **FATHER** God legitimates male supremacy and oppression of women – "as God is male the male becomes god".

She rejects the God-image of Christianity in favour of participation in an **ULTIMATE REALITY** - a God-concept 'beyond and beneath'. The **IMAGE** of **GOD** is the creative potential in all human beings. In this **TRANSFORMATION** of symbols of God, God is transformed from a **NOUN (FATHER, LORD)** to a verb who is "form-destroying, form-creating, transforming power that makes all things new" (Daly, Beyond God the Father). God is **BEING** and **BECOMING**. We might describe this as a rejection of the Christian God and a rediscovery of earlier feminine god-concepts.

Myth of the Feminine

Daly accuses **AUGUSTINE** and **AQUINAS** of misogyny (women hatred) as they deny women the power to reach their full potential.

The male constructs the feminine as the originator of **EVIL** in the myth of the **FALL** and its interpretations. **EVE** is represented as the **SCAPEGOAT** of male sexual guilt. Daly encourages women to enter a new Fall - a **FALL** into **FREEDOM**, involving eating the forbidden fruit of **WISDOM** all over again. Two images of women: the **VIRGIN** and the **WHORE**, represented in the image of the **PURE VIRGIN MARY** and the fallen **MARY MAGDALENE**.

- **MARY** = the impossible virgin (still submissive to the will of the Father-God)

- **MARY MAGDALENE** (the fallen woman) = all other women cast in the image of the fallen **EVE**.

Daly calls women to stop playing the role of meek, subservient 'complement' to men, to re-imagine their power and renew the world.

Yet the virgin **MARY** can be adopted by feminism as a symbol of the **AUTONOMOUS** woman, the first woman to fall into **PARADISE**. Mary echoes back to a pre-Christian era of the **GREAT GODDESS**.

The Scapegoat Christ

Daly believes Jesus was simply a limited human being. It is **IDOLATRY** to suggest a **MALE** saviour can represent the eternal **BEING** which is God. Jesus is portrayed by patriarchy as the **SCAPEGOAT** for the sins originating in **EVE**, and the twin idealisations of **CHRIST** and **MARY** have nothing to do with history.

The projection of our evil onto these twin figures of **PURITY** results from an **INABILITY** to accept our own guilt. Feminism rejects the **SCAPEGOAT** Christ with its projections of **VICTIMHOOD** and the worship of the violence of the **CROSS** as part of the **NECROPHILIA** (love of **DEATH**) of patriarchy.

In the development of patriarchy, the male priest becomes the sole mediator controlling access to the deity. Women need to affirm **BIOPHILIA** (love of life).

A Fall into the Sacred

Women in exercising their **FREEDOM** and **POWER** fall into a new sacred space, a **SECOND COMING**, escaping the false **PARADISE** of patriarchal enslavement. They practise **BECOMING** by renouncing the traditional dichotomy of **HETEROSEXUAL/HOMOSEXUAL**, which are patriarchal classifications, to live in an environment that is "beyond, beneath and all around".

Women empowered cut loose from the **PSYCHOSEXUAL** chains that bind them to a patriarchal set of images, and a patriarchal power structure. Women are by nature **ANTI-CHURCH** with its over-emphasis on sexual and gender differences. Women have to 'live now the freedom we are fighting for', and **FEAR** and **GUILT** are no longer used as weapons of oppression. She calls both men and women to leave the church and become "an **EXODUS** community prepared to get on with the business of **LIVING**". Indeed men may understand the manipulation of **POWER** better as they see it from **WITHIN**.

"Male religion entombs women in sepulchres of silence in order to chant its own eternal and dreary dirge to a past that never was". Mary Daly, Beyond God the Father, page 145

Ultimately Daly believes in a new **COSMIC COVENANT** – which renounces the old order of meaningless desires, violence and war.

Gyn/Ecology

Daly plays on words to encourage women to 'weave tapestries of our own kind". She rages against the oppressive system in which "patriarchy is the homeland of males" and where they oppress and demonise women in rites of **SUTTEE** or **WITCH-BURNING**.

She analyses the **LANGUAGE** of patriarchy and the mind/body/spirit **POLLUTION** this has brought about. **PHALLIC** myths predominate – from the Coca-Cola advert for the **REAL THING** to the Christian hymns glorying in the **DEATH** and real presence of Christ. With spiritual pollution comes pollution of the planet – as the male 'threatens to **TERMINATE** life on the planet through rape (of nature), genocide and war'.

"If life is to survive on this planet, there must be a decontamination of the Earth. I think this will be accompanied by an evolutionary process that will result in a drastic reduction of the population of males." (Gyn/Ecology page 54)

To escape the enslavement and **DENIGRATION** of the male, women need to invent a **NEW LANGUAGE** and set of social relations. Using **CREATIVE ANGER** and **BRILLIANT BRAVERY**, women rediscover 'our **WOMEN-LOVING** love". "We find our original Being and we SPIN our original **INTEGRITY**" and so put **POWER** and JOY back into living.

On contraception she comments, showing her playful use of language:

"It is obvious to Hags that few gynaecologists recommend to their heterosexual patients the most foolproof of solutions, namely Misterectomy. The Spinsters who propose this way by our be-ing, liv-ing, speak-ing can do so with power precisely

Criticisms of Daly

- Black theologian Audre **LOURDE** criticised Daly for refusing to acknowledge the '**HERSTORY** and myth' of women of colour. The severe oppression they have suffered greatly outweighs the discrimination of white women. There's a racial bias to Daly's work and a racist indifference to the plight of minorities who suffer greatest oppression.

- Patriarchy cannot assist in explaining why only a few men in a patriarchy use violence against women and why many males have campaigned for women's rights over the centuries (the first man being Jesus himself who overthrew aspects of anti-women purity code of **LEVITICUS**).

- Daly wanted **WOMEN** to rule men and was herself a lesbian and vegetarian. "I really don't care about men" she commented in an interview. Yet isn't this perpetuating the **DUALISM** she herself rejects as oppressive?

- The **FRAMEWORK** of Patriarchy is assumed in all instances. There is no other explanation given for witch-burning (Christian) or suttee (Hindu). Paradoxically, Enlightenment enquiry provoked an upsurge of interest in alchemy and other forms of magic: it is arguably the flip-side of the stress on autonomous reason. James I wrote a book on witches.

- People who criticise her she calls "**FEMBOTS** doing Daddy's work".

- No analysis of class, wealth or race as instruments of oppression of women.

Confusions to Avoid

1. **Feminists cannot be Christians**. Feminists like Ruether argue that Christianity can be restored to a lost **PROPHETIC** movement, transforming society, but only if patriarchy is rejected. A male saviour is irrelevant to salvation and the male perspective is a gloss overlaying the true gospel, which can be reconstructed as a gospel of liberation and hope. However, both Daphne Hampson and Mary Daly call women out of the church and see Christianity as irredeemably patriarchal. They are post-Christian feminists.

2. **The Church has no response to feminism**. This isn't a fair assessment because the Protestant churches have reformed themselves and allowed women priests and bishops (where appropriate to their order of ministry). The Church of England ordained women **PRIESTS** in 1993 and women **BISHOPS** in 2013. The Roman Catholic Church produced a brave apologetic for its position in not allowing women priests and bishops in Mulieris Dignitatem, which lay great emphasis on the equality of the sexes, but failed to reconcile the **CONTRADICTION** in the Bible between the Paul of Galatians (there is neither male nor female) and the Paul of Ephesians and Corinthians (wives obey your husbands, and "I do not allow women to have authority over a man'). Moreover, the Catholic persistence in advocating the **RHYTHM** method of contraception suggests that the **AUTONOMY** of women and their right to choose is still being overridden by the male perspective.

3. **A male saviour cannot save**. This extreme position, taken by Mary Daly, would appear to overlook the revolutionary attitude of Jesus towards women whom he included in his inner circle and addressed as equals – "daughter, your faith has made you well, go in peace" (Mark 5). Arguably when Jesus 'emptied himself taking the

form of a servant' (Philippians 2:7), he also gave up the genderless **INFINITY** of God (Yahweh – means 'I am who I am'). God cannot have a gender and so if Jesus is one with God his gender must be irrelevant for salvation. Messiah is a genderless idea. Emphasis on the gender of Christ and the virginity of Mary comes later as the male-dominated church hierarchy produces creeds which impose uniformity on belief and cast out so-called heretics, such as the **MONTANISTS**.

Possible Exam Questions

1. 'A male saviour cannot save'. Discuss with reference to the theologies of Rosemary Ruether and Mary Daly.

2. "If God is male the male is God'. Discuss

3. Critically contrast the theologies of Ruether and Daly.

4. "The Church is irrevocably patriarchal'. Discuss

5. "God is genderless, and so the idea of the Father-God is idolatry". Discuss

6. "Only a spirituality of women can save the planet from environmental degradation and war'. Discuss

Key Quotes

"If God is male then the male is God' Mary Daly (1996:76)

"It is obvious to Hags that few gynaecologists recommend to their heterosexual patients the most foolproof of solutions, namely Misterectomy". Mary Daly (Gyn/Ecology p239)

"The dominant Christian tradition, if corrected by feminism, offers viable categories for interpreting human existence and building redemptive communities". Rosemary Ruether, 1985:123

"Some texts, by their very nature, draw part of their meaning from the actions, history and life with which they are inextricably interwoven". Anthony Thiselton, New Horizons pg 66.

"The female is not only secondary to the male but lacks full human status in physical strength, moral self-control, and mental capacity. The lesser "nature" thus confirms the female's subjugation to the male as her "natural" place in the universe". Rosemary Ruether (1985:65)

The Night Before the Exam

I have assumed throughout his book that you are an exam candidate, and so I want to write a chapter for you to read the night before the exam, which distills the advice we have been trying to demonstrate here.

Essentially there are two methods of writing essays on Philosophy, Ethics and Christian Thought.

METHOD 1: The thesis approach **TIDE** (**T**hesis, **I**nterpretation, **D**evelopment, **E**valuation)

In this approach, discussed in the second chapter, we state our thesis (conclusion) early in the first paragraph. We then develop the thesis in the body of the essay, illustrating it briefly and intelligently and presenting contrasting views if we so wish, (which we reject with good reasons). The thesis is then restated in a slightly fuller way (to reflect the careful analysis that precedes it) as a conclusion. **We should use this method when we are confident we understand the question and its implications**.

METHOD 2: The 'ask questions about the question' approach **AQUAQ**

Quite often we may not be very confident about what the question is driving at. If this is the case, then we must adopt the tactic of interrogating the question or asking questions about the question. I suggest we ask three questions and then spend a paragraph answering each one before coming to a conclusion. Each question focuses on one element of the exam question. **We should use this method when we are not fully confident about what the question involves.**

An example might help here. Suppose I have a question on ethics which asks:

"The ethical issues around euthanasia cannot be resolved without first resolving the issue of the sanctity of human life".

What are the ethical issues surrounding euthanasia? How and with what ethical tools are these issues resolved? What is meant by the concept of 'sanctity of life'? These three questions (none of which have a single answer), woven into an opening paragraph, give the answer a clear, relevant structure - and the thesis should emerge as we develop our essay. The conclusion is then presented as our own answer to these three questions, perhaps arrived at by contrasting the views of specific philosophers and setting up two ethical theories to see how the idea of personhood is relevant to each.

An equivalent example in Philosophy might address the title "Religious Language is meaningless.", Discuss. The questions you might ask in your opening paragraph might include: What do we mean by religious language? Are there different rules for religious language when compared to everyday language? How is the word 'meaning' to be understood?

When you arrive in the exam room, you must follow the steps set out here. *It is usually a mistake to launch straight into your answer without first structuring your approach.*

Read every question and highlight key words

Every year candidates make the fundamental error of learning a previous essay off by heart and then regurgitating it in the exam. And every year the examiner complains that candidates did not answer the question. So take a highlighter pen in with you and

1. Highlight all the **trigger/command** words (words like "explain", "to what extent", "discuss"). And then

2. Highlight any words that are **unusual** or unexpected.

If the trigger word is **explain** it is not asking us to **evaluate.** For example "explain the main principles of classical utilitarianism" has the unusual word "classical" in there. By focusing on this word and highlighting it, you are forced to ask the question "what is classical utilitarianism?" and so there is at least a chance that you will avoid the irrelevance of talking about Peter Singer, who is a modern utilitarian.

For Philosophy, sometimes a very specific question is asked to highlight an aspect of an argument, for example, 'Explain Descartes' ontological argument for the existence of God'. It won't gain marks if you go through other ontological arguments as this is not what the question is asking (you could highlight one or two differences, but only to stress the points that Descartes is making). Remember that when a scholar is mentioned in the syllabus, the question can be entirely addressed to that scholar - so the night before go through the syllabus check which scholars might come up.

But (just to be absolutely clear about this) at **A level** we are expected to interweave analysis and evaluation, and this is made clear by trigger words such as "discuss", "assess" or "to what extent".

"Sometimes texts fail me"

Sketch out your thesis/ key questions about the question

Always make sure there is some additional loose paper on your desk (put your hand up before the exam starts and request it). Then sketch out quickly your thesis, the main points you need to develop it, and any illustrations you may use. If you are genuinely unsure about the question, don't worry: every other candidate is probably unsure as well. Then use method 2 and ask three questions about the question and impose your own interpretation on it. You will gain credit by this considered and well-directed line which will then emerge as your answer.

My strong advice would be to practise sequencing ideas before the exam, and to have you own mind-map prepared and memorised which you can quickly sketch on a piece of paper as a memory aid.

Be bold in your answer

It's surprising how many candidates come up with statements such as "there are many arguments for and against the ontological argument, and the issue remains difficult to resolve". This is a form of intellectual cowardice which gains no marks at all. Be bold in what you argue, and try hard to justify your approach with good, solid reasons. It is the quality of the argument which gains credit in philosophical writing, not the conclusion you arrive at. Of course, it essential that the conclusion follows.

Analyse, don't just assert

It is tempting to throw down everything you know about, say, utilitarianism in a series of unconnected assertions.

"Utilitarianism is teleological, consequentialist and relativistic. It sets up the Greatest Happiness Principle. Utilitarians also believe the end justifies the means."

These are just assertions which are peppered liberally with what we call technical language (that is language no-one in the real world ever uses). Notice that the above opening few lines demonstrate no understanding and no analytical ability. Instead we should be aiming to write more like this:

"Utilitarianism is a theory of rational desire which holds to one intrinsic good: pleasure or happiness. By the greatest happiness principle utilitarians seek to maximise this good in two ways: they seek to maximise net happiness (happiness minus misery) for the maximum number of people. So it is an aggregating theory, where goodness is added up from individual desires to produce an overall maximum good in which "everyone counts as one" (Bentham)."

You should avoid phrases like 'this famous philosopher' and 'this issue has been debated for centuries'. Is this true? How would we know? Avoid these kinds of broad, sweeping generalisations.

Illustrate your argument

I remember reading an exam report at University which mentioned that one candidate had been highly commended in an essay on utilitarianism for discussing the case of Captain Oates who, during Scott's doomed Antarctic expedition in 1912, walked out of the storm-bound tent in order to sacrifice himself to save his friends, with the words "I may be gone some considerable time". It's an interesting example because it suggests that a utilitarian could be capable of heroic sacrifice rather than the usual illustration candidates give of torturing a terror suspect to find a bomb location.

Spend a few moments working out which examples you will discuss to illustrate key theories and their application. You can pre-prepare them especially in Ethics, and in Philosophy of Religion you can pre-prepare the contrasting arguments which philosophers bring to many of the syllabus areas.

In Philosophy of Religion this advice applies especially to areas such as religious language and the analogies told by Flew (Wisdom's gardener), Hare (three blik illustrations) and Mitchell, (The Stranger), though be concise in how you illustrate these examples - always make them serve the point you are making and not the other way round.

What is the examiner looking for?

In summary the examiner is looking for three things:

Relevance - every sentence linked to the question set and to your main thesis.

Coherence - every sentence and paragraph should "hang together' or cohere. The linkages should be clear as the analysis proceeds.

Clarity - your style should be clear, and in the context, the philosophical vocabulary you use should be clear. You don't necessarily have to define every technical word, but if it does need a little clarification, you can always use brackets for economy. For example:

"Utilitarianism is a teleological (end-focused) theory combining an idea of intrinsic goodness (pleasure) with a method of assessing that goodness by considering consequences".

An example in philosophy would be:

"The Falsification Principle argues that for any statement to be treated as a proposition we must simply be able to deny at least one state of affairs. In contrast the principle of verification requires us to affirm all outcomes by expanding criteria for verification, (and in doing so in our attempt to verify conclusively, 'dying the death of a thousand qualifications', as Flew notes)."

Appendix of Technical Terms

Here are definitions of every technical term mentioned in the OCR specification H573/1/2/3.

a posteriori - means 'after experience', or 'from observation'. A posteriori arguments include the teleological argument, and the ethical theory of natural law, which derives goodness from observed rational tendencies God has designed into us.

a priori - means 'before experience". A priori arguments proceed by logical deduction, for example the ontological argument for God's existence, or Kant's theory of ethics.

absolutism - 'absolute' means one of three things - a theory is universal (applies to everyone) or that a principle is non-negotiable (unchanging) or that it is objective - tested empirically so beyond dispute.

act utilitarianism - the utility of an act is its ability to maximise happiness and minimise pain - tested by applying the greatest happiness principle to likely consequences of a single action.

agape - one of the four loves of Greek ethics, meaning unconditional commitment to friend and stranger, as in Jesus' saying 'greater agape has no-one than this, that a person lay down his life for his friends" (John 15:13). It is both the foundation principle of situation ethics, and a vital issue in Christian moral principles (Christian Thought).

analogy of attribution - Aquinas' view that you can say God is like blazing sun (attribute of purity and light). But it's an analogy because there isn't a precise one for one likeness between God and the attribute of light. As God is the cause of all good things, God's attributes are simply on a higher level to our own. Hick gave examples of 'upwards' analogy of attribution, such as speaking of a dog's faithfulness as analogical to the faithfulness of God.

anaphatic (or apophatic) way - a philosophical approach to theology which asserts that no finite concepts or attributes can be adequately used of God, but only negative terms, such as immortal, immutable or invisible. Apophasis means 'denial, negation' and so 'apophatic' is another word for anaphatic.

analogy of proper proportion - A plant has a life, a human has life, God has life - there is a proportionate relationship between each life mentioned in the list, with God's being the greatest and the plants being on a proportionately lower level.

attributes - (divine) qualities of God's character such as omnibenevolence, omnipotence and omniscience. Notice these can be expressed positively as in the via positiva or negatively as in the via negativa (God is immortal, so not mortal, invisible, so not visible).

categorical imperative - A term Kant employs to express an unconditional, absolute maxim or command - an imperative like 'never lie!'

category error - applying a category from one form of life to another which it cannot refer to - such as 'what colour is the wind?" The wind never has a colour.

230

cognitive approaches to language - an imposition on the debate on religious and ethical language from the Enlightenment concern for verification and 'meaningfulness' - cognitive approaches examine the truth value of statements according to their verifiability (testability by experience). So 'examination of the truth-aptness of statements'.

conscientia - Aquinas' one of two words for conscience, meaning 'reason making right decisions', he other being 'synderesis', for example, judging what to do in natural law theory when two goods conflict and we need to judge how to apply the principle of double effect means applying the judgement of reason.

corporate social responsibility - a theory developed by Edward Freeman which states that corporations should take responsibility for the consequences of their actions for all stakeholders and for the environment, and not just shareholders.

cosmological - to do with first causes - the cosmological argument is concerned to establish God as first cause of everything (as first muted by Aristotle's prime mover).

divine law - one of the four laws of natural law ethics, sees the inaccessible eternal law revealed to us in two ways by God - by divine law (the Bible) and natural law (morality). Echoes here of Plato's Forms of the good and Kant's noumenal (inaccessible) realm of reality.

efficient cause - one of Aristotle's four causes which implies the process by which something comes into being - eg the sculptor forms the clay to make his art.

ego - one of Freud's three classifications of the human psyche, the ego is the reality principle which forms as we realise how to present ourselves to the public world, even with the contradictions and conflicts within us.

election - the belief that God, with no regard to the will of man, made an eternal choice of certain persons to have eternal life and some to eternal damnation and that number is so fixed that it cannot be changed. Popular view in Calvinism.

emotivism - a theory of ethical language developed by AJ Ayer from the logical positivists of the Vienna Circle, which concludes that all ethical statements are simply expressions of emotion and have no factual (cognitive, truth-apt) content.

empiricism - the view that the meaningfulness and truth conditions of experience are required to test our knowledge of reality. Their views affect both issues of language and of testability, but as the empiricist Hume concedes there is a problem in induction - we cannot finally prove the sun will rise tomorrow.

eternal law - one fo the four laws of Aquinas' natural law which refers to the inaccessible mind and purposeful design of God, whose blueprint is only partially revealed to us.

exclusivism - a view in the debate about theological pluralism which states that Jesus is the only 'way, the truth and the life' as in John 14:6.

extramarital sex - sexual relations outside marriage between at least one married person and another (irrespective of gender).

fall - the Fall of humankind in Genesis 3 occurred when Eve disobeyed God by taking the fruit fro the tree of knowledge and giving it to Adam, who disobeys by eating it. In consequence, they are expelled from Eden, Eve gets pain in childbirth and Adam finds weeds growing in the garden as God's curse - also Adam 'has dominion' over Eve and she 'desires him' - Augustine sees this as the moment lust (cupiditas) enters the world.

fallacy - a mistake in deductive logic when one thing doesn't follow from another. In the naturalistic fallacy (meta-ethics) the fallacy is that we move from is statements to ought statements without supplying an answer to the question - this may be pleasurable, but what exactly makes it good?

falsificationism - conditions by which a proposition may be considered false, for example, the proposition 'the sun will rise tomorrow' can be falsified because the sun may not rise tomorrow.

five ways - the five proofs in Aquinas for the existence of God which include - the unmoved mover, the first cause, the argument from necessity (contingency), the argument from degree, and the argument from ends (the teleological argument). All these are forms of cosmological argument. Richard Dawkins criticisms of Aquinas' argument has been challenged by Keith ward and Alister McGrath.

formal cause - the concept in the mind of the sculptor before he takes the clay (material cause), sculpts (efficient cause) and produces a work of art (final cause). the formal cause of the existence of the universe is part of God's eternal law in natural law ethics.

formula of kingdom of ends - Kant's formal principe, that defines goodness, that we should so act as to imagine ourselves a lawmaker in a kingdom of ends, with the consistent rules that would follow.

formula of law of nature (law) - Kant's formula that we should act according to a maxim which can be willed as a universal law for the whole fo humanity.

formula of the end in itself (ends) - Kant's formula, often misquoted, that we should treat people not simply as a means to an end, but always also as an end in themselves. He never said as Fletcher states - don't treat people as means, but only as ends.

globalisation - the process of opening up global markets and global culture so that people trade, interchange and share products, views, and values freely and without restrictions.

grace - God's generous gifts to humanity of love, sustaining power, and life itself. Jesus is described as 'full of grace and truth' (John 1:14). Closely linked to the character of God int he Old Testament of hesed (Hebrew - steadfast love) and emeth (Hebrew - truth or faithfulness).

hedonic calculus - Bentham's way of calculating the balance of pleasure over pain in an action by seven criteria - things such as intensity, extent and duration of the pleasure.

hypothetical imperative - a command with an 'if' in it - if you are faced with an axe murderer asking after your friend, you should lie (a famous Kantian example). Kant felt morality was based on categorical absolutes, not conditional statements with an 'if' making them relative to circumstances.

id - Freud's term for the part of the psyche which follows the pleasure principle of satisfying needs and desires, typified by the screaming baby.

inclusivism - a term in religious pluralism which means that all ways (religions) lead to God, and no one path excludes others. Hick's universal pluralism is an example.

innate - means 'born with' and so in natural law ethics we are all born with a tendency to do good and avoid evil a kind of inbuilt knowledge called synderesis.

intuitionism - a theory of goodness that holds that we know right and wrong by intuition, a kind of inbuilt perception. GE Moore argues that good is an indefinable, non-reducible, simple property of an action which we just recognise like the colour yellow.

invincible ignorance - ignorance of sin and morality which Aquinas believes gives us an excuse, for example, because we have never heard of Jesus or the Bible.

limited election - the argument that only certain people will be saved - either those predestined (Calvin) or those who have repented and chosen to believe (general Protestant view)

material cause - the stuff something is made of, such as clay in a sculpture.

materialism - a Marxist idea that human beings have been reduced to an object which is in fundamental conflict with other objects, particularly the capitalist against the worker where both are 'objectified'. Also refers more generally to a human desire and obsession to get wealth.

messiah - the 'anointed one', and the hope of Israel that one day 'a son is born, a son is given who shall be called wonderful counsellor, Mighty God, Prince of Peace'. In the Person of Christ section of Christian Thought, the debate about whether Jesus thought himself the special one (Messiah) in a divine sense and what the title 'Son of God' actually meant.

meta-ethics - 'beyond ethics' so the language and meaning of ethical terms, and questions of the foundation of ethics, whether it is naturalistic (something in the world) or non-naturalistic.

metaphysics - beyond physics and so that which is not observable/measurable by science, such as truth, beauty and love (includes God, of course).

mystical experience - experience that cannot be explained by science or medicine, such as the visions of St Teresa of Avila, or Paul's meeting Christ on the road to Damascus in Acts.

natural knowledge - knowledge that can be gained from observing nature. The teleological argument, that God has designed patterns into nature, is an inference from natural knowledge.

natural law - a theory of ethics originating from Aristotle and developed by Aquinas, that human beings have a true rational purpose designed into them, observable a posteriori by the goals we by our nature's pursue. The 'unofficial moral theology of the Catholic Church' (Singer).

natural religion - religion based on reason rather than divine revelation, especially deism which became popular during the Enlightenment.

naturalism - a debate in meta-ethics about the foundation of ethics, whether it exists in the natural world, or as part of our experience (such as pleasure and pain) or whether it's source is a priori (so non-natural, as Kant agues).

nature of attributes of God - attributes of God typically include his omniscience, omnipotence and omnibenevolence (which are linked to his powers) or faithfulness, steadfast-love and generosity (related to his moral character and holiness).

non-cognitive approaches to language - non-cognitive means 'not truth-apt' ie not verifiable by reference to something else such as observation or experience.

normative means of salvation - the ways by which God saves us, where 'normative' means 'those defined as true and accepted'. In Christianity the normative means of salvation is the cross of Christ, by which he paid the price as a ransom for sin (Mark 10:45).

omnibenevolence - all-loving attribute of God

omnipotence - all-powerful attribute of God

omniscience - all-knowing attribute of God

ontological - means 'of the essence' as in the ontological argument for the existence of God which derives from his essence as ever-existing and perfect.

original sin - sin coming from the choice of Adam and Eve in the Garden to disobey God and eat the fruit of the tree of knowledge. Augustine believed this original sin was transmitted ever-after by the male semen. It's a debate in Knowledge of God (Christian Thought) how much we can 'see' God ourselves in nature, and how much original sin permanently blinds us.

personalism - one of the working principles of Situation ethics, meaning 'related to the effect on the individual'. Fletcher argues ethics should be related to individual needs and desires, not imposed as law.

pluralism - means 'many views of truth and goodness'.

positivism - has two meanings, rather different. Fletcher cites positivism as a working principle of situation ethics, meaning 'received by faith and then lived by'. Whereas in logical positivism in meta-ethics and religious language it means 'provable by a principle of verification'.

postulates - things put forward as self-evident, as assumptions, as in Kant's ethical theory which postulates God, immortality and freedom.

pragmatism - one of Fletcher's four working principles in situation ethics, meaning 'practical, based on a real case-by-case approach to ethics'.

primary precept - the five precepts mentioned by Aquinas as the natural rational goals of human beings (preserve life, order society, worship God, educate and reproduce).

prime mover - an Aristotelean idea that something (God) put the world and cosmos into existence. Became associated with Deism in the eighteenth century as God gets progressively distanced from his creation.

purgatory - a state of being between death and heaven when the soul is purified (or purged) of sin.

ratio - the reason by which we work out the eternal law of God evidenced in experience and by observation. Synderesis in contrast, in natural law ethics, is intuitive reason.

rationalism - a principle of the Enlightenment which has as its motto 'dare to reason' and which exalts reason over metaphysics, and so closely linked to scepticism and secularism (Christian Thought specification). In meta-ethics and religious language debates, influences of rationalists like David Hume cause people to doubt the meaningfulness of religious language.

relativism - means one of three things, relative to consequences, subjective (up to me) or particular to culture (as in 'cultural relativism').

repentance - Greek 'metanoia' means to change direction by renouncing one way and actively embracing another. The first call of Jesus in Mark's gospel is 'repent, for the Kingdom of Heaven is at hand'. In Liberation Theology it means taking up the cause of justice and revolution and overturning social evils.

rule utilitarianism - a theory of ethics normally attributed to JS Mill which argues that maximising happiness involves the recognition of certain (non-absolute) social rules which past experience confirms as good.

salvation - the process of being saved by the activity (grace) of God.

sanctity of life - the specialness and uniqueness of human life based either on the will of God in creating us and sustaining us, or some rational principle as in Kantian ethics, where it is seen as inconsistent to will your own death..

secondary precept - applications by human reason of primary precepts (primary goods of natural law) to specific circumstances.

secularism - the progressive separation of private religion and public human affairs, and the evacuation of metaphysics from the realm of public debate.

sinful - sin is lawlessness, and falling short, and disobeying God.

son of god - title given to Jesus which might mean 'special anointed one' or possibly just 'the human one'.

soul - part of a human being that is metaphysical and separate from the body. Dualism is the belief we have a body and a soul and the soul goes on to eternal existence after death as a different substance. Monism argues body and soul are one.

stakeholders - all those who have an interest in the activities of a corporation, includes shareholders, employees, the local community, suppliers, the Government etc.

substance dualism - states that two sorts of substances exist: the mental and the physical. Substance dualism is a fundamentally ontological position: it states that the mental and the physical are separate substances with independent existence.

summum bonum - the greatest good, a term used in ethics (eg Kant) for the ultimate goal or result of good actions.

superego -that part of the Freudian psyche which mediates between right and wrong and resolves conflicts between ego and id.

synderesis - a term in natural law ethics meaning we have natural innate disposition to 'do good and avid evil'. Aquinas also calls it the 'intuitive knowledge of first principles' or the primary precepts.

teleological - telos means end or purpose. So a teleological argument looks at the purpose in patterns of design in the world, as in Paley's watchmaker analogy. Teleological ethics is the ethics of purpose - as in utilitarian ethics (happiness) or situation ethics (love).

teleology - the study of purpose in nature or in ethics.

telos - Greek for purpose or end (goal)

The Forms - Plato's word for the reality behind and beyond reality which we only see as shadows in a cave. The Theory of Forms is Plato's answer to the problem "how one unchanging reality or essential being can appear in so many changing phenomena."

theodicies- rational philosophies which provide an explanation for the presence of evil in the face of the providence and goodness of God.

universalist belief - the belief that all people everywhere will eventually be saved, irrespective of their faith position.

utility - means 'usefulness' as in utilitarianism which states that we can make a practical calculation of happiness of the greatest number, a view made popular by Jeremy Bentham and John Stuart Mill (19th century).

verificationism - a philosophical theory that holds that for propositions to meaningful they must be susceptible to rational proof by observation.

via negativa (anaphatic way) - a philosophical approach to theology which asserts that no finite concepts or attributes can be adequately used of God, but only negative terms, such as immortal, invisible. Apophasis means 'denial, negation' and so 'apophatic' is another word for anaphatic.

via positiva (cataphatic way) - uses "positive" terminology to describe or refer to the divine – specifically, God – i.e. terminology that describes or refers to what the divine is believed to be.

vincible ignorance - ignorance that a person could remove by applying reasonable diligence in the given set of circumstances, so blameworthy ignorance, echoing Paul in Romans 2, 'the Gentiles are without excuse' because we all have the moral law written on our hearts.

whistle-blowing - the practice in business ethics whereby an employee reveals malpractice, now protected as a right in UK law.

working principles - the four principles in situation ethics which define how agape love applies in practice: personalism, positivism, pragmatism and relativism.

About the Authors

Peter Baron

Peter is well-known in the UK as a trainer, educator and writer on Philosophy and Ethics as well as a first-rate teacher.

He read Politics, Philosophy and Economics at New College, Oxford and afterwards obtained an MLitt for a research degree in Hermeneutics at Newcastle University. He qualified as an Economics teacher in 1982, and taught ethics at Wells Cathedral School in Somerset from 2006-2012. From 2012 he ahs been a freelance writer and speaker.

In 2007 he set up a philosophy and ethics community dedicated to enlarging the teaching of philosophy in schools by applying the theory of multiple intelligences to the analysis of philosophical and ethical problems. So far over 700 schools have joined the community and over 40,000 individuals use his website every month.

Daniella Dunsmore

Daniella trained in Theology at Cambridge University. She is currently subject leader in Religious Studies at Thetford Grammar School, speaks at Conferences, and is a Teach First Ambassador.

Andrew Capone

Andrew is the Head of RE at St Simon Stock Catholic School, Maidstone. He has a Masters of Arts in Classical History and a Joint Bachelors of Arts in Philosophy and Religious Studies. He also offers personal tuition, analytical marking and consultation to RE and Philosophy teachers.

He is always willing to discuss and share work and resources, and support both students and teachers of the subject. Philosophy is a subject to be shared.

About Peped

Links, reviews, news and revision materials available on peped.org

peped.org allows students and teachers to explore Philosophy of Religion, Christian Thought, and Ethics through handouts, film clips, presentations, case studies, extracts, games and academic articles.

Pitched just right, and so much more than a text book, here is a place to engage with critical reflection whatever your level. Marked student essays are also posted.

Published by Active Education

www.peped.org

First published in 2018

ISBN: 9781724092540

Cartoons used with permission © Becky Dyer

All images © their respective owners

Printed in Great Britain
by Amazon